"Fear of knowledge is natural; al[...]
and there is nothing we can do ab[...]
how frightening learning is, it is n[...]
of a man without knowledge."
—don Juan Matus

Also by Carlos Castaneda

Journey to Ixtlan

THE LESSONS
OF DON JUAN

by
CARLOS CASTANEDA

WASHINGTON SQUARE PRESS
New York   London   Toronto   Sydney

Washington Square Press
A Division of Simon & Schuster, Inc.
1230 Avenue of the Americas
New York, NY 10020

First Washington Square Press trade paperback printing February 1991

WASHINGTON SQUARE PRESS and colophon are registered
trademarks of Simon & Schuster, Inc.

For information about special discounts for bulk purchases,
please contact Simon & Schuster Special Sales at
1-800-456-6798 or business@simonandschuster.com

Manufactured in the United States of America

50 49 48 47 46 45 44

ISBN-13: 978-0-671-73246-2
ISBN-10:   0-671-73246-3

CONTENTS

PART TWO
Journey to Ixtlan

INTRODUCTION

ON SATURDAY, MAY 22, 1971, I went to Sonora, Mexico, to see don Juan Matus, a Yaqui Indian sorcerer, with whom I had been associated since 1961. I thought that my visit on that day was going to be in no way different from the scores of times I had gone to see him in the ten years I had been his apprentice. The events that took place on that day and on the following days, however, were momentous to me. On that occasion my apprenticeship came to an end. This was not an arbitrary withdrawal on my part but a bona fide termination.

I have already presented the case of my apprenticeship in two previous works: *The Teachings of Don Juan* and *A Separate Reality*.

My basic assumption in both books has been that the articulation points in learning to be a sorcerer were the states of nonordinary reality produced by the ingestion of psychotropic plants.

In this respect don Juan was an expert in the use of three such plants: *Datura inoxia,* commonly known as jimson weed; *Lophophora williamsii,* known as peyote; and a hallucinogenic mushroom of the genus *Psilocybe.*

My perception of the world through the effects of those psychotropics had been so bizarre and impressive that I was forced to assume that such states were the only avenue to communicating and learning what don Juan was attempting to teach me.

That assumption was erroneous.

For the purpose of avoiding any misunderstandings

about my work with don Juan I would like to clarify
the following issues at this point.

So far I have made no attempt whatsoever to place
don Juan in a cultural milieu. The fact that he considers
himself to be a Yaqui Indian does not mean that his
knowledge of sorcery is known to or practiced by the
Yaqui Indians in general.

All the conversations that don Juan and I have had
throughout the apprenticeship were conducted in Spanish, and only because of his thorough command of the
language was I capable of obtaining complex explanations of his system of beliefs.

I have maintained the practice of referring to that system as sorcery and I have also maintained the practice
of referring to don Juan as a sorcerer, because these were
categories he himself used.

Since I was capable of writing down most of what he
said in the beginning of the apprenticeship, and everything that was said in the later phases of it, I gathered
voluminous field notes. In order to render those notes
readable and still preserve the dramatic unity of don
Juan's teachings, I have had to edit them, but what I
have deleted is, I believe, immaterial to the points I want
to raise.

In the case of my work with don Juan I have limited
my efforts solely to viewing him as a sorcerer and to ac-
quiring *membership* in his knowledge.

For the purpose of presenting my argument I must
first explain the basic premise of sorcery as don Juan
presented it to me. He said that for a sorcerer, the world
of everyday life is not real, or out there, as we believe
it is. For a sorcerer, reality, or the world we all know,
is only a description.

For the sake of validating this premise don Juan concentrated the best of his efforts into leading me to a
genuine conviction that what I held in mind as the world
at hand was merely a description of the world; a description that had been pounded into me from the moment I was born.

He pointed out that everyone who comes into contact

with a child is a teacher who incessantly describes the world to him, until the moment when the child is capable of perceiving the world as it is described. According to don Juan, we have no memory of that portentous moment, simply because none of us could possibly have had any point of reference to compare it to anything else. From that moment on, however, the child is a *member*. He knows the description of the world; and his *membership* becomes full-fledged, I suppose, when he is capable of making all the proper perceptual interpretations which, by conforming to that description, validate it.

For don Juan, then, the reality of our day-to-day life consists of an endless flow of perceptual interpretations which we, the individuals who share a specific *membership*, have learned to make in common.

The idea that the perceptual interpretations that make up the world have a flow is congruous with the fact that they run uninterruptedly and are rarely, if ever, open to question. In fact, the reality of the world we know is so taken for granted that the basic premise of sorcery, that our reality is merely one of many descriptions, could hardly be taken as a serious proposition.

Fortunately, in the case of my apprenticeship, don Juan was not concerned at all with whether or not I could take his proposition seriously, and he proceeded to elucidate his points, in spite of my opposition, my disbelief, and my inability to understand what he was saying. Thus, as a teacher of sorcery, don Juan endeavored to describe the world to me from the very first time we talked. My difficulty in grasping his concepts and methods stemmed from the fact that the units of his description were alien and incompatible with those of my own.

His contention was that he was teaching me how to "see" as opposed to merely "looking," and that "stopping the world" was the first step to "seeing."

For years I had treated the idea of "stopping the world" as a cryptic metaphor that really did not mean anything. It was only during an informal conversation that took place towards the end of my apprenticeship that I came to fully realize its scope and importance as one of the main propositions of don Juan's knowledge.

Don Juan and I had been talking about different things in a relaxed and unstructured manner. I told him about a friend of mine and his dilemma with his nine-year-old son. The child, who had been living with the mother for the past four years, was then living with my friend, and the problem was what to do with him? According to my friend, the child was a misfit in school; he lacked concentration and was not interested in anything. He was given to tantrums, disruptive behavior, and to running away from home.

"Your friend certainly does have a problem," don Juan said, laughing.

I wanted to keep on telling him all the "terrible" things the child had done, but he interrupted me.

"There is no need to say any more about that poor little boy," he said. "There is no need for you or for me to regard his actions in our thoughts one way or another."

His manner was abrupt and his tone was firm, but then he smiled.

"What can my friend do?" I asked.

"The worst thing he could do is to force the child to agree with him," don Juan said.

"What do you mean?"

"I mean that that child shouldn't be spanked or scared by his father when he doesn't behave the way he wants him to."

"How can he teach him anything if he isn't firm with him?"

"Your friend should let someone else spank the child."

"He can't let anyone else touch his little boy!" I said, surprised at his suggestion.

Don Juan seemed to enjoy my reaction and giggled.

"Your friend is not a warrior," he said. "If he were, he would know that the worst thing one can do is to confront human beings bluntly."

"What does a warrior do, don Juan?"

"A warrior proceeds strategically."

"I still don't understand what you mean."

"I mean that if your friend were a warrior he would help his child to *stop the world.*"

"How can my friend do that?"

"He would need personal power. He would need to be a sorcerer."

"But he isn't."

"In that case he must use ordinary means to help his son to change his idea of the world. It is not *stopping the world,* but it will work just the same."

I asked him to explain his statements.

"If I were your friend," don Juan said, "I would start by hiring someone to spank the little guy. I would go to skid row and hire the worst-looking man I could find."

"To scare a little boy?"

"Not just to scare a little boy, you fool. That little fellow must be *stopped,* and being beaten by his father won't do it.

"If one wants to *stop* our fellow men one must always be outside the circle that presses them. That way one can always direct the pressure."

The idea was preposterous, but somehow it was appealing to me.

Don Juan was resting his chin on his left palm. His left arm was propped against his chest on a wooden box that served as a low table. His eyes were closed but his eyeballs moved. I felt he was looking at me through his eyelids. The thought scared me.

"Tell me more about what my friend should do with his little boy," I said.

"Tell him to go to skid row and very carefully select an ugly-looking derelict," he went on. "Tell him to get a young one. One who still has some strength left in him."

Don Juan then delineated a strange strategy. I was to instruct my friend to have the man follow him or wait for him at a place where he would go with his son. The man, in response to a prearranged cue to be given after any objectionable behavior on the part of the child, was supposed to leap from a hiding place, pick the child up, and spank the living daylights out of him.

"After the man scares him, your friend must help the little boy regain his confidence, in any way he can. If he follows this procedure three or four times I assure you that that child will feel differently towards everything. He will change his idea of the world."

"What if the fright injures him?"

"Fright never injures anyone. What injures the spirit is having someone always on your back, beating you, telling you what to do and what not to do.

"When that boy is more contained you must tell your friend to do one last thing for him. He must find some way to get to a dead child, perhaps in a hospital, or at the office of a doctor. He must take his son there and show the dead child to him. He must let him touch the corpse once with his left hand, on any place except the corpse's belly. After the boy does that he will be renewed. The world will never be the same for him."

I realized then that throughout the years of our association don Juan had been employing with me, although on a different scale, the same tactics he was suggesting my friend should use with his son. I asked him about it. He said that he had been trying all along to teach me how to "stop the world."

"You haven't yet," he said, smiling. "Nothing seems to work, because you are very stubborn. If you were less stubborn, however, by now you would probably have *stopped the world* with any of the techniques I have taught you."

"What techniques, don Juan?"

"Everything I have told you to do was a technique for *stopping the world.*"

A few months after that conversation don Juan accomplished what he had set out to do, to teach me to "stop the world."

That monumental event in my life compelled me to reexamine in detail my work of ten years. It became evident to me that my original assumption about the role of psychotropic plants was erroneous. They were not the

essential feature of the sorcerer's description of the
world, but were only an aid to cement, so to speak, parts
of the description which I had been incapable of perceiving otherwise. My insistence on holding on to my
standard version of reality rendered me almost deaf
and blind to don Juan's aims. Therefore, it was simply
my lack of sensitivity which had fostered their use.

In reviewing the totality of my field notes I became
aware that don Juan had given me the bulk of the new
description at the very beginning of our association in
what he called "techniques for stopping the world." I
had discarded those parts of my field notes in my earlier
works because they did not pertain to the use of psychotropic plants. I have now rightfully reinstated them in the
total scope of don Juan's teachings and they comprise
the first seventeen chapters of this work. The last three
chapters are the field notes covering the events that cul-
minated in my "stopping the world."

In summing up I can say that when I began the apprenticeship, there was another reality, that is to say,
there was a sorcery description of the world, which I did
not know.

Don Juan, as a sorcerer and a teacher, taught me that
description. The ten-year apprenticeship I have under-
gone consisted, therefore, in setting up that unknown
reality by unfolding its description, adding increasingly
more complex parts as I went along.

The termination of the apprenticeship meant that I
had learned a new description of the world in a convincing and authentic manner and thus I had become capable of eliciting a new perception of the world, which
matched its new description. In other words, I had gained
membership.

Don Juan stated that in order to arrive at "seeing" one
first had to "stop the world." "Stopping the world" was
indeed an appropriate rendition of certain states of
awareness in which the reality of everyday life is altered
because the flow of interpretation, which ordinarily runs
uninterruptedly, has been stopped by a set of circumstances alien to that flow. In my case the set of circum-

stances alien to my normal flow of interpretations was the sorcery description of the world. Don Juan's precondition for "stopping the world" was that one had to be convinced; in other words, one had to learn the new description in a total sense, for the purpose of pitting it against the old one, and in that way break the dogmatic certainty, which we all share, that the validity of our perceptions, or our reality of the world, is not to be questioned.

After "stopping the world" the next step was "seeing." By that don Juan meant what I would like to categorize as "responding to the perceptual solicitations of a world outside the description we have learned to call reality."

My contention is that all these steps can only be understood in terms of the description to which they belong; and since it was a description that he endeavored to give me from the beginning, I must then let his teachings be the only source of entrance into it. Thus, I have left don Juan's words to speak for themselves.

—C.C.
1972

Journey to Ixtlan

THE LESSONS
OF DON JUAN

PART ONE
"Stopping the World"

1

REAFFIRMATIONS
FROM THE WORLD AROUND US

"I understand you know a great deal about plants, sir," I said to the old Indian in front of me.

A friend of mine had just put us in contact and left the room and we had introduced ourselves to each other. The old man had told me that his name was Juan Matus.

"Did your friend tell you that?" he asked casually.

"Yes, he did."

"I pick plants, or rather, they let me pick them," he said softly.

We were in the waiting room of a bus depot in Arizona. I asked him in very formal Spanish if he would allow me to question him. I said, "Would the gentleman [caballero] permit me to ask some questions?"

"Caballero," which is derived from the word "caballo," horse, originally meant horseman or a nobleman on horseback.

He looked at me inquisitively.

"I'm a horseman without a horse," he said with a big smile and then he added, "I've told you that my name is Juan Matus."

I liked his smile. I thought that, obviously he was a man that could appreciate directness and I decided to boldly tackle him with a request.

I told him I was interested in collecting and studying medicinal plants. I said that my special interest was the uses of the hallucinogenic cactus, peyote, which I had studied at length at the university in Los Angeles.

I thought that my presentation was very serious. I was very contained and sounded perfectly credible to myself.

The old man shook his head slowly, and I, encouraged by his silence, added that it would no doubt be profitable for us to get together and talk about peyote.

It was at that moment that he lifted his head and looked me squarely in the eyes. It was a formidable look. Yet it was not menacing or awesome in any way. It was a look that went through me. I became tongue-tied at once and could not continue with the harangues about myself. That was the end of our meeting. Yet he left on a note of hope. He said that perhaps I could visit him at his house someday.

It would be difficult to assess the impact of don Juan's look if my inventory of experience is not somehow brought to bear on the uniqueness of that event. When I began to study anthropology and thus met don Juan, I was already an expert in "getting around." I had left my home years before and that meant in my evaluation that I was capable of taking care of myself. Whenever I was rebuffed I could usually cajole my way in or make concessions, argue, get angry, or if nothing succeeded I would whine or complain; in other words, there was always something I knew I could do under the circumstances, and never in my life had any human being stopped my momentum so swiftly and so definitely as don Juan did that afternoon. But it was not only a matter of being silenced; there had been times when I had been unable to say a word to my opponent because of some inherent respect I felt for him, still my anger or frustration was manifested in my thoughts. Don Juan's look, however, numbed me to the point that I could not think coherently.

I became thoroughly intrigued with that stupendous look and decided to search for him.

I prepared myself for six months, after that first meeting, reading up on the uses of peyote among the American Indians, especially about the peyote cult of the Indians of the Plains. I became acquainted with every work available, and when I felt I was ready I went back to Arizona.

Saturday, December 17, 1960

I found his house after making long and taxing inquiries among the local Indians. It was early afternoon when I arrived and parked in front of it. I saw him sitting on a wooden milk crate. He seemed to recognize me and greeted me as I got out of my car.

We exchanged social courtesies for a while and then, in plain terms, I confessed that I had been very devious with him the first time we had met. I had boasted that I knew a great deal about peyote, when in reality I knew nothing about it. He stared at me. His eyes were very kind.

I told him that for six months I had been reading to prepare myself for our meeting and that this time I really knew a great deal more.

He laughed. Obviously, there was something in my statement which was funny to him. He was laughing at me and I felt a bit confused and offended.

He apparently noticed my discomfort and assured me that although I had had good intentions there was really no way to prepare myself for our meeting.

I wondered if it would have been proper to ask whether that statement had any hidden meaning, but I did not; yet he seemed to be attuned to my feelings and proceeded to explain what he had meant. He said that my endeavors reminded him of a story about some people a certain king had persecuted and killed once upon a time. He said that in the story the persecuted people were indistinguishable from their persecutors, except that they insisted on pronouncing certain words in a peculiar manner proper only to them; that flaw, of course, was the giveaway. The king posted roadblocks at critical points where an official would ask every man passing by to pronounce a key word. Those who could pronounce it the way the king pronounced it would live, but those who could not were immediately put to death. The point of the story was that one day a young man decided to prepare himself for passing the roadblock by learning to pronounce the test word just as the king liked it.

Don Juan said, with a broad smile, that in fact it took the young man "six months" to master such a pronunciation. And then came the day of the great test; the young man very confidently came upon the roadblock and waited for the official to ask him to pronounce the word.

At that point don Juan very dramatically stopped his recounting and looked at me. His pause was very studied and seemed a bit corny to me, but I played along. I had heard the theme of the story before. It had to do with Jews in Germany and the way one could tell who was a Jew by the way they pronounced certain words. I also knew the punch line: the young man was going to get caught because the official had forgotten the key word and asked him to pronounce another word which was very similar but which the young man had not learned to say correctly.

Don Juan seemed to be waiting for me to ask what happened, so I did.

"What happened to him?" I asked, trying to sound naïve and interested in the story.

"The young man, who was truly foxy," he said, "realized that the official had forgotten the key word, and before the man could say anything else he confessed that he had prepared himself for six months."

He made another pause and looked at me with a mischievous glint in his eyes. This time he had turned the tables on me. The young man's confession was a new element and I no longer knew how the story would end.

"Well, what happened then?" I asked, truly interested.

"The young man was killed instantly, of course," he said and broke into a roaring laughter.

I liked very much the way he had entrapped my interest; above all I liked the way he had linked that story to my own case. In fact, he seemed to have constructed it to fit me. He was making fun of me in a very subtle and artistic manner. I laughed with him.

Afterwards I told him that no matter how stupid I

sounded I was really interested in learning something about plants.

"I like to walk a great deal," he said.

I thought he was deliberately changing the topic of conversation to avoid answering me. I did not want to antagonize him with my insistence.

He asked me if I wanted to go with him on a short hike in the desert. I eagerly told him that I would love to walk in the desert.

"This is no picnic," he said in a tone of warning.

I told him that I wanted very seriously to work with him. I said that I needed information, any kind of information, on the uses of medicinal herbs, and that I was willing to pay him for his time and effort.

"You'll be working for me," I said. "And I'll pay you wages."

"How much would you pay me?" he asked.

I detected a note of greed in his voice.

"Whatever you think is appropriate," I said.

"Pay me for my time . . . with your time," he said.

I thought he was a most peculiar fellow. I told him I did not understand what he meant. He replied that there was nothing to say about plants, thus to take my money would be unthinkable for him.

He looked at me piercingly.

"What are you doing in your pocket?" he asked, frowning. "Are you playing with your whanger?"

He was referring to my taking notes on a minute pad inside the enormous pockets of my windbreaker.

When I told him what I was doing he laughed heartily.

I said that I did not want to disturb him by writing in front of him.

"If you want to write, write," he said. "You don't disturb me."

We hiked in the surrounding desert until it was almost dark. He did not show me any plants nor did he talk about them at all. We stopped for a moment to rest by some large bushes.

"Plants are very peculiar things," he said without looking at me. "They are alive and they feel."

At the very moment he made that statement a strong gust of wind shook the desert chaparral around us. The bushes made a rattling noise.

"Do you hear that?" he asked me, putting his right hand to his ear as if he were aiding his hearing. "The leaves and the wind are agreeing with me."

I laughed. The friend who had put us in contact had already told me to watch out, because the old man was very eccentric. I thought the "agreement with the leaves" was one of his eccentricities.

We walked for a while longer but he still did not show me any plants, nor did he pick any of them. He simply breezed through the bushes touching them gently. Then he came to a halt and sat down on a rock and told me to rest and look around.

I insisted on talking. Once more I let him know that I wanted very much to learn about plants, especially peyote. I pleaded with him to become my informant in exchange for some sort of monetary reward.

"You don't have to pay me," he said. "You can ask me anything you want. I will tell you what I know and then I will tell you what to do with it."

He asked me if I agreed with the arrangement. I was delighted. Then he added a cryptic statement: "Perhaps there is nothing to learn about plants, because there is nothing to say about them."

I did not understand what he had said or what he had meant by it.

"What did you say?" I asked.

He repeated the statement three times and then the whole area was shaken by the roar of an Air Force jet flying low.

"There! The world has just agreed with me," he said, putting his left hand to his ear.

I found him very amusing. His laughter was contagious.

"Are you from Arizona, don Juan?" I asked, in an effort to keep the conversation centered around his being my informant.

He looked at me and nodded affirmatively. His eyes seemed to be tired. I could see the white underneath his pupils.

"Were you born in this locality?"

He nodded his head again without answering me. It seemed to be an affirmative gesture, but it also seemed to be the nervous headshake of a person who is thinking.

"And where are you from yourself?" he asked.

"I come from South America," I said.

"That's a big place. Do you come from all of it?"

His eyes were piercing again as he looked at me.

I began to explain the circumstances of my birth, but he interrupted me.

"We are alike in this respect," he said. "I live here now but I'm really a Yaqui from Sonora."

"Is that so! I myself come from—"

He did not let me finish.

"I know, I know," he said. "You are who you are, from wherever you are, as I am a Yaqui from Sonora."

His eyes were very shiny and his laughter was strangely unsettling. He made me feel as if he had caught me in a lie. I experienced a peculiar sensation of guilt. I had the feeling he knew something I did not know or did not want to tell.

My strange embarrassment grew. He must have noticed it, for he stood up and asked me if I wanted to go eat in a restaurant in town.

Walking back to his home and then driving into town made me feel better, but I was not quite relaxed. I somehow felt threatened, although I could not pinpoint the reason.

I wanted to buy him some beer in the restaurant. He said that he never drank, not even beer. I laughed to myself. I did not believe him; the friend who had put us in contact had told me that "the old man was plastered out of his mind most of the time." I really did not mind if he was lying to me about not drinking. I liked him; there was something very soothing about his person.

I must have had a look of doubt on my face, for he

then went on to explain that he used to drink in his youth, but that one day he simply dropped it.

"People hardly ever realize that we can cut anything from our lives, any time, just like that." He snapped his fingers.

"Do you think that one can stop smoking or drinking that easily?" I asked.

"Sure!" he said with great conviction. "Smoking and drinking are nothing. Nothing at all if we want to drop them."

At that very moment the water that was boiling in the coffee percolator made a loud perking sound.

"Hear that!" don Juan exclaimed with a shine in his eyes. "The boiling water agrees with me."

Then he added after a pause, "A man can get agreements from everything around him."

At that crucial instant the coffee percolator made a truly obscene gurgling sound.

He looked at the percolator and softly said, "Thank you," nodded his head, and then broke into a roaring laughter.

I was taken aback. His laughter was a bit too loud, but I was genuinely amused by it all.

My first real session with my "informant" ended then. He said goodbye at the door of the restaurant. I told him I had to visit some friends and that I would like to see him again at the end of the following week.

"When will you be home?" I asked.

He scrutinized me.

"Whenever you come," he replied.

"I don't know exactly when I can come."

"Just come then and don't worry."

"What if you're not in?"

"I'll be there," he said, smiling, and walked away.

I ran after him and asked him if he would mind my bringing a camera with me to take pictures of him and his house.

"That's out of the question," he said with a frown.

"How about a tape recorder? Would you mind that?"

"I'm afraid there's no possibility of that either."

I became annoyed and began to fret. I said I saw no logical reason for his refusal.

Don Juan shook his head negatively.

"Forget it," he said forcefully. "And if you still want to see me don't ever mention it again."

I staged a weak final complaint. I said that pictures and recordings were indispensable to my work. He said that there was only one thing which was indispensable for anything we did. He called it "the spirit."

"One can't do without the spirit," he said. "And you don't have it. Worry about that and not about pictures."

"What do you . . . ?"

He interrupted me with a movement of his hand and walked backwards a few steps.

"Be sure to come back," he said softly and waved goodbye.

2

ERASING PERSONAL HISTORY

Thursday, December 22, 1960

Don Juan was sitting on the floor, by the door of his house, with his back against the wall. He turned over a wooden milk crate and asked me to sit down and make myself at home. I offered him some cigarettes. I had brought a carton of them. He said he did not smoke but he accepted the gift. We talked about the coldness of the desert nights and other ordinary topics of conversation.

I asked him if I was interfering with his normal routine. He looked at me with a sort of frown and said he had no routines, and that I could stay with him all afternoon if I wanted to.

I had prepared some genealogy and kinship charts that I wanted to fill out with his help. I had also compiled, from the ethnographic literature, a long list of culture traits that were purported to belong to the Indians of the area. I wanted to go through the list with him and mark all the items that were familiar to him.

I began with the kinship charts.

"What did you call your father?" I asked.

"I called him Dad," he said with a very serious face.

I felt a little bit annoyed, but I proceeded on the assumption that he had not understood.

I showed him the chart and explained that one space was for the father and another space was for the mother. I gave as an example the different words used in English and in Spanish for father and mother.

I thought that perhaps I should have taken mother first.

"What did you call your mother?" I asked.

"I called her Mom," he replied in a naïve tone.

"I mean what other words did you use to call your father and mother? How did you call them?" I said, trying to be patient and polite.

He scratched his head and looked at me with a stupid expression.

"Golly!" he said. "You got me there. Let me think."

After a moment's hesitation he seemed to remember something and I got ready to write.

"Well," he said, as if he were involved in serious thought, "how else did I call them? I called them Hey, hey, Dad! Hey, hey, Mom!"

I laughed against my desire. His expression was truly comical and at that moment I did not know whether he was a preposterous old man pulling my leg or whether he was really a simpleton. Using all the patience I had, I explained to him that these were very serious questions and that it was very important for my work to fill out the forms. I tried to make him understand the idea of a genealogy and personal history.

"What were the names of your father and mother?" I asked.

He looked at me with clear kind eyes.

"Don't waste your time with that crap," he said softly but with unsuspected force.

I did not know what to say; it was as if someone else had uttered those words. A moment before, he had been a fumbling stupid Indian scratching his head, and then in an instant he had reversed the roles; I was the stupid one, and he was staring at me with an indescribable look that was not a look of arrogance, or defiance, or hatred, or contempt. His eyes were kind and clear and penetrating.

"I don't have any personal history," he said after a long pause. "One day I found out that personal history was no longer necessary for me and, like drinking, I dropped it."

I did not quite understand what he meant by that. I suddenly felt ill at ease, threatened. I reminded him that he had assured me that it was all right to ask him questions. He reiterated that he did not mind at all.

"I don't have personal history any more," he said and looked at me probingly. "I dropped it one day when I felt it was no longer necessary."

I stared at him, trying to detect the hidden meanings of his words.

"How can one drop one's personal history?" I asked in an argumentative mood.

"One must first have the desire to drop it," he said. "And then one must proceed harmoniously to chop it off, little by little."

"Why should anyone have such a desire?" I exclaimed.

I had a terribly strong attachment to my personal history. My family roots were deep. I honestly felt that without them my life had no continuity or purpose.

"Perhaps you should tell me what you mean by dropping one's personal history," I said.

"To do away with it, that's what I mean," he replied cuttingly.

I insisted that I must not have understood the proposition.

"Take you for instance," I said. "You are a Yaqui. You can't change that."

"Am I?" he asked, smiling. "How do you know that?"

"True!" I said. "I can't know that with certainty, at this point, but you know it and that is what counts. That's what makes it personal history."

I felt I had driven a hard nail in.

"The fact that I know whether I am a Yaqui or not does not make it personal history," he replied. "Only when someone else knows that does it become personal history. And I assure you that no one will ever know that for sure."

I had written down what he had said in a clumsy way. I stopped writing and looked at him. I could not figure him out. I mentally ran through my impressions of him; the mysterious and unprecedented way he had looked at me during our first meeting, the charm with which he had claimed that he received agreement from everything around him, his annoying humor and his alertness, his look of bona fide stupidity when I asked about his father and mother, and then the unsuspected force of his statements which had snapped me apart.

"You don't know what I am, do you?" he said as if he were reading my thoughts. "You will never know who or what I am, because I don't have a personal history."

He asked me if I had a father. I told him I did. He said that my father was an example of what he had in mind. He urged me to remember what my father thought of me.

"Your father knows everything about you," he said. "So he has you all figured out. He knows who you are and what you do, and there is no power on earth that can make him change his mind about you."

Don Juan said that everybody that knew me had an idea about me, and that I kept feeding the idea with everything I did. "Don't you see?" he asked dramatically. "You must renew your personal history by telling your parents, your relatives, and your friends everything you do. On the other hand, if you have no personal history, no explanations are needed; nobody is angry or disillusioned with your acts. And above all no one pins you down with their thoughts."

Suddenly the idea became clear in my mind. I had almost known it myself, but I had never examined it. Not having personal history was indeed an appealing concept, at least on the intellectual level; it gave me, however, a sense of loneliness which I found threatening and distasteful. I wanted to discuss my feelings with him, but I kept myself in check; something was terribly incongruous in the situation at hand. I felt ridiculous trying to get into a philosophical argument with an old Indian who obviously did not have the "sophistication" of a university student. Somehow he had led me away from my original intention of asking him about his genealogy.

"I don't know how we ended up talking about this when all I wanted was some names for my charts," I said, trying to steer the conversation back to the topic I wanted.

"It's terribly simple," he said. "The way we ended up talking about it was because I said that to ask questions about one's past is a bunch of crap."

His tone was firm. I felt there was no way to make him budge, so I changed my tactics.

"Is this idea of not having personal history something that the Yaquis do?" I asked.

"It's something that I do."

"Where did you learn it?"

"I learned it during the course of my life."

"Did your father teach you that?"

"No. Let's say that I learned it by myself and now I am going to give you its secret, so you won't go away empty-handed today."

He lowered his voice to a dramatic whisper. I laughed at his histrionics. I had to admit that he was stupendous at that. The thought crossed my mind that I was in the presence of a born actor.

"Write it down," he said patronizingly. "Why not? You seem to be more comfortable writing."

I looked at him and my eyes must have betrayed my confusion. He slapped his thighs and laughed with great delight.

"It is best to erase all personal history," he said

slowly, as if giving me time to write it down in my clumsy way, "because that would make us free from the encumbering thoughts of other people."

I could not believe that he was actually saying that. I had a very confusing moment. He must have read in my face my inner turmoil and used it immediately.

"Take yourself, for instance," he went on saying. "Right now you don't know whether you are coming or going. And that is so, because I have erased my personal history. I have, little by little, created a fog around me and my life. And now nobody knows for sure who I am or what I do."

"But, you yourself know who you are, don't you?" I interjected.

"You bet I . . . don't," he exclaimed and rolled on the floor, laughing at my surprised look.

He had paused long enough to make me believe that he was going to say that he did know, as I was anticipating it. His subterfuge was very threatening to me. I actually became afraid.

"That is the little secret I am going to give you today," he said in a low voice. "Nobody knows my personal history. Nobody knows who I am or what I do. Not even I."

He squinted his eyes. He was not looking at me but beyond me over my right shoulder. He was sitting cross-legged, his back was straight and yet he seemed to be so relaxed. At that moment he was the very picture of fierceness. I fancied him to be an Indian chief, a "red-skinned warrior" in the romantic frontier sagas of my childhood. My romanticism carried me away and the most insidious feeling of ambivalence enveloped me. I could sincerely say that I liked him a great deal and in the same breath I could say that I was deadly afraid of him.

He maintained that strange stare for a long moment.

"How can I know who I am, when I am all this?" he said, sweeping the surroundings with a gesture of his head.

Then he glanced at me and smiled.

"Little by little you must create a fog around yourself;

you must erase everything around you until nothing can be taken for granted, until nothing is any longer for sure, or real. Your problem now is that you're too real. Your endeavors are too real; your moods are too real. Don't take things so for granted. You must begin to erase yourself."

"What for?" I asked belligerently.

It became clear to me then that he was prescribing behavior for me. All my life I had reached a breaking point when someone attempted to tell me what to do; the mere thought of being told what do to put me immediately on the defensive.

"You said that you wanted to learn about plants," he said calmly. "Do you want to get something for nothing? What do you think this is? We agreed that you would ask me questions and I'd tell you what I know. If you don't like it, there is nothing else we can say to each other."

His terrible directness made me feel peeved, and begrudgingly I conceded that he was right.

"Let's put it this way then," he went on. "If you want to learn about plants, since there is really nothing to say about them, you must, among other things, erase your personal history."

"How?" I asked.

"Begin with simple things, such as not revealing what you really do. Then you must leave everyone who knows you well. This way you'll build up a fog around yourself."

"But that's absurd," I protested. "Why shouldn't people know me? What's wrong with that?"

"What's wrong is that once they know you, you are an affair taken for granted and from that moment on you won't be able to break the tie of their thoughts. I personally like the ultimate freedom of being unknown. No one knows me with steadfast certainty, the way people know you, for instance."

"But that would be lying."

"I'm not concerned with lies or truths," he said severely. "Lies are lies only if you have personal history."

I argued that I did not like to deliberately mystify people or mislead them. His reply was that I misled everybody anyway.

The old man had touched a sore spot in my life. I did not pause to ask him what he meant by that or how he knew that I mystified people all the time. I simply reacted to his statement, defending myself by means of an explanation. I said that I was painfully aware that my family and my friends believed I was unreliable, when in reality I had never told a lie in my life.

"You always knew how to lie," he said. "The only thing that was missing was that you didn't know why to do it. Now you do."

I protested.

"Don't you see that I'm really sick and tired of people thinking that I'm unreliable?" I said.

"But you are unreliable," he replied with conviction.

"Damn it to hell, man, I am not!" I exclaimed.

My mood, instead of forcing him into seriousness, made him laugh hysterically. I really despised the old man for all his cockiness. Unfortunately he was right about me.

After a while I calmed down and he continued talking.

"When one does not have personal history," he explained, "nothing that one says can be taken for a lie. Your trouble is that you have to explain everything to everybody, compulsively, and at the same time you want to keep the freshness, the newness of what you do. Well, since you can't be excited after explaining everything you've done, you lie in order to keep on going."

I was truly bewildered by the scope of our conversation. I wrote down all the details of our exchange in the best way I could, concentrating on what he was saying rather than pausing to deliberate on my prejudices or on his meanings.

"From now on," he said, "you must simply show people whatever you care to show them, but without ever telling exactly how you've done it."

"I can't keep secrets!" I exclaimed. "What you are saying is useless to me."

"Then change!" he said cuttingly and with a fierce glint in his eyes.

He looked like a strange wild animal. And yet he was so coherent in his thoughts and so verbal. My annoyance gave way to a state of irritating confusion.

"You see," he went on, "we only have two alternatives; we either take everything for sure and real, or we don't. If we follow the first, we end up bored to death with ourselves and with the world. If we follow the second and erase personal history, we create a fog around us, a very exciting and mysterious state in which nobody knows where the rabbit will pop out, not even ourselves."

I contended that erasing personal history would only increase our sensation of insecurity.

"When nothing is for sure we remain alert, perennially on our toes," he said. "It is more exciting not to know which bush the rabbit is hiding behind than to behave as though we know everything."

He did not say another word for a very long time; perhaps an hour went by in complete silence. I did not know what to ask. Finally he got up and asked me to drive him to the nearby town.

I did not know why but our conversation had drained me. I felt like going to sleep. He asked me to stop on the way and told me that if I wanted to relax, I had to climb to the flat top of a small hill on the side of the road and lie down on my stomach with my head towards the east.

He seemed to have a feeling of urgency. I did not want to argue or perhaps I was too tired to even speak. I climbed the hill and did as he had prescribed.

I slept only two or three minutes, but it was sufficient to have my energy renewed.

We drove to the center of town, where he told me to let him off.

"Come back," he said as he stepped out of the car. "Be sure to come back."

3

LOSING SELF-IMPORTANCE

I had the opportunity of discussing my two previous visits to don Juan with the friend who had put us in contact. It was his opinion that I was wasting my time. I related to him, in every detail, the scope of our conversation. He thought I was exaggerating and romanticizing a silly old fogy.

There was very little room in me for romanticizing such a preposterous old man. I sincerely felt that his criticism about my personality had seriously undermined my liking him. Yet I had to admit that they had always been apropros, sharply delineated, and true to the letter.

The crux of my dilemma at that point was my unwillingness to accept that don Juan was very capable of disrupting all my preconceptions about the world, and my unwillingness to agree with my friend who believed that "the old Indian was just nuts."

I felt compelled to pay him another visit before I made up my mind.

Wednesday, December 28, 1960

Immediately after I arrived at his house he took me for a walk in the desert chaparral. He did not even look at the bag of groceries that I had brought him. He seemed to have been waiting for me.

We walked for hours. He did not collect or show me any plants. He did, however, teach me an "appropriate form of walking." He said that I had to curl my fingers gently as I walked so I would keep my attention on the trail and the surroundings. He claimed that my ordinary way of walking was debilitating and that one should never carry anything in the hands. If things had to be carried one should use a knapsack or any sort of carrying net or shoulder bag. His idea was that by forcing the hands into a specific position one was capable of greater stamina and greater awareness.

I saw no point in arguing and curled my fingers as he had prescribed and kept on walking. My awareness was in no way different, nor was my stamina.

We started our hike in the morning and we stopped to rest around noon. I was perspiring and tried to drink from my canteen, but he stopped me by saying that it was better to have only a sip of water. He cut some leaves from a small yellowish bush and chewed them. He gave me some and remarked that they were excellent, and if I chewed them slowly my thirst would vanish. It did not, but I was not uncomfortable either.

He seemed to have read my thoughts and explained that I had not felt the benefits of the "right way of walking" or the benefits of chewing the leaves because I was young and strong and my body did not notice anything because it was a bit stupid.

He laughed. I was not in a laughing mood and that seemed to amuse him even more. He corrected his previous statement, saying that my body was not really stupid but somehow dormant.

At that moment an enormous crow flew right over us, cawing. That startled me and I began to laugh. I thought that the occasion called for laughter, but to my utter amazement he shook my arm vigorously and hushed me up. He had a most serious expression.

"That was not a joke," he said severely, as if I knew what he was talking about.

I asked for an explanation. I told him that it was incongruous that my laughing at the crow had made him angry when we had laughed at the coffee percolator.

"What you saw was not just a crow!" he exclaimed.

"But I saw it and it was a crow," I insisted.

"You saw nothing, you fool," he said in a gruff voice.

His rudeness was uncalled for. I told him that I did not like to make people angry and that perhaps it would be better if I left, since he did not seem to be in a mood to have company.

He laughed uproariously, as if I were a clown performing for him. My annoyance and embarrassment grew in proportion.

"You're very violent," he commented casually. "You're taking yourself too seriously."

"But weren't you doing the same?" I interjected. "Taking yourself seriously when you got angry at me?"

He said that to get angry at me was the farthest thing from his mind. He looked at me piercingly.

"What you saw was not an agreement fom the world," he said. "Crows flying or cawing are never an agreement. That was an omen!"

"An omen of what?"

"A very important indication about you," he replied cryptically.

At that very instant the wind blew the dry branch of a bush right to our feet.

"That was an agreement!" he exclaimed and looked at me with shiny eyes and broke into a belly laugh.

I had the feeling that he was teasing me by making up the rules of his strange game as we went along, thus it was all right for him to laugh, but not for me. My annoyance mushroomed again and I told him what I thought of him.

He was not cross or offended at all. He laughed and his laughter caused me even more anguish and frustration. I thought that he was deliberately humiliating me. I decided right then that I had had my fill of "field work."

I stood up and said that I wanted to start walking back to his house because I had to leave for Los Angeles.

"Sit down!" he said imperatively. "You get peeved like an old lady. You cannot leave now, because we're not through yet."

I hated him. I thought he was a contemptuous man.

He began to sing an idiotic Mexican folk song. He was obviously imitating some popular singer. He elongated certain syllables and contracted others and made the song into a most farcical affair. It was so comical that I ended up laughing.

"You see, you laugh at the stupid song," he said. "But the man who sings it that way and those who pay to listen to him are not laughing; they think it is serious."

"What do you mean?" I asked.

I thought he had deliberately concocted the example to tell me that I had laughed at the crow because I had not taken it seriously, the same way I had not taken the song seriously. But he baffled me again. He said I was like the singer and the people who liked his songs, conceited and deadly serious about some nonsense that no one in his right mind should give a damn about.

He then recapitulated, as if to refresh my memory, all he had said before on the topic of "learning about plants." He stressed emphatically that if I really wanted to learn, I had to remodel most of my behavior.

My sense of annoyance grew, until I had to make a supreme effort to even take notes.

"You take yourself too seriously," he said slowly. "You are too damn important in your own mind. That must be changed! You are so goddamn important that you feel justified to be annoyed with everything. You're so damn important that you can afford to leave if things don't go your way. I suppose you think that shows you have character. That's nonsense! You're weak, and conceited!"

I tried to stage a protest but he did not budge. He pointed out that in the course of my life I had not ever finished anything because of that sense of disproportionate importance that I attached to myself.

I was flabbergasted at the certainty with which he made his statements. They were true, of course, and that made me feel not only angry but also threatened.

"Self-importance is another thing that must be dropped, just like personal history," he said in a dramatic tone.

I certainly did not want to argue with him. It was obvious that I was at a terrible disadvantage; he was not going to walk back to his house until he was ready and I did not know the way. I had to stay with him.

He made a strange and sudden movement, he sort of sniffed the air around him, his head shook slightly and rhythmically. He seemed to be in a state of unusual alertness. He turned and stared at me with a look of bewilderment and curiosity. His eyes swept up and down my body as if he were looking for something specific; then he stood up abruptly and began to walk fast. He was almost running. I followed him. He kept a very accelerated pace for nearly an hour.

Finally he stopped by a rocky hill and we sat in the shade of a bush. The trotting had exhausted me completely although my mood was better. It was strange the way I had changed. I felt almost elated, but when we had started to trot, after our argument, I was furious with him.

"This is very weird," I said, "but I feel really good."

I heard the cawing of a crow in the distance. He lifted his finger to his right ear and smiled.

"That was an omen," he said.

A small rock tumbled downhill and made a crashing sound when it landed in the chaparral.

He laughed out loud and pointed his finger in the direction of the sound.

"And that was an agreement," he said.

He then asked me if I was ready to talk about my self-importance. I laughed; my feeling of anger seemed so far away that I could not even conceive how I had become so cross with him.

"I can't understand what's happening to me," I said. "I got angry and now I don't know why I am not angry any more."

"The world around us is very mysterious," he said. "It doesn't yield its secrets easily."

I liked his cryptic statements. They were challenging and mysterious. I could not determine whether they were filled with hidden meanings or whether they were just plain nonsense.

"If you ever come back to the desert here," he said, "stay away from that rocky hill where we stopped today. Avoid it like the plague."

"Why? What's the matter?"

"This is not the time to explain it," he said. "Now we are concerned with losing self-importance. As long as you feel that you are the most important thing in the world you cannot really appreciate the world around you. You are like a horse with blinders, all you see is yourself apart from everything else."

He examined me for a moment.

"I am going to talk to my little friend here," he said, pointing to a small plant.

He kneeled in front of it and began to caress it and to talk to it. I did not understand what he was saying at first, but then he switched languages and talked to the plant in Spanish. He babbled inanities for a while. Then he stood up.

"It doesn't matter what you say to a plant," he said. "You can just as well make up words; what's important is the feeling of liking it, and treating it as an equal."

He explained that a man who gathers plants must apologize every time for taking them and must assure them that someday his own body will serve as food for them.

"So, all in all, the plants and ourselves are even," he said. "Neither we nor they are more or less important.

"Come on, talk to the little plant," he urged me. "Tell it that you don't feel important any more."

"I went as far as kneeling in front of the plant but I could not bring myself to speak to it. I felt ridiculous and laughed. I was not angry, however.

Don Juan patted me on the back and said that it was all right, that at least I had contained my temper.

"From now on talk to the little plants," he said. "Talk until you lose all sense of importance. Talk to them until you can do it in front of others.

"Go to those hills over there and practice by yourself."

I asked if it was all right to talk to the plants silently, in my mind.

He laughed and tapped my head.

"No!" he said. "You must talk to them in a loud and clear voice if you want them to answer you."

I walked to the area in question, laughing to myself about his eccentricities. I even tried to talk to the plants, but my feeling of being ludicrous was overpowering.

After what I thought was an appropriate wait I went back to where don Juan was. I had the certainty that he knew I had not talked to the plants.

He did not look at me. He signaled me to sit down by him.

"Watch me carefully," he said. "I'm going to have a talk with my little friend."

He kneeled down in front of a small plant and for a few minutes he moved and contorted his body, talking and laughing.

I thought he was out of his mind.

"This little plant told me to tell you that she is good to eat," he said as he got up from his kneeling position. "She said that a handful of them would keep a man healthy. She also said that there is a batch of them growing over there."

Don Juan pointed to an area on a hillside perhaps two hundred yards away.

"Let's go and find out," he said.

I laughed at his histrionics. I was sure we would find the plants, because he was an expert in the terrain and knew where the edible and medicinal plants were.

As we walked towards the area in question he told me casually that I should take notice of the plant because it was both a food and a medicine.

I asked him, half in jest, if the plant had just told him that. He stopped walking and examined me with an air of disbelief. He shook his head from side to side.

"Ah!" he exclaimed, laughing. "Your cleverness makes you more silly than I thought. How can the little plant tell me now what I've known all my life?"

He proceeded then to explain that he knew all along the different properties of that specific plant, and that the plant had just told him that there was a batch of them growing in the area he had pointed to, and that she did not mind if he told me that.

Upon arriving at the hillside I found a whole cluster of the same plants. I wanted to laugh but he did not give me time. He wanted me to thank the batch of plants. I felt excruciatingly self-conscious and could not bring myself to do it.

He smiled benevolently and made another of his cryptic statements. He repeated it three or four times as if to give me time to figure out its meaning.

"The world around us is a mystery," he said. "And men are no better than anything else. If a little plant is generous with us we must thank her, or perhaps she will not let us go."

The way he looked at me when he said that gave me a chill. I hurriedly leaned over the plants and said, "Thank you," in a loud voice.

He began to laugh in controlled and quiet spurts.

We walked for another hour and then started on our way back to his house. At a certain time I dropped behind and he had to wait for me. He checked my fingers to see if I had curled them. I had not. He told me imperatively that whenever I walked with him I had to observe and copy his mannerisms or not come along at all.

"I can't be waiting for you as though you're a child," he said in a scolding tone.

That statement sunk me into the depths of embarrassment and bewilderment. How could it be possible that such an old man could walk so much better than I? I thought I was athletic and strong, and yet he had actually had to wait for me to catch up with him.

I curled my fingers and strangely enough I was able to keep his tremendous pace without any effort. In fact, at times I felt that my hands were pulling me forward.

I felt elated. I was quite happy walking inanely with the strange old Indian. I began to talk and asked repeatedly if he would show me some peyote plants. He looked at me but did not say a word.

4

DEATH IS AN ADVISER

Wednesday, January 25, 1961

"Would you teach me someday about peyote?" I asked.

He did not answer and, as he had done before, simply looked at me as if I were crazy.

I had mentioned the topic to him, in casual conversation, various times already, and every time he frowned and shook his head. It was not an affirmative or a negative gesture; it was rather a gesture of despair and disbelief.

He stood up abruptly. We had been sitting on the ground in front of his house. An almost imperceptible shake of his head was the invitation to follow hiim.

We went into the desert chaparral in a southerly direction. He mentioned repeatedly as we walked that I had to be aware of the uselessness of my self-importance and of my personal history.

"Your friends," he said, turning to me abruptly. "Those who have known you for a long time, you must leave them quickly."

I thought he was crazy and his insistence was idiotic, but I did not say anything. He peered at me and began to laugh.

After a long hike we came to a halt. I was about to sit down to rest but he told me to go some twenty yards away and talk to a batch of plants in a loud and clear voice. I felt ill at ease and apprehensive. His weird demands were more than I could bear and I told him once more that I could not speak to plants, because I felt ridiculous. His only comment was that my feeling of self-importance was immense. He seemed to have made a sudden decision and said that I should not try to talk to plants until I felt easy and natural about it.

"You want to learn about them and yet you don't want to do any work," he said accusingly. "What are you trying to do?"

My explanation was that I wanted bona fide information about the uses of plants, thus I had asked him to be my informant. I had even offered to pay him for his time and trouble.

"You should take the money," I said. "This way we both would feel better. I could then ask you anything I want to because you would be working for me and I would pay you for it. What do you think of that?"

He looked at me contemptuously and made an obscene sound with his mouth, making his lower lip and his tongue vibrate by exhaling with great force.

"That's what I think of it," he said and laughed hysterically at the look of utmost surprise that I must have had on my face.

It was obvious to me that he was not a man I could easily contend with. In spite of his age, he was ebullient and unbelievably strong. I had had the idea that, being so old, he could have been the perfect "informant" for me. Old people, I had been led to believe, made the best informants because they were too feeble to do anything else except talk. Don Juan, on the other hand, was a miserable subject. I felt he was unmanageable and dangerous. The friend who had introduced us was right. He was an eccentric old Indian; and although he was not plastered out of his mind most of the time, as my friend had told me, he was worse yet, he was crazy. I again felt the terrible doubt and apprehension I had experienced before. I thought I had overcome that. In fact, I had had no trouble at all convincing myself that I wanted to visit him again. The idea had crept into my mind, however, that perhaps I was a bit crazy myself when I realized that I liked to be with him. His idea that my feeling of self-importance was an obstacle had really made an impact on me. But all that was apparently only an intellectual exercise on my part; the moment I was confronted with his odd behavior, I began to experience apprehension and I wanted to leave.

I said that I believed we were so different that there was no possibility of our getting along.

"One of us has to change," he said, staring at the ground. "And you know who."

He began humming a Mexican folk song and then lifted his head abruptly and looked at me. His eyes were fierce and burning. I wanted to look away or close my eyes, but to my utter amazement I could not break away from his gaze.

He asked me to tell him what I had seen in his eyes. I said that I saw nothing, but he insisted that I had to voice what his eyes had made me feel aware of. I struggled to make him understand that the only thing his eyes made me aware of was my embarrassment, and that the way he was looking at me was very discomforting.

He did not let go. He kept a steady stare. It was not an outright menacing or mean look; it was rather a mysterious but unpleasant gaze.

He asked me if he reminded me of a bird.

"A bird?" I exclaimed.

He giggled like a child and moved his eyes away from me.

"Yes," he said softly. "A bird, a very funny bird!"

He locked his gaze on me again and commanded me to remember. He said with an extraordinary conviction that he "knew" I had seen that look before.

My feelings of the moment were that the old man provoked me, against my honest desire, every time he opened his mouth. I stared back at him in obvious defiance. Instead of getting angry he began to laugh. He slapped his thigh and yelled as if he were riding a wild horse. Then he became serious and told me that it was of utmost importance that I stop fighting him and remember that funny bird he was talking about.

"Look into my eyes," he said.

His eyes were extraordinarily fierce. There was a feeling

about them that actually reminded me of something but I was not sure what it was. I pondered upon it for a moment and then I had a sudden realization; it was not the shape of his eyes nor the shape of his head, but some cold fierceness in his gaze that had reminded me of the look in the eyes of a falcon. At the very moment of that realization he was looking at me askew and for an instant my mind experienced a total chaos. I thought I had seen a falcon's features instead of don Juan's. The image was too fleeting and I was too upset to have paid more attention to it.

In a very excited tone I told him that I could have sworn I had seen the features of a falcon on his face. He had another attack of laughter.

I have seen the look in the eyes of falcons. I used to hunt them when I was a boy, and in the opinion of my grandfather I was good. He had a Leghorn chicken farm and falcons were a menace to his business. Shooting them was not only functional but also "right." I had forgotten until that moment that the fierceness of their eyes had haunted me for years, but it was so far in my past that I thought I had lost the memory of it.

"I used to hunt falcons," I said.

"I know it," don Juan replied matter-of-factly.

His tone carried such a certainty that I began to laugh. I thought he was a preposterous fellow. He had the gall to sound as if he knew I had hunted falcons. I felt supremely contemptuous of him.

"Why do you get so angry?" he asked in a tone of genuine concern.

I did not know why. He began to probe me in a very unusual manner. He asked me to look at him again and tell him about the "very funny bird" he reminded me of. I struggled against him and out of contempt said that there was nothing to talk about. Then I felt compelled to ask him why he had said he knew I used to hunt falcons. Instead of answering me he again commented on my behavior. He said I was a violent fellow that was capable of "frothing at the mouth" at the drop of a hat. I protested that that was not true; I had always had the idea I was rather congenial and easygoing. I said it was his fault for forcing me out of control with his unexpected words and actions.

"Why the anger?" he asked.

I took stock of my feelings and reactions. I really had no need to be angry with him.

He again insisted that I should look into his eyes and tell him about the "strange falcon." He had changed his wording; he had said before, "a very funny bird," then he substituted it with "strange falcon." The change in wording summed up a change in my own mood. I had suddenly become sad.

He squinted his eyes until they were two slits and said in an overdramatic voice that he was "seeing" a very strange falcon. He repeated his statement three times as if he were actually seeing it there in front of him.

"Don't you remember it?" he asked.

I did not remember anything of the sort.

"What's strange about the falcon?" I asked.

"You must tell me that," he replied.

I insisted that I had no way of knowing what he was referring to, therefore I could not tell him anything.

"Don't fight me!" he said. "Fight your sluggishness and remember."

I seriously struggled for a moment to figure him out. It did not occur to me that I could just as well have tried to remember.

"There was a time when you saw a lot of birds," he said as though cuing me.

I told him that when I was a child I had lived on a farm and had hunted hundreds of birds.

He said that if that was the case I should not have any difficulty remembering all the funny birds I had hunted.

He looked at me with a question in his eyes, as if he had just given me the last clue.

"I have hunted so many birds," I said, "that I can't recall anything about them."

"This bird is special," he replied almost in a whisper. "This bird is a falcon."

I became involved again in figuring out what he was driving at. Was he teasing me? Was he serious? After a long interval he urged me again to remember. I felt that it was useless for me to try to end his play; the only other thing I could do was to join him.

"Are you talking about a falcon that I have hunted?" I asked.

"Yes," he whispered with his eyes closed.

"So this happened when I was a boy?"

"Yes."

"But you said you're seeing a falcon in front of you now."

"I am."

"What are you trying to do to me?"

"I'm trying to make you remember."

"What? For heaven's sakes!"

"A falcon swift as light," he said, looking at me in the eyes. I felt my heart had stopped.

"Now look at me," he said.

But I did not. I heard his voice as a faint sound. Some stupendous recollection had taken me wholly. The white falcon!

It all began with my grandfather's explosion of anger upon taking a count of his young Leghorn chickens. They had been disappearing in a steady and disconcerting manner. He personally organized and carried out a meticulous vigil, and after days of steady watching we finally saw a big white bird flying away with a young Leghorn chicken in its claws. The bird was fast and apparently knew its route. It swooped down from behind some trees, grabbed the chicken and flew away through an opening between two ranches. It happened so fast that my grandfather had hardly seen it, but I did and I knew that it was indeed a falcon. My grandfather said that if that was the case it had to be an albino.

We started a campaign against the albino falcon and twice I thought I had gotten it. It even dropped its prey, but it got away. It was too fast for me. It was also very intelligent; it never came back to hunt on my grandfather's farm.

I would have forgotten about it had my grandfather not needled me to hunt the bird. For two months I chased the albino falcon all over the valley where I lived. I learned its habits and I could almost intuit its route of flight, yet its speed and the suddenness of its appearance would always baffle me. I could boast that I had prevented it from taking its prey, perhaps every time we had met, but I could never bag it.

In the two months that I carried on the strange war against the albino falcon I came close to it only once. I had been chasing it all day and I was tired. I had sat down to rest and fell asleep under a tall eucalyptus tree. The sudden cry of a falcon woke me up. I opened my eyes without making any other movement and I saw a whitish bird perched in the highest branches of the eucalyptus tree. It was the albino falcon. The chase was over. It was going to be a difficult shot; I was lying on my back and the bird had its back turned to me. There was a sudden gust of wind and I used it to muffle the noise of lifting my .22 long rifle to take aim. I wanted to wait until the bird had turned or until it had begun to fly so I would not miss it. But the albino bird remained motionless. In order to take a better shot I would have needed to move and the falcon was too fast for that. I thought that my best alternative was to wait. And I did, a long, interminable time. Perhaps what affected me was the long wait, or perhaps it was the loneliness of the spot where the bird and I were; I suddenly felt a chill up my spine and in an unprecedented action I stood up and left. I did not even look to see if the bird had flown away.

I never attached any significance to my final act with the albino falcon. However, it was terribly strange that I did not shoot it. I had shot dozens of falcons before. On the farm where I grew up, shooting birds or hunting any kind of animal was a matter of course.

Don Juan listened attentively as I told him the story of the albino falcon.

"How did you know about the white falcon?" I asked when I had finished.

"I saw it," he replied.

"Where?"

"Right here in front of you."

I was not in an argumentative mood any more.

"What does all this mean?" I asked.

He said that a white bird like that was an omen, and that not shooting it down was the only right thing to do.

"Your death gave you a little warning," he said with a mysterious tone. "It always comes as a chill."

"What are you talking about?" I said nervously.

He really made me nervous with his spooky talk.

"You know a lot about birds," he said. "You've killed too many of them. You know how to wait. You have waited patiently for hours. I know that. I am seeing it."

His words caused a great turmoil in me. I thought that what annoyed me the most about him was his certainty. I could not stand his dogmatic assuredness about the issues in my own life that I was not sure of myself. I became engulfed in my feelings of dejection and I did not see him leaning over me until he actually had whispered something in my ear. I did not understand at first and he repeated it. He told me to turn around casually and look at a boulder to my left. He said that my death was there staring at me and if I turned when he signaled me I might be capable of seeing it.

He signaled me with his eyes. I turned and I thought I saw a flickering movement over the boulder. A chill ran through my body, the muscles of my abdomen contracted involuntarily and I experienced a jolt, a spasm. After a moment I regained my composure and I explained away the sensation of seeing the flickering shadow as an optical illusion caused by turning my head so abruptly.

"Death is our eternal companion," don Juan said with a most serious air. "It is always to our left, at an arm's length. It was watching you when you were watching the white falcon; it whispered in your ear and you felt its chill, as you felt it today. It has always been watching you. It always will until the day it taps you."

He extended his arm and touched me lightly on the shoulder and at the same time he made a deep clicking sound with his tongue. The effect was devastating; I almost got sick to my stomach.

"You're the boy who stalked game and waited patiently, as death waits; you know very well that death is to our left, the same way you were to the left of the white falcon."

His words had the strange power to plunge me into an unwarranted terror; my only defense was my compulsion to commit to writing everything he said.

"How can anyone feel so important when we know that death is stalking us?" he asked.

I had the feeling my answer was not really needed. I could not have said anything anyway. A new mood had possessed me.

"The thing to do when you're impatient," he proceeded, "is to turn to your left and ask advice from your death. An immense amount of pettiness is dropped if your death makes a gesture to you, or if you catch a glimpse of it, or if you just have the feeling that your companion is there watching you."

He leaned over again and whispered in my ear that if I turned to my left suddenly, upon seeing his signal, I could again see my death on the boulder.

His eyes gave me an almost imperceptible signal, but I did not dare to look.

I told him that I believed him and that he did not have to press the issue any further because I was terrified. He had one of his roaring belly laughs.

He replied that the issue of our death was never pressed far enough. And I argued that it would be meaningless for me to dwell upon my death, since such a thought would only bring discomfort and fear.

"You're full of crap!" he exclaimed. "Death is the only wise adviser that we have. Whenever you feel, as you always do, that everything is going wrong and you're about to be annihilated, turn to your death and ask if that is so. Your death will tell you that you're wrong; that nothing really matters outside its touch. Your death will tell you, 'I haven't touched you yet.'"

He shook his head and seemed to be waiting for my

reply. I had none. My thoughts were running rampant.
He had delivered a staggering blow to my egotism. The
pettiness of being annoyed with him was monstrous in
the light of my death.

I had the feeling he was fully aware of my change of
mood. He had turned the tide in his favor. He smiled
and began to hum a Mexican tune.

"Yes," he said softly after a long pause. "One of us
here has to change, and fast. One of us here has to learn
again that death is the hunter, and that it is always to
one's left. One of us here has to ask death's advice and
drop the cursed pettiness that belongs to men that live
their lives as if death will never tap them."

We remained quiet for more than an hour, then we
started walking again. We meandered in the desert chaparral for hours. I did not ask him if there was any purpose to it; it did not matter. Somehow he had made me
recapture an old feeling, something I had quite forgotten,
the sheer joy of just moving around without attaching
any intellectual purpose to it.

I wanted him to let me catch a glimpse of whatever I
had seen on the boulder.

"Let me see that shadow again," I said.

"You mean your death, don't you?" he replied with a
touch of irony in his voice.

For a moment I felt reluctant to voice it.

"Yes," I finally said. "Let me see my death once
again."

"Not now," he said. "You're too solid."

"I beg your pardon?"

He began to laugh and for some unknown reason his
laughter was no longer offensive and insidious, as it had
been in the past. I did not think that it was different,
from the point of view of its pitch, or its loudness, or the
spirit of it; the new element was my mood. In view of
my impending death my fears and annoyance were nonsense.

"Let me talk to plants then," I said.

He roared with laughter.

"You're too good now," he said, still laughing. "You

go from one extreme to the other. Be still. There is no need to talk to plants unless you want to know their secrets, and for that you need the most unbending intent. So save your good wishes. There is no need to see your death either. It is sufficient that you feel its presence around you."

5

ASSUMING RESPONSIBILITY

Tuesday, April 11, 1961

I arrived at don Juan's house in the early morning on Sunday, April 9.

"Good morning, don Juan," I said. "Am I glad to see you!"

He looked at me and broke into a soft laughter. He had walked to my car as I was parking it and held the door open while I gathered some packages of food that I had brought for him.

We walked to the house and sat down by the door.

This was the first time I had been really aware of what I was doing there. For three months I had actually looked forward to going back to the "field." It was as if a time bomb set within myself had exploded and suddenly I had remembered something transcendental to me. I had remembered that once in my life I had been very patient and very efficient.

Before don Juan could say anything I asked him the question that had been pressing hard in my mind. For three months I had been obsessed with the memory of the albino falcon. How did he know about it when I myself had forgotten?

He laughed but did not answer. I pleaded with him to tell me.

"It was nothing," he said with his usual conviction. "Anyone could tell that you're strange. You're just numb, that's all."

I felt that he was again getting me off guard and pushing me into a corner in which I did not care to be.

"Is it possible to see our death?" I asked, trying to remain within the topic.

"Sure," he said, laughing. "It is here with us."

"How do you know that?"

"I'm an old man; with age one learns all kinds of things."

"I know lots of old people, but they have never learned this. How come you did?"

"Well, let's say that I know all kinds of things because I don't have a personal history, and because I don't feel more important than anything else, and because my death is sitting with me right here."

He extended his left arm and moved his fingers as if he were actually petting something.

I laughed. I knew where he was leading me. The old devil was going to clobber me again, probably with my self-importance, but I did not mind this time. The memory that once I had had a superb patience had filled me with a strange, quiet euphoria that had dispelled most of my feelings of nervousness and intolerance towards don Juan; what I felt instead was a sensation of wonder about his acts.

"Who are you, really?" I asked.

He seemed surprised. He opened his eyes to an enormous size and blinked like a bird, closing his eyelids as if they were a shutter. They came down and went up again and his eyes remained in focus. His maneuver startled me and I recoiled, and he laughed with childlike abandon.

"For you I am Juan Matus, and I am at your service," he said with exaggerated politeness.

I then asked my other burning question: "What did you do to me the first day we met?"

I was referring to the look he had given me.

"Me? Nothing," he replied with a tone of innocence.

I described to him the way I had felt when he had looked at me and how incongruous it had been for me to be tongue-tied by it.

He laughed until tears rolled down his cheeks. I again felt a surge of animosity towards him. I thought that I was being so serious and thoughtful and he was being so "Indian" in his coarse ways.

He apparently detected my mood and stopped laughing all of a sudden.

After a long hesitation I told him that his laughter had annoyed me because I was seriously trying to understand what had happened to me.

"There is nothing to understand," he replied, undisturbed.

I reviewed for him the sequence of unusual events that had taken place since I had met him, starting with the mysterious look he had given me, to remembering the albino falcon and seeing on the boulder the shadow he had said was my death.

"Why are you doing all this to me?" I asked.

There was no belligerence in my question. I was only curious as to why it was me in particular.

"You asked me to tell you what I know about plants," he said.

I noticed a tinge of sarcasm in his voice. He sounded as if he were humoring me.

"But what you have told me so far has nothing to do with plants," I protested.

His reply was that it took time to learn about them.

My feeling was that it was useless to argue with him. I realized then the total idiocy of the easy and absurd resolutions I had made. While I was at home I had promised myself that I was never going to lose my temper or feel annoyed with don Juan. In the actual situation, however, the minute he rebuffed me I had another attack of peevishness. I felt there was no way for me to interact with him and that angered me.

"Think of your death now," don Juan said suddenly. "It is at arm's length. It may tap you any moment, so really you have no time for crappy thoughts and moods. None of us have time for that.

"Do you want to know what I did to you the first day we met? I *saw* you, and I *saw* that you thought you were lying to me. But you weren't, not really."

I told him that his explanation confused me even more. He replied that that was the reason he did not want to explain his acts, and that explanations were not necessary. He said that the only thing that counted was action, acting instead of talking.

He pulled out a straw mat and lay down, propping his head up with a bundle. He made himself comfortable and then he told me that there was another thing I had to perform if I really wanted to learn about plants.

"What was wrong with you when I *saw* you, and what is wrong with you now, is that you don't like to take responsibility for what you do," he said slowly, as if to give me time to understand what he was saying. "When you were telling me all those things in the bus depot you were aware that they were lies. Why were you lying?"

I explained that my objective had been to find a "key informant" for my work.

Don Juan smiled and began humming a Mexican tune.

"When a man decides to do something he must go all the way," he said, "but he must take responsibility for what he does. No matter what he does, he must know first why he is doing it, and then he must proceed with his actions without having doubts or remorse about them."

He examined me. I did not know what to say. Finally I ventured an opinion, almost as a protest.

"That's an impossibility!" I said.

He asked me why, and I said that perhaps ideally that was what everybody thought they should do. In practice, however, there was no way to avoid doubts and remorse.

"Of course there is a way," he replied with conviction.

"Look at me," he said. "I have no doubts or remorse. Everything I do is my decision and my responsibility. The simplest thing I do, to take you for a walk in the desert, for instance, may very well mean my death. Death is stalking me. Therefore, I have no room for doubts or remorse. If I have to die as a result of taking you for a walk, then I must die.

"You, on the other hand, feel that you are immortal, and the decisions of an immortal man can be canceled or regretted or doubted. In a world where death is the hunter, my friend, there is not time for regrets or doubts. There is only time for decisions."

I argued, in sincerity, that in my opinion that was an unreal world, because it was arbitrarily made by taking an idealized form of behavior and saying that that was the way to proceed.

I told him the story of my father, who used to give me endless lectures about the wonders of a healthy mind in a healthy body, and how young men should temper their bodies with hardships and with feats of athletic competition. He was a young man; when I was eight years old he was only twenty-seven. During the summertime, as a rule, he would come from the city, where he taught school, to spend at least a month with me at my grandparents' farm, where I lived. It was a hellish month for me. I told don Juan one instance of my father's behavior that I thought would apply to the situation at hand.

Almost immediately upon arriving at the farm my father would insist on taking a long walk with me at his side, so we could talk things over, and while we were talking he would make plans for us to go swimming, every day at six A.M. At night he would set the alarm for five-thirty to have plenty of time, because at six sharp we had to be in the water. And when the alarm would go off in the morning, he would jump out of bed, put on his glasses, go to the window and look out.

I had even memorized the ensuing monologue.

"Uhm . . . A bit cloudy today. Listen, I'm going to lie down again for just five minutes. O.K.? No more than five! I'm just going to stretch my muscles and fully wake up."

He would invariably fall asleep again until ten, sometimes until noon.

I told don Juan that what annoyed me was his refusal to give up his obviously phony resolutions. He would repeat this ritual every morning until I would finally hurt his feelings by refusing to set the alarm clock.

"They were not phony resolutions," don Juan said, obviously taking sides with my father. "He just didn't know how to get out of bed, that's all."

"At any rate," I said, "I'm always leery of unreal resolutions."

"What would be a resolution that is real then?" don Juan asked with a coy smile.

"If my father would have said to himself that he could not go swimming at six in the morning but perhaps at three in the afternoon."

"Your resolutions injure the spirit," don Juan said with an air of great seriousness.

I thought I even detected a note of sadness in his tone. We were quiet for a long time. My peevishness had vanished. I thought of my father.

"He didn't want to swim at three in the afternoon. Don't you see?" don Juan said.

His words made me jump.

I told him that my father was weak, and so was his world of ideal acts that he never performed. I was almost shouting.

Don Juan did not say a word. He shook his head slowly in a rhythmical way. I felt terribly sad. Thinking of my father always gave me a consuming feeling.

"You think you were stronger, don't you?" he asked in a casual tone.

I said I did, and I began to tell him all the emotional turmoil that my father had put me through, but he interrupted me.

"Was he mean to you?" he asked.

"No."

"Was he petty with you?"

"No."

"Did he do all he could for you?"

"Yes."

"Then what was wrong with him?"

Again I began to shout that he was weak, but I caught myself and lowered my voice. I felt a bit ludicrous being cross-examined by don Juan.

"What are you doing all this for?" I said. "We were supposed to be talking about plants."

I felt more annoyed and despondent than ever. I told him that he had no business or the remotest qualifications to pass judgment on my behavior, and he exploded into a belly laugh.

"When you get angry you always feel righteous, don't you?" he said and blinked like a bird.

He was right. I had the tendency to feel justified at being angry.

"Let's not talk about my father," I said, feigning a happy mood. "Let's talk about plants."

"No, let's talk about your father," he insisted. "That is the place to begin today. If you think that you were so much stronger than he, why didn't you go swimming at six in the morning in his place?"

I told him that I could not believe he was seriously asking me that. I had always thought that swimming at six in the morning was my father's business and not mine.

"It was also your business from the moment you accepted his idea," don Juan snapped at me.

I said that I had never accepted it, that I had always known my father was not truthful to himself. Don Juan asked me matter-of-factly why I had not voiced my opinions at the time.

"You don't tell your father things like that," I said as a weak explanation.

"Why not?"

"That was not done in my house, that's all."

"You have done worse things in your house," he declared like a judge from the bench. "The only thing you never did was to shine your spirit."

There was such a devastating force in his words that

they echoed in my mind. He brought all my defenses down. I could not argue with him. I took refuge in writing my notes.

I tried a last feeble explanation and said that all my life I had encountered people of my father's kind, who had, like my father, hooked me somehow into their schemes, and as a rule I had always been left dangling.

"You are complaining," he said softly. "You have been complaining all your life because you don't assume responsibility for your decisions. If you would have assumed responsibility for your father's idea of swimming at six in the morning you would have swum, by yourself if necessary, or you would have told him to go to hell the first time he opened his mouth after you knew his devices. But you didn't say anything. Therefore, you were as weak as your father.

"To assume the responsibility of one's decisions means that one is ready to die for them."

"Wait, wait!" I said. "You are twisting this around."

He did not let me finish. I was going to tell him that I had used my father only as an example of an unrealistic way of acting, and that nobody in his right mind would be willing to die for such an idiotic thing.

"It doesn't matter what the decision is," he said. "Nothing could be more or less serious than anything else. Don't you see? In a world where death is the hunter there are no small or big decisions. There are only decisions that we make in the face of our inevitable death."

I could not say anything. Perhaps an hour went by. Don Juan was perfectly motionless on his mat although he was not sleeping.

"Why do you tell me all this, don Juan?" I asked. "Why are you doing this to me?"

"You came to me," he said. "No, that was not the case, you were brought to me. And I have had a gesture with you."

"I beg your pardon?"

"You could have had a gesture with your father by swimming for him, but you didn't, perhaps because you were too young. I have lived longer than you. I have

nothing pending. There is no hurry in my life, therefore
I can properly have a gesture with you."

In the afternoon we went for a hike. I easily kept his
pace and marveled again at his stupendous physical prowess. He walked so nimbly and with such sure steps that
next to him I was like a child. We went in an easterly
direction. I noticed then that he did not like to talk while
he walked. If I spoke to him he would stop walking in
order to answer me.

After a couple of hours we came to a hill; he sat down
and signaled me to sit by him. He announced in a mock-
dramatic tone that he was going to tell me a story.

He said that once upon a time there was a young man,
a destitute Indian who lived among the white men in a
city. He had no home, no relatives, no friends. He had
come into the city to find his fortune and had found only
misery and pain. From time to time he made a few cents
working like a mule, barely enough for a morsel; otherwise
he had to beg or steal food.

Don Juan said that one day the young man went to
the market place. He walked up and down the street in
a haze, his eyes wild upon seeing all the good things that
were gathered there. He was so frantic that he did not
see where he was walking, and ended up tripping over
some baskets and falling on top of an old man.

The old man was carrying four enormous gourds and
had just sat down to rest and eat. Don Juan smiled knowingly and said that the old man found it quite strange that
the young man had stumbled on him. He was not angry
at being disturbed but amazed at why this particular
young man had fallen on top of him. The young man,
on the other hand, was angry and told him to get out of
his way. He was not concerned at all about the ultimate
reason for their meeting. He had not noticed that their
paths had actually crossed.

Don Juan mimicked the motions of someone going after something that was rolling over. He said that the old
man's gourds had turned over and were rolling down the

street. When the young man saw the gourds he thought he had found his food for the day.

He helped the old man up and insisted on helping him carry the heavy gourds. The old man told him that he was on his way to his home in the mountains and the young man insisted on going with him, at least part of the way.

The old man took the road to the mountains and as they walked he gave the young man part of the food he had bought at the market. The young man ate to his heart's content and when he was quite satisfied he began to notice how heavy the gourds were and clutched them tightly.

Don Juan opened his eyes and smiled with a devilish grin and said that the young man asked, "What do you carry in these gourds?" The old man did not answer but told him that he was going to show him a companion or friend who could alleviate his sorrows and give him advice and wisdom about the ways of the world.

Don Juan made a majestic gesture with both hands and said that the old man summoned the most beautiful deer that the young man had ever seen. The deer was so tame that it came to him and walked around him. It glittered and shone. The young man was spellbound and knew right away that it was a "spirit deer." The old man told him then that if he wished to have that friend and its wisdom all he had to do was to let go of the gourds.

Don Juan's grin portrayed ambition; he said that the young man's petty desires were pricked upon hearing such a request. Don Juan's eyes became small and devilish as he voiced the young man's question: "What do you have in these four enormous gourds?"

Don Juan said that the old man very serenely replied that he was carrying food: "pinole" and water. He stopped narrating the story and walked around in a circle a couple of times. I did not know what he was doing. But apparently it was part of the story. The circle seemed to portray the deliberations of the young man.

Don Juan said that, of course, the young man had not believed a word. He calculated that if the old man, who was obviously a wizard, was willing to give a "spirit deer" for his gourds, then the gourds must have been filled with power beyond belief.

Don Juan contorted his face again into a devilish grin and said that the young man declared that he wanted to have the gourds. There was a long pause that seemed to mark the end of the story. Don Juan remained quiet, yet I was sure he wanted me to ask about it, and I did.

"What happened to the young man?"

"He took the gourds," he replied with a smile of satisfaction.

There was another long pause. I laughed. I thought that this had been a real "Indian story."

Don Juan's eyes were shining as he smiled at me. There was an air of innocence about him. He began to laugh in soft spurts and asked me, "Don't you want to know about the gourds?"

"Of course I want to know. I thought that was the end of the story."

"Oh no," he said with a mischievous light in his eyes. "The young man took his gourds and ran away to an isolated place and opened them."

"What did he find?" I asked.

Don Juan glanced at me and I had the feeling he was aware of my mental gymnastics. He shook his head and chuckled.

"Well," I urged him. "Were the gourds empty?"

"There was only food and water inside the gourds," he said. "And the young man, in a fit of anger, smashed them against the rocks."

I said that his reaction was only natural—anyone in his position would have done the same.

Don Juan's reply was that the young man was a fool who did not know what he was looking for. He did not know what "power" was, so he could not tell whether or not he had found it. He had not taken responsibility for his decision, therefore he was angered by his blunder. He expected to gain something and got nothing instead. Don Juan speculated that if I were the young man and if I had followed my inclinations I would have ended up angry and remorseful, and would, no doubt, have spent the rest of my life feeling sorry for myself for what I had lost.

Then he explained the behavior of the old man. He had cleverly fed the young man so as to give him the "daring of a satisfied stomach," thus the young man upon finding only food in the gourds smashed them in a fit of anger.

"Had he been aware of his decision and assumed responsibility for it," don Juan said, "he would have taken the food and would've been more than satisfied with it. And perhaps he might even have realized that that food was power too."

6

BECOMING A HUNTER

Friday, June 23, 1961

As soon as I sat down I bombarded don Juan with questions. He did not answer me and made an impatient gesture with his hand to be quiet. He seemed to be in a serious mood.

"I was thinking that you haven't changed at all in the time you've been trying to learn about plants," he said in an accusing tone.

He began reviewing in a loud voice all the changes of personality he had recommended I should undertake. I told him that I had considered the matter very seriously and found that I could not possibly fulfill them because each of them ran contrary to my core. He replied that to merely consider them was not enough, and that whatever he had said to me was not said just for fun. I again insisted that, although I had done very little in matters of adjusting my personal life to his ideas, I really wanted to learn the uses of plants.

After a long, uneasy silence I boldly asked him, "Would you teach me about peyote, don Juan?"

He said that my intentions alone were not enough, and that to know about peyote—he called it "Mescalito" for the first time—was a serious matter. It seemed that there was nothing else to say.

In the early evening, however, he set up a test for me; he put forth a problem without giving me any clues to its solution: to find a beneficial place or spot in the area right in front of his door where we always sat to talk, a spot where I could allegedly feel perfectly happy and invigorated. During the course of the night, while I attempted to find the "spot" by rolling on the ground, I twice detected a change of coloration on the uniformly dark dirt floor of the designated area.

The problem exhausted me and I fell asleep on one of the places where I had detected the change in color. In the morning don Juan woke me up and announced that I had had a very successful experience. Not only had I found the beneficial spot I was looking for, but I had also found its opposite, an enemy or negative spot and the colors associated with both.

Saturday, June 24, 1961

We went into the desert chaparral in the early morning. As we walked, don Juan explained to me that finding a "beneficial" or an "enemy" spot was an important need for a man in the wilderness. I wanted to steer the conversation to the topic of peyote, but he flatly refused to talk about it. He warned me that there should be no mention of it, unless he himself brought up the subject.

We sat down to rest in the shade of some tall bushes in an area of thick vegetation. The desert chaparral around us was not quite dry yet; it was a warm day and the flies kept on pestering me but they did not seem to bother don Juan. I wondered whether he was just ignoring them but then I noticed they were not landing on his face at all.

"Sometimes it is necessary to find a beneficial spot quickly, out in the open," don Juan went on. "Or maybe it is necessary to determine quickly whether or not the spot where one is about to rest is a bad one. One time, we sat to rest by some hill and you got very angry and upset. That spot was your enemy. A little crow gave you a warning, remember?"

I remembered that he had made a point of telling me to avoid that area in the future. I also remembered that I had become angry because he had not let me laugh.

"I thought that the crow that flew overhead was an omen for me alone," he said. "I would never have suspected that the crows were friendly towards you too."

"What are you talking about?"

"The crow was an omen," he went on. "If you knew about crows you would have avoided the place like the plague. Crows are not always available to give warning though, and you must learn to find, by yourself, a proper place to camp or to rest."

After a long pause don Juan suddenly turned to me and said that in order to find the proper place to rest all I had to do was to cross my eyes. He gave me a knowing look and in a confidential tone told me that I had done precisely that when I was rolling on his porch, and thus I had been capable of finding two spots and their colors. He let me know that he was impressed by my accomplishment.

"I really don't know what I did," I said.

"You crossed your eyes," he said emphatically. "That's the technique; you must have done that, although you don't remember it."

Don Juan then described the technique, which he said took years to perfect, and which consisted of gradually forcing the eyes to see separately the same image. The lack of image conversion entailed a double perception of the world; this double perception, according to don Juan, allowed one the opportunity of judging changes in the surroundings, which the eyes were ordinarily incapable of perceiving.

Don Juan coaxed me to try it. He assured me that it was not injurious to the sight. He said that I should begin by looking in short glances, almost with the corners of my eyes. He pointed to a large bush and showed me how. I had a strange feeling, seeing don Juan's eyes taking incredibly fast glances at the bush. His eyes reminded me of those of a shifty animal that cannot look straight.

We walked for perhaps an hour while I tried not to focus my sight on anything. Then don Juan asked me to start separating the images perceived by each of my eyes. After another hour or so I got a terrible headache and had to stop.

"Do you think you could find, by yourself, a proper place for us to rest?" he asked.

I had no idea what the criterion for a "proper place" was. He patiently explained that looking in short glances allowed the eyes to pick out unusual sights.

"Such as what?" I asked.

"They are not sights proper," he said. "They are more like feelings. If you look at a bush or a tree or a rock where you may like to rest, your eyes can make you feel whether or not that's the best resting place."

I again urged him to describe what those feelings were but he either could not describe them or he simply did not want to. He said that I should practice by picking out a place and then he would tell me whether or not my eyes were working.

At one moment I caught sight of what I thought was a pebble which reflected light. I could not see it if I focused my eyes on it, but if I swept the area with fast glances I could detect a sort of faint glitter. I pointed out the place to don Juan. It was in the middle of an open unshaded flat area devoid of thick bushes. He laughed uproariously and then asked me why I had picked that specific spot. I explained that I was seeing a glitter.

"I don't care what you see," he said. "You could be seeing an elephant. How you feel is the important issue."

I did not feel anything at all. He gave me a mysterious look and said that he wished he could oblige me and sit down to rest with me there, but he was going to sit somewhere else while I tested my choice.

I sat down while he looked at me curiously from a distance of thirty or forty feet away. After a few minutes he began to laugh loudly. Somehow his laughter made me nervous. It put me on edge. I felt he was making fun of me and I got angry. I began to question my motives for being there. There was definitely something wrong in the way my total endeavor with don Juan was proceeding. I felt that I was just a pawn in his clutches.

Suddenly don Juan charged at me, at full speed, and pulled me by the arm, dragging me bodily for ten or twelve feet. He helped me to stand up and wiped some perspiration from his forehead. I noticed then that he had exerted himself to his limit. He patted me on the back and said that I had picked the wrong place and that he had to rescue me in a real hurry, because he saw that the spot where I was sitting was about to take over my entire feelings. I laughed. The image of don Juan charging at me was very funny. He had actually run like a young man. His feet moved as if he were grabbing the soft reddish dirt of the desert in order to catapult himself over me. I had seen him laughing at me and then in a matter of seconds he was dragging me by the arm.

After a while he urged me to continue looking for a proper place to rest. We kept on walking but I did not detect or "feel" anything at all. Perhaps if I had been more relaxed I would have noticed or felt something. I had ceased, however, to be angry with him. Finally he pointed to some rocks and we came to a halt.

"Don't feel disappointed," don Juan said. "It takes a long time to train the eyes properly."

I did not say anything. I was not going to be disappointed about something I did not understand at all. Yet, I had to admit that three times already since I had begun to visit don Juan I had become very angry and had been agitated to the point of being nearly ill while sitting on places that he called bad.

"The trick is to feel with your eyes," he said. "Your

problem now is that you don't know what to feel. It'll come to you, though, with practice."

"Perhaps you should tell me, don Juan, what I am supposed to feel."

"That's impossible."

"Why?"

"No one can tell you what you are supposed to feel. It is not heat, or light, or glare, or color. It is something else."

"Can't you describe it?"

"No. All I can do is give you the technique. Once you learn to separate the images and see two of everything, you must focus your attention in the area between the two images. Any change worthy of notice would take place there, in that area."

"What kind of changes are they?"

"That is not important. The feeling that you get is what counts. Every man is different. You saw glitter today, but that did not mean anything, because the feeling was missing. I can't tell you how to feel. You must learn that yourself."

We rested in silence for some time. Don Juan covered his face with his hat and remained motionless as if he were asleep. I became absorbed in writing my notes, until he made a sudden movement that made me jolt. He sat up abruptly and faced me, frowning.

"You have a knack for hunting," he said. "And that's what you should learn, hunting. We are not going to talk about plants any more."

He puffed out his jaw for an instant, then candidly added, "I don't think we ever have, anyway, have we?" and laughed.

We spent the rest of the day walking in every direction while he gave me an unbelievably detailed explanation about rattlesnakes. The way they nest, the way they move around, their seasonal habits, their quirks of behavior. Then he proceeded to corroborate each of the points he had made and finally he caught and killed a large snake; he cut its head off, cleaned its viscera, skinned it, and roasted the meat. His movements had such a grace and skill that it was a sheer pleasure just to be around him. I had listened to him and watched him, spellbound. My concentration had been so complete that the rest of the world had practically vanished for me.

Eating the snake was a hard reentry into the world of ordinary affairs. I felt nauseated when I began to chew a bite of snake meat. It was an ill-founded queasiness, as the meat was delicious, but my stomach seemed to be rather an independent unit. I could hardly swallow at all. I thought don Juan would have a heart attack from laughing so hard.

Afterwards we sat down for a leisurely rest in the shade of some rocks. I began to work on my notes, and the quantity of them made me realize that he had given me an astonishing amount of information about rattlesnakes.

"Your hunter's spirit has returned to you," don Juan said suddenly and with a serious face. "Now you're hooked."

"I beg your pardon?"

I wanted him to elaborate on his statement that I was hooked, but he only laughed and repeated it.

"How am I hooked?" I insisted.

"Hunters will always hunt," he said. "I am a hunter myself."

"Do you mean you hunt for a living?"

"I hunt in order to live. I can live off the land, anywhere."

He indicated the total surroundings with his head.

"To be a hunter means that one knows a great deal," he went on. "It means that one can see the world in different ways. In order to be a hunter one must be in perfect balance with everything else, otherwise hunting would become a meaningless chore. For instance, today we took a little snake. I had to apologize to her for cutting her life off so suddenly and so definitely; I did what I did knowing that my own life will also be cut off someday in very much the same fashion, suddenly and definitely. So, all in all, we and the snakes are on a par. One of them fed us today."

"I had never conceived a balance of that kind when I used to hunt," I said.

"That's not true. You didn't just kill animals. You and your family all ate the game."

His statements carried the conviction of someone who had been there. He was, of course, right. There had been times when I had provided the incidental wild meat for my family.

After a moment's hesitation I asked, "How did you know that?"

"There are certain things that I just know," he said. "I can't tell you how though."

I told him that my aunts and uncles would very seriously call all the birds I would bag "pheasants."

Don Juan said he could easily imagine them calling a sparrow a "tiny pheasant" and added a comical rendition of how they would chew it. The extraordinary movements of his jaw gave me the feeling that he was actually chewing a whole bird, bones and all.

"I really think that you have a touch for hunting," he said, staring at me. "And we have been barking up the wrong tree. Perhaps you will be willing to change your way of life in order to become a hunter."

He reminded me that I had found out, with just a little exertion on my part, that in the world there were good and bad spots for me; he added that I had also found out the specific colors associated with them.

"That means that you have a knack for hunting," he declared. "Not everyone who tried would find their colors and their spots at the same time."

To be a hunter sounded very nice and romantic, but it was an absurdity to me, since I did not particularly care to hunt.

"You don't have to care to hunt or to like it," he replied to my complaint. "You have a natural inclination. I think the best hunters never like hunting; they do it well, that's all."

I had the feeling don Juan was capable of arguing his way out of anything, and yet he maintained that he did not like to talk at all.

"It is like what I have told you about hunters," he said. "I don't necessarily like to talk. I just have a knack for it and I do it well, that's all."

I found his mental agility truly funny.

"Hunters must be exceptionally tight individuals," he continued. "A hunter leaves very little to chance. I have been trying all along to convince you that you must learn to live in a different way. So far I have not succeeded. There was nothing you could've grabbed on to. Now it's different. I have brought back your old hunter's spirit, perhaps through it you will change."

I protested that I did not want to become a hunter. I reminded him that in the beginning I had just wanted him to tell me about medicinal plants, but he had made me stray so far away from my original purpose that I could not clearly recall any more whether or not I had really wanted to learn about plants.

"Good," he said. "Really good. If you don't have such a clear picture of what you want, you may become more humble.

"Let's put it this way. For your purposes it doesn't really matter whether you learn about plants or about hunting. You've told me that yourself. You are interested in anything that anyone can tell you. True?"

I had said that to him in trying to define the scope of anthropology and in order to draft him as my informant.

Don Juan chuckled, obviously aware of his control over the situation.

"I am a hunter," he said, as if he were reading my thoughts. "I leave very little to chance. Perhaps I should explain to you that I learned to be a hunter. I have not always lived the way I do now. At one point in my life I had to change. Now I'm pointing the direction to you. I'm guiding you. I know what I'm talking about; someone taught me all this. I didn't figure it out for myself."

"Do you mean that you had a teacher, don Juan?"

"Let's say that someone taught me to hunt the way I want to teach you now," he said and quickly changed the topic.

"I think that once upon a time hunting was one of the

greatest acts a man could perform," he said. "All hunters were powerful men. In fact, a hunter had to be powerful to begin with in order to withstand the rigors of that life."

Suddenly I became curious. Was he referring to a time perhaps prior to the Conquest? I began to probe him.

"When was the time you are talking about?"

"Once upon a time."

"When? What does 'once upon a time' mean?"

"It means once upon a time, or maybe it means now, today. It doesn't matter. At one time everybody knew that a hunter was the best of men. Now not everyone knows that, but there are a sufficient number of people who do. I know it, someday you will. See what I mean?"

"Do the Yaqui Indians feel that way about hunters? That's what I want to know."

"Not necessarily."

"Do the Pima Indians?"

"Not all of them. But some."

I named various neighboring groups. I wanted to commit him to a statement that hunting was a shared belief and practice of some specific people. But he avoided answering me directly, so I changed the subject.

"Why are you doing all this for me, don Juan?" I asked.

He took off his hat and scratched his temples in feigned bafflement.

"I'm having a gesture with you," he said softly. "Other people have had a similar gesture with you; someday you yourself will have the same gesture with others. Let's say that it is my turn. One day I found out that if I wanted to be a hunter worthy of self-respect I had to change my way of life. I used to whine and complain a great deal. I had good reasons to feel shortchanged. I am an Indian and Indians are treated like dogs. There was nothing I could do to remedy that, so all I was left with was my sorrow. But then my good fortune spared me and someone taught me to hunt. And I realized that the way I lived was not worth living . . . so I changed it."

"But I am happy with my life, don Juan. Why should I have to change it?"

He began to sing a Mexican song, very softly, and then hummed the tune. His head bobbed up and down as he followed the beat of the song.

"Do you think that you and I are equals?" he asked in a sharp voice.

His question caught me off guard. I experienced a peculiar buzzing in my ears as though he had actually shouted his words, which he had not done; however, there had been a metallic sound in his voice that was reverberating in my ears.

I scratched the inside of my left ear with the small finger of my left hand. My ears itched all the time and I had developed a rhythmical nervous way of rubbing the inside of them with the small finger of either hand. The movement was more properly a shake of my whole arm.

Don Juan watched my movements with apparent fascination.

"Well . . . are we equals?" he asked.

"Of course we're equals," I said.

I was, naturally, being condescending. I felt very warm towards him even though at times I did not know what to do with him; yet I still held in the back of my mind, although I would never voice it, the belief that I, being a university student, a man of the sophisticated Western world, was superior to an Indian.

"No," he said calmly, "we are not."

"Why, certainly we are," I protested.

"No," he said in a soft voice. "We are not equals. I am a hunter and a warrior, and you are a pimp."

My mouth fell open. I could not believe that don Juan had actually said that. I dropped my notebook and stared at him dumbfoundedly and then, of course, I became furious.

He looked at me with calm and collected eyes. I avoided his gaze. And then he began to talk. He enunciated his words clearly. They poured out smoothly and deadly. He said that I was pimping for someone else.

That I was not fighting my own battles but the battles of some unknown people. That I did not want to learn about plants or about hunting or about anything. And that his world of precise acts and feelings and decisions was infinitely more effective than the blundering idiocy I called "my life."

After he finished talking I was numb. He had spoken without belligerence or conceit but with such power, and yet such calmness, that I was not even angry any more.

We remained silent. I felt embarrassed and could not think of anything appropriate to say. I waited for him to break the silence. Hours went by. Don Juan became motionless by degrees, until his body had acquired a strange, almost frightening rigidity; his silhouette became difficult to make out as it got dark, and finally when it was pitch black around us he seemed to have merged into the blackness of the stones. His state of motionlessness was so total that it was as if he did not exist any longer.

It was midnight when I finally realized that he could and would stay motionless there in that wilderness, in those rocks, perhaps forever if he had to. His world of precise acts and feelings and decisions was indeed superior.

I quietly touched his arm and tears flooded me.

7

BEING INACCESSIBLE

Thursday, June 29, 1961

Again don Juan, as he had done every day for nearly a week, held me spellbound with his knowledge of specific details about the behavior of game. He first explained and then corroborated a number of hunting tactics based on what he called "the quirks of quails." I became so utterly involved in his explanations that a whole day went by and I had not noticed the passage of time. I even forgot to eat lunch. Don Juan made joking remarks that it was quite unusual for me to miss a meal.

By the end of the day he had caught five quail in a most ingenious trap, which he had taught me to assemble and set up.

"Two are enough for us," he said and let three of them loose.

He then taught me how to roast quail. I had wanted to cut some shrubs and make a barbecue pit, the way my grandfather used to make it, lined with green branches and leaves and sealed with dirt, but don Juan said that there was no need to injure the shrubs, since we had already injured the quail.

After we finished eating we walked very leisurely towards a rocky area. We sat on a sandstone hillside and I said jokingly that if he would have left the matter up to me I would have cooked all five of the quail, and that my barbecue would have tasted much better than his roast.

"No doubt," he said. "But if you would have done all that, we might have never left this place in one piece."

"What do you mean?" I asked. "What would have prevented us?"

"The shrubs, the quail, everything around would have pitched in."

"I never know when you are talking seriously," I said. He made a gesture of feigned impatience and smacked his lips.

"You have a weird notion of what it means to talk seriously," he said. "I laugh a great deal because I like to laugh, yet everything I say is deadly serious, even if you don't understand it. Why should the world be only as you think it is? Who gave you the authority to say so?"

"There is no proof that the world is otherwise," I said.

It was getting dark. I was wondering if it was time to go back to his house, but he did not seem to be in a hurry and I was enjoying myself.

The wind was cold. Suddenly he stood up and told me that we had to climb to the hilltop and stand up on an area clear of shrubs.

"Don't be afraid," he said. "I'm your friend and I'll see that nothing bad happens to you."

"What do you mean?" I asked, alarmed.

Don Juan had the most insidious facility to shift me from sheer enjoyment to sheer fright.

"The world is very strange at this time of the day," he said. "That's what I mean. No matter what you see, don't be afraid."

"What am I going to see?"

"I don't know yet," he said, peering into the distance towards the south.

He did not seem to be worried. I also kept on looking in the same direction.

Suddenly he perked up and pointed with his left hand towards a dark area in the desert shrubbery.

"There it is," he said, as if he had been waiting for something which had suddenly appeared.

"What is it?" I asked.

"There it is," he repeated. "Look! Look!"

I did not see anything, just the shrubs.

"It is here now," he said with great urgency in his voice. "It is here."

A sudden gust of wind hit me at that instant and made my eyes burn. I stared towards the area in question. There was absolutely nothing out of the ordinary.

"I can't see a thing," I said.

"You just felt it," he replied. "Right now. It got into your eyes and kept you from seeing."

"What are you talking about?"

"I have deliberately brought you to a hilltop," he said. "We are very noticeable here and something is coming to us."

"What? The wind?"

"Not just the wind," he said sternly. "It may seem to be wind to you, because wind is all you know."

I strained my eyes staring into the desert shrubs. Don Juan stood silently by me for a moment and then walked into the nearby chaparral and began to tear some big branches from the surrounding shrubs; he gathered eight of them and made a bundle. He ordered me to do the same and to apologize to the plants in a loud voice for mutilating them.

When we had two bundles he made me run with them to the hilltop and lie down on my back between two large rocks. With tremendous speed he arranged the branches of my bundle to cover my entire body, then he covered himself in the same manner and whispered through the leaves that I should watch how the so-called wind would cease to blow once we had become unnoticeable.

At one moment, to my utter amazement, the wind actually ceased to blow as don Juan had predicted. It happened so gradually that I would have missed the change had I not been deliberately waiting for it. For a while the wind had hissed through the leaves over my face and then gradually it became quiet all around us.

I whispered to don Juan that the wind had stopped and he whispered back that I should not make any overt noise or movement, because what I was calling the wind was not wind at all but something that had a volition of its own and could actually recognize us.

I laughed out of nervousness.

In a muffled voice don Juan called my attention to the quietness around us and whispered that he was going to stand up and I should follow him, putting the branches aside very gently with my left hand.

We stood up at the same time. Don Juan stared for a moment into the distance towards the south and then turned around abruptly and faced the west.

"Sneaky. Really sneaky," he muttered, pointing to an area towards the southwest.

"Look! Look!" he urged me.

I stared with all the intensity I was capable of. I wanted to see whatever he was referring to, but I did not notice anything at all. Or rather I did not notice anything I had not seen before; there were just shrubs which seemed to be agitated by a soft wind; they rippled.

"It's here," don Juan said.

At that moment I felt a blast of air in my face. It seemed that the wind had actually begun to blow after we stood up. I could not believe it; there had to be a logical explanation for it.

Don Juan chuckled softly and told me not to tax my brain trying to reason it out.

"Let's go gather the shrubs once more," he said. "I hate to do this to these little plants, but we must *stop* you."

He picked up the branches we had used to cover ourselves and piled small rocks and dirt over them. Then, repeating the same movements we had made before, each of us gathered eight new branches. In the meantime the wind kept on blowing ceaselessly. I could feel it ruffling the hair around my ears. Don Juan whispered that once he had covered me I should not make the slightest movement or sound. He very quickly put the branches over my body and then he lay down and covered himself.

We stayed in that position for about twenty minutes and during that time a most extraordinary phenomenon occurred; the wind again changed from a hard continuous gust to a mild vibration.

I held my breath, waiting for don Juan's signal. At a given moment he gently shoved off the branches. I did the same and we stood up. The hilltop was very quiet. There was only a slight, soft vibration of leaves in the surrounding chaparral.

Don Juan's eyes were fixedly staring at an area in the shrubs south of us.

"There it is again!" he exclaimed in a loud voice.

I involuntarily jumped, nearly losing my balance, and he ordered me in a loud imperative voice to look.

"What am I supposed to see?" I asked desperately.

He said that it, the wind or whatever, was like a cloud or a whorl that was quite a ways above the shrubs, twirling its way to the hilltop where we were.

I saw a ripple forming on the bushes in the distance.

"There it comes," don Juan said in my ear. "Look how it is searching for us."

Right then a strong steady gust of wind hit my face, as it had hit it before. This time, however, my reaction was different. I was terrified. I had not seen what don Juan had described, but I had seen a most eerie wave rippling the shrubs. I did not want to succumb to my fear and deliberately sought any kind of suitable explanation. I said to myself that there must be continuous air currents in the area, and don Juan, being thoroughly acquainted with the whole region, was not only aware of that but was capable of mentally plotting their occurrence. All he had to do was to lie down, count, and wait for the wind to taper off; and once he stood up he had only to wait again for its reoccurrence.

Don Juan's voice shook me out of my mental deliberations. He was telling me that it was time to leave. I stalled; I wanted to stay to make sure that the wind would taper off.

"I didn't see anything, don Juan," I said.

"You noticed something unusual though."

"Perhaps you should tell me again what I was supposed to see."

"I've already told you," he said. "Something that hides

in the wind and looks like a whorl, a cloud, a mist, a face that twirls around."

Don Juan made a gesture with his hands to depict a horizontal and a vertical motion.

"It moves in a specific direction," he went on. "It either tumbles or it twirls. A hunter must know all that in order to move correctly."

I wanted to humor him, but he seemed to be trying so hard to make his point that I did not dare. He looked at me for a moment and I moved my eyes away.

"To believe that the world is only as you think it is, is stupid," he said. "The world is a mysterious place. Especially in the twilight."

He pointed towards the wind with a movement of his chin.

"This can follow us," he said. "It can make us tired or it might even kill us."

"That wind?"

"At this time of the day, in the twilight, there is no wind. At this time there is only power."

We sat on the hilltop for an hour. The wind blew hard and constantly all that time.

Friday, June 30, 1961

In the late afternoon, after eating, don Juan and I moved to the area in front of his door. I sat on my "spot" and began working on my notes. He lay down on his back with his hands folded over his stomach. We had stayed around the house all day on account of the "wind." Don Juan explained that we had disturbed the wind deliberately and that it was better not to fool around with it. I had even had to sleep covered with branches.

A sudden gust of wind made don Juan get up in one incredibly agile jump.

"Damn it," he said. "The wind is looking for you."

"I can't buy that, don Juan," I said, laughing. "I really can't."

I was not being stubborn, I just found it impossible to

endorse the idea that the wind had its own volition and was looking for me, or that it had actually spotted us and rushed to us on top of the hill. I said that the idea of a "willful wind" was a view of the world that was rather simplistic.

"What is the wind then?" he asked in a challenging tone.

I patiently explained to him that masses of hot and cold air produced different pressures and that the pressure made the masses of air move vertically and horizontally. It took me a long while to explain all the details of basic meteorology.

"You mean that all there is to the wind is hot and cold air?" he asked in a tone of bafflement.

"I'm afraid so." I said and silently enjoyed my triumph.

Don Juan seemed to be dumbfounded. But then he looked at me and began to laugh uproariously.

"Your opinions are final opinions." he said with a note of sarcasm. "They are the last word. aren't they? For a hunter. however. your opinions are pure crap. It makes no difference whether the pressure is one or two or ten; if you would live out here in the wilderness you would know that during the twilight the wind becomes power. A hunter that is worth his salt knows that, and acts accordingly."

"How does he act?"

"He uses the twilight and that power hidden in the wind."

"How?"

"If it is convenient to him, the hunter hides from the power by covering himself and remaining motionless until the twilight is gone and the power has sealed him into its protection."

Don Juan made a gesture of enveloping something with his hands.

"Its protection is like a . . ."

He paused in search of a word and I suggested "cocoon."

"That is right," he said. "The protection of the power seals you like in a cocoon. A hunter can stay out in the open and no puma or coyote or slimy bug could bother him. A mountain lion could come up to the hunter's nose and sniff him, and if the hunter does not move, the lion would leave. I can guarantee you that.

"If the hunter, on the other hand, wants to be noticed all he has to do is to stand on a hilltop at the time of the twilight and the power will nag him and seek him all night. Therefore, if a hunter wants to travel at night or if he wants to be kept awake he must make himself available to the wind.

"Therein lies the secret of great hunters. To be available and unavailable at the precise turn of the road."

I felt a bit confused and asked him to recapitulate his point. Don Juan very patiently explained that he had used the twilight and the wind to point out the crucial importance of the interplay between hiding and showing oneself.

"You must learn to become deliberately available and unavailable," he said. "As your life goes now, you are unwittingly available at all times."

I protested. My feeling was that my life was becoming increasingly more and more secretive. He said I had not understood his point, and that to be unavailable did not mean to hide or to be secretive but to be inaccessible.

"Let me put it in another way," he proceeded patiently. "It makes no difference to hide if everyone knows that you are hiding.

"Your problems right now stem from that. When you are hiding, everyone knows that you are hiding, and when you are not, you are available for everyone to take a poke at you."

I was beginning to feel threatened and hurriedly tried to defend myself.

"Don't explain yourself," don Juan said dryly. "There is no need. We are fools, all of us, and you cannot be different. At one time in my life I, like you, made myself available over and over again until there was nothing of me left for anything except perhaps crying. And that I did, just like yourself."

Don Juan sized me up for a moment and then sighed loudly.

"I was younger than you, though," he went on, "but one day I had enough and I changed. Let's say that one day, when I was becoming a hunter, I learned the secret of being available and unavailable."

I told him that his point was bypassing me. I truly could not understand what he meant by being available. He had used the Spanish idioms "ponerse al alcance" and "ponerse en el medio del camino," to put oneself within reach, and to put oneself in the middle of a trafficked way.

"You must take yourself away," he explained. "You must retrieve yourself from the middle of a trafficked way. Your whole being is there, thus it is of no use to hide; you would only imagine that you are hidden. Being in the middle of the road means that everyone passing by watches your comings and goings."

His metaphor was interesting, but at the same time it was also obscure.

"You are talking in riddles," I said.

He stared at me fixedly for a long moment and then began to hum a tune. I straightened my back and sat attentively. I knew that when don Juan hummed a Mexican tune he was about to clobber me.

"Hey," he said, smiling, and peered at me. "Whatever happened to your blond friend? That girl that you used to really like."

I must have looked at him like a confounded idiot. He laughed with great delight. I did not know what to say.

"You told me about her," he said reassuringly.

But I did not remember ever telling him about anybody, much less about a blond girl.

"I've never mentioned anything like that to you," I said.

"Of course you have," he said as if dismissing the argument.

I wanted to protest, but he stopped me, saying that it did not matter how he knew about her, that the important issue was that I had liked her.

I sensed a surge of animosity towards him building up within myself.

"Don't stall," don Juan said dryly. "This is a time when you should cut off your feelings of importance.

"You once had a woman, a very dear woman, and then one day you lost her."

I began to wonder if I had ever talked about her to don Juan. I concluded that there had never been an opportunity. Yet I might have. Every time he drove with me we had always talked incessantly about everything. I did not remember everything we had talked about because I could not take notes while driving. I felt somehow appeased by my conclusions. I told him that he was right. There had been a very important blond girl in my life.

"Why isn't she with you?" he asked.

"She left."

"Why?"

"There were many reasons."

"There were not so many reasons. There was only one. You made yourself too available."

I earnestly wanted to know what he meant. He again had touched me. He seemed to be cognizant of the effect of his touch and puckered up his lips to hide a mischievous smile.

"Everyone knew about you two," he said with unshaken conviction.

"Was it wrong?"

"It was deadly wrong. She was a fine person."

I expressed the sincere feeling that his fishing in the dark was odious to me, especially the fact that he always made his statements with the assurance of someone who had been at the scene and had seen it all.

"But that's true," he said with a disarming candor. "I have *seen* it all. She was a fine person."

I knew that it was meaningless to argue, but I was angry with him for touching that sore spot in my life and I said that the girl in question was not such a fine person after all, that in my opinion she was rather weak.

"So are you," he said calmly. "But that is not important. What counts is that you have looked for her everywhere;

that makes her a special person in your world, and for a special person one should have only fine words."

I felt embarrassed; a great sadness had begun to engulf me.

"What are you doing to me, don Juan?" I asked. "You always succeed in making me sad. Why?"

"You are now indulging in sentimentality," he said accusingly.

"What is the point of all this, don Juan?"

"Being inaccessible is the point," he declared. "I brought up the memory of this person only as a means to show you directly what I couldn't show you with the wind.

"You lost her because you were accessible; you were always within her reach and your life was a routine one."

"No!" I said. "You're wrong. My life was never a routine."

"It was and it is a routine," he said dogmatically. "It is an unusual routine and that gives you the impression that it is not a routine, but I assure you it is."

I wanted to sulk and get lost in moroseness, but somehow his eyes made me feel restless; they seemed to push me on and on.

"The art of a hunter is to become inaccessible," he said. "In the case of that blond girl it would've meant that you had to become a hunter and meet her sparingly. Not the way you did. You stayed with her day after day, until the only feeling that remained was boredom. True?"

I did not answer. I felt I did not have to. He was right.

"To be inaccessible means that you touch the world around you sparingly. You don't eat five quail; you eat one. You don't damage the plants just to make a barbecue pit. You don't expose yourself to the power of the wind unless it is mandatory. You don't use and squeeze people until they have shriveled to nothing, especially the people you love."

"I have never used anyone," I said sincerely.

But don Juan maintained that I had, and thus I could bluntly state that I became tired and bored with people.

"To be unavailable means that you deliberately avoid

exhausting yourself and others," he continued. "It means that you are not hungry and desperate, like the poor bastard that feels he will never eat again and devours all the food he can, all five quail!"

Don Juan was definitely hitting me below the belt. I laughed and that seemed to please him. He touched my back lightly.

"A hunter knows he will lure game into his traps over and over again, so he doesn't worry. To worry is to become accessible, unwittingly accessible. And once you worry you cling to anything out of desperation; and once you cling you are bound to get exhausted or to exhaust whoever or whatever you are clinging to."

I told him that in my day-to-day life it was inconceivable to be inaccessible. My point was that in order to function I had to be within reach of everyone that had something to do with me.

"I've told you already that to be inaccessible does not mean to hide or to be secretive," he said calmly. "It doesn't mean that you cannot deal with people either. A hunter uses his world sparingly and with tenderness, regardless of whether the world might be things, or plants, or animal, or people, or power. A hunter deals intimately with his world and yet he is inaccessible to that same world."

"That's a contradiction," I said. "He cannot be inaccessible if he is there in his world, hour after hour, day after day."

"You did not understand," don Juan said patiently. "He is inaccessible because he's not squeezing his world out of shape. He taps it lightly, stays for as long as he needs to, and then swiftly moves away leaving hardly a mark."

8

DISRUPTING THE ROUTINES OF LIFE

Sunday, July 16, 1961

We spent all morning watching some rodents that looked like fat squirrels; don Juan called them water rats. He pointed out that they were very fast in getting out of danger, but after they had outrun any predator they had the terrible habit of stopping, or even climbing a rock, to stand on their hind legs to look around and groom themselves.

"They have very good eyes," don Juan said. "You must move only when they are on the run, therefore, you must learn to predict when and where they will stop, so you would also stop at the same time."

I became engrossed in observing them and I had what would have been a field day for hunters as I spotted so many of them. And finally I could predict their movements almost every time.

Don Juan then showed me how to make traps to catch them. He explained that a hunter had to take time to observe their eating or their nesting places in order to determine where to locate his traps; he would then set them during the night and all he had to do the next day was to scare them off so they would scatter away into his catching devices.

We gathered some sticks and proceeded to build the hunting contraptions. I had mine almost finished and was excitedly wondering whether or not it would work when suddenly don Juan stopped and looked at his left wrist, as if he were checking a watch which he had never had, and said that according to his timepiece it was lunchtime. I was holding a long stick, which I was trying to make into a hoop by bending it in a circle. I automatically put it down with the rest of my hunting paraphernalia.

Don Juan looked at me with an expression of curiosity. Then he made the wailing sound of a factory siren at lunchtime. I laughed. His siren sound was perfect. I walked towards him and noticed that he was staring at me. He shook his head from side to side.

"I'll be damned," he said.

"What's wrong?" I asked.

He again made the long wailing sound of a factory whistle.

"Lunch is over," he said. "Go back to work."

I felt confused for an instant, but then I thought that he was joking, perhaps because we really had nothing to make lunch with. I had been so engrossed with the rodents that I had forgotten we had no provisions. I picked up the stick again and tried to bend it. After a moment don Juan again blew his "whistle."

"Time to go home," he said.

He examined his imaginary watch and then looked at me and winked.

"It's five o'clock," he said with an air of someone revealing a secret. I thought that he had suddenly become fed up with hunting and was calling the whole thing off. I simply put everything down and began to get ready to leave. I did not look at him. I presumed that he also was preparing his gear. When I was through I looked up and saw him sitting cross-legged a few feet away.

"I'm through," I said. "We can go anytime."

He got up and climbed a rock. He stood there, five or six feet above the ground, looking at me. He put his hands on either side of his mouth and made a very prolonged and piercing sound. It was like a magnified factory siren. He turned around in a complete circle, making the wailing sound.

"What are you doing, don Juan?" I asked.

He said that he was giving the signal for the whole

world to go home. I was completely baffled. I could not figure out whether he was joking or whether he had simply flipped his lid. I watched him intently and tried to relate what he was doing to something he may have said before. We had hardly talked at all during the morning and I could not remember anything of importance.

Don Juan was still standing on top of the rock. He looked at me, smiled and winked again. I suddenly became alarmed. Don Juan put his hands on both sides of his mouth and let out another long whistlelike sound.

He said that it was eight o'clock in the morning and that I had to set up my gear again because we had a whole day ahead of us.

I was completely confused by then. In a matter of minutes my fear mounted to an irresistible desire to run away from the scene. I thought don Juan was crazy. I was about to flee when he slid down from the rock and came to me, smiling.

"You think I'm crazy, don't you?" he asked.

I told him that he was frightening me out of my wits with his unexpected behavior.

He said that we were even. I did not understand what he meant. I was deeply preoccupied with the thought that his acts seemed thoroughly insane. He explained that he had deliberately tried to scare me out of my wits with the heaviness of his unexpected behavior because I myself was driving him up the walls with the heaviness of my expected behavior. He added that my routines were as insane as his blowing his whistle.

I was shocked and asserted that I did not really have any routines. I told him that I believed my life was in fact a mess because of my lack of healthy routines.

Don Juan laughed and signaled me to sit down by him. The whole situation had mysteriously changed again. My fear had vanished as soon as he had begun to talk.

"What are my routines?" I asked.

"Everything you do is a routine."

"Aren't we all that way?"

"Not all of us. I don't do things out of routine."

"What prompted all this, don Juan? What did I do or what did I say that made you act the way you did?"

"You were worrying about lunch."

"I did not say anything to you; how did you know that I was worrying about lunch?"

"You worry about eating every day around noontime, and around six in the evening, and around eight in the morning," he said with a malicious grin. "You worry about eating at those times even if you're not hungry.

"All I had to do to show your routine spirit was to blow my whistle. Your spirit is trained to work with a signal."

He stared at me with a question in his eyes. I could not defend myself.

"Now you're getting ready to make hunting into a routine," he went on. "You have already set your pace in hunting; you talk at a certain time, eat at a certain time, and fall asleep at a certain time."

I had nothing to say. The way don Juan had described my eating habits was the pattern I used for everything in my life. Yet I strongly felt that my life was less routine than that of most of my friends and acquaintances.

"You know a great deal about hunting now," don Juan continued. "It'll be easy for you to realize that a good hunter knows one thing above all—he knows the routines of his prey. That's what makes him a good hunter.

"If you would remember the way I have proceeded in teaching you hunting, you would perhaps understand what I mean. First I taught you how to make and set up your traps, then I taught you the routines of the game you were after, and then we tested the traps against their routines. Those parts are the outside forms of hunting.

"Now I have to teach you the final, and by far the most difficult, part. Perhaps years will pass before you can say that you understand it and that you're a hunter."

Don Juan paused as if to give me time. He took off his hat and imitated the grooming movements of the rodents we had been observing. It was very funny to me. His round head made him look like one of those rodents.

"To be a hunter is not just to trap game," he went on. "A hunter that is worth his salt does not catch game because he sets his traps, or because he knows the routines of his prey, but because he himself has no routines. This is his advantage. He is not at all like the animals he is after, fixed by heavy routines and predictable quirks; he is free, fluid, unpredictable."

What don Juan was saying sounded to me like an arbitrary and irrational idealization. I could not conceive of a life without routines. I wanted to be very honest with him and not just agree or disagree with him. I felt that what he had in mind was not possible to accomplish by me or by anyone.

"I don't care how you feel," he said. "In order to be a hunter you must disrupt the routines of your life. You have done well in hunting. You have learned quickly and now you can see that you are like your prey, easy to predict."

I asked him to be specific and give me concrete examples.

"I am talking about hunting," he said calmly. "Therefore I am concerned with the things animals do; the places they eat; the place, the manner, the time they sleep; where they nest; how they walk. These are the routines I am pointing out to you so you can become aware of them in your own being.

"You have observed the habits of animals in the desert. They eat and drink at certain places, they nest at specific spots, they leave their tracks in specific ways; in fact, everything they do can be foreseen or reconstructed by a good hunter.

"As I told you before, in my eyes you behave like your prey. Once in my life someone pointed out the same thing to me, so you're not unique in that. All of us behave like the prey we are after. That, of course, also makes us prey for something or someone else. Now, the concern of a hunter, who knows all this, is to stop being a prey himself. Do you see what I mean?"

I again expressed the opinion that his proposition was unattainable.

"It takes time," don Juan said. "You could begin by not eating lunch every single day at twelve o'clock."

He looked at me and smiled benevolently. His expression was very funny and made me laugh.

"There are certain animals, however, that are impossible to track," he went on. "There are certain types of deer, for instance, which a fortunate hunter might be able to come across, by sheer luck, once in his lifetime."

Don Juan paused dramatically and looked at me piercingly. He seemed to be waiting for a question, but I did not have any.

"What do you think makes them so difficult to find and so unique?" he asked.

I shrugged my shoulders because I did not know what to say.

"They have no routines," he said in a tone of revelation. "That's what makes them magical."

"A deer has to sleep at night," I said. "Isn't that a routine?"

"Certainly, if the deer sleeps every night at a specific time and in one specific place. But those magical beings do not behave like that. In fact, someday you may verify this for yourself. Perhaps it'll be your fate to chase one of them for the rest of your life."

"What do you mean by that?"

"You like hunting; perhaps someday, in some place in the world, your path may cross the path of a magical being and you might go after it.

"A magical being is a sight to behold. I was fortunate enough to cross paths with one. Our encounter took place after I had learned and practiced a great deal of hunting. Once I was in a forest of thick trees in the mountains of central Mexico when suddenly I heard a sweet whistle. It was unknown to me; never in all my years of roaming in the wilderness had I heard such a sound. I could not place it in the terrain; it seemed to come from different places. I thought that perhaps I was surrounded by a herd or a pack of some unknown animals.

"I heard the tantalizing whistle once more; it seemed to come from everywhere. I realized then my good fortune. I knew it was a magical being, a deer. I also knew that a magical deer is aware of the routines of ordinary men and the routines of hunters.

"It is very easy to figure out what an average man would do in a situation like that. First of all his fear would immediately turn him into a prey. Once he becomes a prey he has two courses of action left. He either flees or he makes his stand. If he is not armed he would ordinarily flee into the open field to run for his life. If he is armed he would get his weapon ready and would then make his stand either by freezing on the spot or by dropping to the ground.

"A hunter, on the other hand, when he stalks in the wilderness would never walk into any place without figuring out his points of protection, therefore he would immediately take cover. He might drop his poncho on the ground or he might hang it from a branch as a decoy and then he would hide and wait until the game makes its next move.

"So, in the presence of the magical deer I didn't behave like either. I quickly stood on my head and began to wail softly; I actually wept tears and sobbed for such a long time that I was about to faint. Suddenly I felt a soft breeze; something was sniffing my hair behind my right ear. I tried to turn my head to see what it was, and I tumbled down and sat up in time to see a radiant creature staring at me. The deer looked at me and I told him I would not harm him. And the deer talked to me."

Don Juan stopped and looked at me. I smiled involuntarily. The idea of a talking deer was quite incredible, to put it mildly.

"He talked to me," don Juan said with a grin.

"The deer talked?"

"He did."

Don Juan stood and picked up his bundle of hunting paraphernalia.

"Did it really talk?" I asked in a tone of perplexity.

Don Juan roared with laughter.

"What did it say?" I asked half in jest.

I thought he was pulling my leg. Don Juan was quiet

for a moment, as if he were trying to remember, then his eyes brightened as he told me what the deer had said.

"The magical deer said, 'Hello friend,'" don Juan went on. "And I answered, 'Hello.' Then he asked me, 'Why are you crying?' and I said, 'Because I'm sad.' Then the magical creature came to my ear and said as clearly as I am speaking now, 'Don't be sad.'"

Don Juan stared into my eyes. He had a glint of sheer mischievousness. He began to laugh uproariously.

I said that his dialogue with the deer had been sort of dumb.

"What did you expect?" he asked, still laughing. "I'm an Indian."

His sense of humor was so outlandish that all I could do was laugh with him.

"You don't believe that a magical deer talks, do you?"

"I'm sorry but I just can't believe things like that can happen," I said.

"I don't blame you," he said reassuringly. "It's one of the darndest things."

9

THE LAST BATTLE ON EARTH

Monday, July 24, 1961

Around mid-afternoon, after we had roamed for hours in the desert, don Juan chose a place to rest in a shaded area. As soon as we sat down he began talking. He said that I had learned a great deal about hunting, but I had not changed as much as he had wished.

"It's not enough to know how to make and set up

traps," he said. "A hunter must live as a hunter in order to draw the most out of his life. Unfortunately, changes are difficult and happen very slowly; sometimes it takes years for a man to become convinced of the need to change. It took me years, but maybe I didn't have a knack for hunting. I think for me the most difficult thing was to really want to change."

I assured him that I understood his point. In fact, since he had begun to teach me how to hunt I also had begun to reassess my actions. Perhaps the most dramatic discovery for me was that I liked don Juan's ways. I liked don Juan as a person. There was something solid about his behavior; the way he conducted himself left no doubts about his mastery, and yet he had never exercised his advantage to demand anything from me. His interest in changing my way of life, I felt, was akin to an impersonal suggestion, or perhaps it was akin to an authoritative commentary on my failures. He had made me very aware of my failings, yet I could not see how his ways would remedy anything in me. I sincerely believed that, in light of what I wanted to do in my life, his ways would have brought me misery and hardship, hence the impasse. However, I had learned to respect his mastery, which had always been expressed in terms of beauty and precision.

"I have decided to shift my tactics," he said.

I asked him to explain; his statement was vague and I was not sure whether or not he was referring to me.

"A good hunter changes his ways as often as he needs," he replied. "You know that yourself."

"What do you have in mind, don Juan?"

"A hunter must not only know about the habits of his prey, he also must know that there are powers on this earth that guide men and animals and everything that is living."

He stopped talking. I waited but he seemed to have come to the end of what he wanted to say.

"What kind of powers are you talking about?" I asked after a long pause.

"Powers that guide our lives and our deaths."

Don Juan stopped talking and seemed to be having tremendous difficulty in deciding what to say. He rubbed his hands and shook his head, puffing out his jaws. Twice he signaled me to be quiet as I started to ask him to explain his cryptic statements.

"You won't be able to stop yourself easily," he finally said. "I know that you're stubborn, but that doesn't matter. The more stubborn you are the better it'll be when you finally succeed in changing yourself."

"I am trying my best," I said.

"No. I disagree. You're not trying your best. You just said that because it sounds good to you; in fact, you've been saying the same thing about everything you do. You've been trying your best for years to no avail. Something must be done to remedy that."

I felt compelled, as usual, to defend myself. Don Juan seemed to aim, as a rule, at my very weakest points. I remembered then that every time I had attempted to defend myself against his criticisms I had ended up feeling like a fool, and I stopped myself in the midst of a long explanatory speech.

Don Juan examined me with curiosity and laughed. He said in a very kind tone that he had already told me that all of us were fools. I was not an exception.

"You always feel compelled to explain your acts, as if you were the only man on earth who's wrong," he said. "It's your old feeling of importance. You have too much of it; you also have too much personal history. On the other hand, you don't assume responsibility for your acts; you're not using your death as an adviser, and above all, you are too accessible. In other words, your life is as messy as it was before I met you."

Again I had a genuine surge of pride and wanted to argue that he was wrong. He gestured to me to be quiet.

"One must assume responsibility for being in a weird world," he said. "We are in a weird world, you know."

I nodded my head affirmatively.

"We're not talking about the same thing," he said. "For you the world is weird because if you're not bored with it you're at odds with it. For me the world is weird because it is stupendous, awesome, mysterious, unfathomable; my interest has been to convince you that you must assume responsibility for being here, in this marvelous world, in this marvelous desert, in this marvelous time. I wanted to convince you that you must learn to make every act count, since you are going to be here for only a short while, in fact, too short for witnessing all the marvels of it."

I insisted that to be bored with the world or to be at odds with it was the human condition.

"So, change it," he replied dryly. "If you do not respond to that challenge you are as good as dead."

He dared me to name an issue, an item in my life that had engaged all my thoughts. I said art. I had always wanted to be an artist and for years I had tried my hand at that. I still had the painful memory of my failure.

"You have never taken the responsibility for being in this unfathomable world," he said in an indicting tone. "Therefore, you were never an artist, and perhaps you'll never be a hunter."

"This is my best, don Juan."

"No. You don't know what your best is."

"I am doing all I can."

"You're wrong again. You can do better. There is one simple thing wrong with you—you think you have plenty of time."

He paused and looked at me as if waiting for my reaction.

"You think you have plenty of time," he repeated.

"Plenty of time for what, don Juan?"

"You think your life is going to last forever."

"No. I don't."

"Then, if you don't think your life is going to last forever, what are you waiting for? Why the hesitation to change?"

"Has it ever occurred to you, don Juan, that I may not want to change?"

"Yes, it has occurred to me. I did not want to change either, just like you. However, I didn't like my life; I was tired of it, just like you. Now I don't have enough of it."

I vehemently asserted that his insistence about changing my way of life was frightening and arbitrary. I said that I really agreed with him. at a certain level, but the mere fact that he was always the master that called the shots made the situation untenable for me.

"You don't have time for this display, you fool," he said in a severe tone. "This, whatever you're doing now, may be your last act on earth. It may very well be your last battle. There is no power which could guarantee that you are going to live one more minute."

"I know that," I said with contained anger.

"No. You don't. If you knew that you would be a hunter."

I contended that I was aware of my impending death but it was useless to talk or think about it, since I could not do anything to avoid it. Don Juan laughed and said I was like a comedian going mechanically through a routine.

"If this were your last battle on earth, I would say that you are an idiot," he said calmly. "You are wasting your last act on earth in some stupid mood."

We were quiet for a moment. My thoughts ran rampant. He was right. of course.

"You have no time, my friend, no time. None of us have time," he said.

"I agree, don Juan, but—"

"Don't just agree with me," he snapped. "You must, instead of agreeing so easily, act upon it. Take the challenge. Change."

"Just like that?"

"That's right. The change I'm talking about never takes place by degrees: it happens suddenly. And you are not preparing yourself for that sudden act that will bring a total change."

I believed he was expressing a contradiction. I explained to him that if I were preparing myself to change I was certainly changing by degrees.

"You haven't changed at all," he said. "That is why

you believe you're changing little by little. Yet, perhaps you will surprise yourself someday by changing suddenly and without a single warning. I know this is so, and thus I don't lose sight of my interest in convincing you."

I could not persist in my arguing. I was not sure of what I really wanted to say. After a moment's pause don Juan went on explaining his point.

"Perhaps I should put it in a different way," he said. "What I recommend you to do is to notice that we do not have any assurance that our lives will go on indefinitely. I have just said that change comes suddenly and unexpectedly, and so does death. What do you think we can do about it?"

I thought he was asking a rhetorical question, but he made a gesture with his eyebrows urging me to answer.

"To live as happily as possible," I said.

"Right! But do you know anyone who lives happily?"

My first impulse was to say yes; I thought I could use a number of people I knew as examples. On second thought, however, I knew my effort would only be an empty attempt at exonerating myself.

"No," I said. "I really don't."

"I do," don Juan said. "There are some people who are very careful about the nature of their acts. Their happiness is to act with the full knowledge that they don't have time; therefore, their acts have a peculiar power; their acts have a sense of . . ."

Don Juan seemed to be at a loss for words. He scratched his temples and smiled. Then suddenly he stood up as if he were through with our conversation. I beseeched him to finish what he was telling me. He sat down and puckered up his lips.

"Acts have power," he said. "Especially when the person acting knows that those acts are his last battle. There is a strange consuming happiness in acting with the full knowledge that whatever one is doing may very well be one's last act on earth. I recommend that you reconsider your life and bring your acts into that light."

I disagreed with him. Happiness for me was to assume that there was an inherent continuity to my acts and that

I would be able to continue doing, at will, whatever I was doing at the moment, especially if I was enjoying it. I told him that my disagreement was not a banal one but stemmed from the conviction that the world and myself had a determinable continuity.

Don Juan seemed to be amused by my efforts to make sense. He laughed, shook his head, scratched his hair, and finally when I talked about a "determinable continuity" threw his hat to the ground and stomped on it.

I ended up laughing at his clowning.

"You don't have time, my friend," he said. "That is the misfortune of human beings. None of us have sufficient time, and your continuity has no meaning in this awesome, mysterious world.

"Your continuity only makes you timid," he said. "Your acts cannot possibly have the flair, the power, the compelling force of the acts performed by a man who knows that he is fighting his last battle on earth. In other words, your continuity does not make you happy or powerful."

I admitted that I was afraid of thinking I was going to die and accused him of causing great apprehension in me with his constant talk and concern about death.

"But we are all going to die," he said.

He pointed towards some hills in the distance.

"There is something out there waiting for me, for sure; and I will join it, also for sure. But perhaps you're different and death is not waiting for you at all."

He laughed at my gesture of despair.

"I don't want to think about it, don Juan."

"Why not?"

"It is meaningless. If it is out there waiting for me why should I worry about it?"

"I didn't say that you have to worry about it."

"What am I supposed to do then?"

"Use it. Focus your attention on the link between you and your death, without remorse or sadness or worrying. Focus your attention on the fact you don't have time and let your acts flow accordingly. Let each of your acts be your last battle on earth. Only under those conditions will your acts have their rightful power. Otherwise they will be, for as long as you live, the acts of a timid man."

"Is it so terrible to be a timid man?"

"No. It isn't if you are going to be immortal, but if you are going to die there is no time for timidity, simply because timidity makes you cling to something that exists only in your thoughts. It soothes you while everything is at a lull, but then the awesome, mysterious world will open its mouth for you, as it will open for every one of us, and then you will realize that your sure ways were not sure at all. Being timid prevents us from examining and exploiting our lot as men."

"It is not natural to live with the constant idea of our death, don Juan."

"Our death is waiting and this very act we're performing now may well be our last battle on earth," he replied in a solemn voice. "I call it a battle because it is a struggle. Most people move from act to act without any struggle or thought. A hunter, on the contrary, assesses every act; and since he has an intimate knowledge of his death, he proceeds judiciously, as if every act were his last battle. Only a fool would fail to notice the advantage a hunter has over his fellow men. A hunter gives his last battle its due respect. It's only natural that his last act on earth should be the best of himself. It's pleasurable that way. It dulls the edge of his fright."

"You are right," I conceded. "It's just hard to accept."

"It'll take years for you to convince yourself and then it'll take years for you to act accordingly. I only hope you have time left."

"I get scared when you say that," I said.

Don Juan examined me with a serious expression on his face.

"I've told you, this is a weird world," he said. "The forces that guide men are unpredictable, awesome, yet their splendor is something to witness."

He stopped talking and looked at me again. He seemed to be on the verge of revealing something to me, but he checked himself and smiled.

"Is there something that guides us?" I asked.

"Certainly. There are powers that guide us."

"Can you describe them?"

"Not really, except to call them forces, spirits, airs, winds, or anything like that."

I wanted to probe him further, but before I could ask anything else he stood up. I stared at him, flabbergasted. He had stood up in one single movement; his body simply jerked up and he was on his feet.

I was still pondering upon the unusual skill that would be needed in order to move with such speed when he told me in a dry tone of command to stalk a rabbit, catch it, kill it, skin it, and roast the meat before the twilight.

He looked up at the sky and said that I might have enough time.

I automatically started off, proceeding the way I had done scores of times. Don Juan walked beside me and followed my movements with a scrutinizing look. I was very calm and moved carefully and I had no trouble at all in catching a male rabbit.

"Now kill it," don Juan said dryly.

I reached into the trap to grab hold of the rabbit. I had it by the ears and was pulling it out when a sudden sensation of terror invaded me. For the first time since don Juan had begun to teach me to hunt it occurred to me that he had never taught me how to kill game. In the scores of times we had roamed in the desert he himself had only killed one rabbit, two quail and one rattlesnake.

I dropped the rabbit and looked at don Juan.

"I can't kill it," I said.

"Why not?"

"I've never done that."

"But you've killed hundreds of birds and other animals."

"With a gun, not with my bare hands."

"What difference does it make? This rabbit's time is up."

Don Juan's tone shocked me; it was so authoritative, so knowledgeable, it left no doubts in my mind that he knew that the rabbit's time was up.

"Kill it!" he commanded with a ferocious look in his eyes.

"I can't."

He yelled at me that the rabbit had to die. He said that its roaming in that beautiful desert had come to an end. I had no business stalling, because the power or the spirit that guides rabbits had led that particular one into my trap, right at the edge of the twilight.

A series of confusing thoughts and feelings overtook me, as if the feelings had been out there waiting for me. I felt with agonizing clarity the rabbit's tragedy, to have fallen into my trap. In a matter of seconds my mind swept across the most crucial moments of my own life, the many times I had been the rabbit myself.

I looked at it, and it looked at me. The rabbit had backed up against the side of the cage; it was almost curled up, very quiet and motionless. We exchanged a somber glance, and that glance, which I fancied to be of silent despair, cemented a complete identification on my part.

"The hell with it," I said loudly. "I won't kill anything. That rabbit goes free."

A profound emotion made me shiver. My arms trembled as I tried to grab the rabbit by the ears; it moved fast and I missed. I again tried and fumbled once more. I became desperate. I had the sensation of nausea and quickly kicked the trap in order to smash it and let the rabbit go free. The cage was unsuspectedly strong and did not break as I thought it would. My despair mounted to an unbearable feeling of anguish. Using all my strength, I stomped on the edge of the cage with my right foot. The sticks cracked loudly. I pulled the rabbit out. I had a moment of relief, which was shattered to bits in the next instant. The rabbit hung limp in my hand. It was dead.

I did not know what to do. I became preoccupied with finding out how it had died. I turned to don Juan. He was staring at me. A feeling of terror sent a chill through my body.

I sat down by some rocks. I had a terrible headache. Don Juan put his hand on my head and whispered in my

ear that I had to skin the rabbit and roast it before the
twilight was over.

I felt nauseated. He very patiently talked to me as if he
were talking to a child. He said that the powers that
guided men or animals had led that particular rabbit to
me, in the same way they will lead me to my own death.
He said the rabbit's death had been a gift for me in exactly the same way my own death will be a gift for something or someone else.

I was dizzy. The simple events of that day had crushed
me. I tried to think that it was only a rabbit; I could
not, however, shake off the uncanny identification I had
had with it.

Don Juan said that I needed to eat some of its meat, if
only a morsel, in order to validate my finding.

"I can't do that," I protested meekly.

"We are dregs in the hands of those forces," he snapped
at me. "So stop your self-importance and use this gift
properly."

I picked up the rabbit; it was warm.

Don Juan leaned over and whispered in my ear, "Your
trap was his last battle on earth. I told you, he had no
more time to roam in this marvelous desert."

10

BECOMING ACCESSIBLE TO POWER

Thursday, August 17, 1961

As soon as I got out of my car I complained to don Juan
that I was not feeling well.

"Sit down, sit down," he said softly and almost led me

by the hand to his porch. He smiled and patted me on the back.

Two weeks before, on August 4th, don Juan, as he had said, changed his tactics with me and allowed me to ingest some peyote buttons. During the height of my hallucinatory experience I played with a dog that lived in the house where the peyote session took place. Don Juan interpreted my interaction with the dog as a very special event. He contended that at moments of power, such as the one I had been living then, the world of ordinary affairs did not exist and nothing could be taken for granted, that the dog was not really a dog but the incarnation of Mescalito, the power of deity contained in peyote.

The post-effects of that experience were a general sense of fatigue and melancholy, plus the incidence of exceptionally vivid dreams and nightmares.

"Where's your writing gear?" don Juan asked as I sat down on the porch.

I had left my notebooks in my car. Don Juan walked back to the car and carefully pulled out my briefcase and brought it to my side.

He asked if I usually carried my briefcase when I walked. I said I did.

"That's madness," he said. "I've told you never to carry anything in your hands when you walk. Get a knapsack."

I laughed. The idea of carrying my notes in a knapsack was ludicrous. I told him that ordinarily I wore a suit and a knapsack over a three-piece suit would be a preposterous sight.

"Put your coat on over the knapsack," he said. "It is better that people think you're a hunchback than to ruin your body carrying all this around."

He urged me to get out my notebook and write. He seemed to be making a deliberate effort to put me at ease.

I complained again about the feeling of physical discomfort and the strange sense of unhappiness I was experiencing.

Don Juan laughed and said, "You're beginning to learn."

We then had a long conversation. He said that Mescalito, by allowing me to play with him, had pointed me
out as a "chosen man" and that, although he was baffled
by the omen because I was not an Indian, he was going
to pass on to me some secret knowledge. He said that he
had had a "benefactor" himself, who taught him how to
become a "man of knowledge."

I sensed that something dreadful was about to happen.
The revelation that I was his chosen man, plus the un-
questionable strangeness of his ways and the devastating
effect that peyote had had on me, created a state of unbearable apprehension and indecision. But don Juan dis-
regarded my feelings and recommended that I should only
think of the wonder of Mescalito playing with me.

"Think about nothing else," he said. "The rest will
come to you of itself."

He stood up and patted me gently on the head and
said in a very soft voice, "I am going to teach you how
to become a warrior in the same manner I have taught
you how to hunt. I must warn you, though, learning how
to hunt has not made you into a hunter, nor would learning how to become a warrior make you one."

I experienced a sense of frustration, a physical discomfort that bordered on anguish. I complained about the vivid dreams and nightmares I was having. He seemed to deliberate for a moment and sat down again.

"They're weird dreams," I said.

"You've always had weird dreams," he retorted.

"I'm telling you, this time they are truly more weird
than anything I've ever had."

"Don't concern yourself. They are only dreams. Like
the dreams of any ordinary dreamer, they don't have power. So what's the use of worrying about them or talking
about them?"

"They bother me, don Juan. Isn't there something I
can do to stop them?"

"Nothing. Let them pass," he said. "Now it's time for
you to become accessible to power, and you are going to
begin by tackling *dreaming*."

The tone of voice he used when he said "dreaming"

made me think that he was using the word in a very particular fashion. I was pondering about a proper question to ask when he began to talk again.

"I've never told you about *dreaming,* because until now I was only concerned with teaching you how to be a hunter," he said. "A hunter is not concerned with the manipulation of power, therefore his dreams are only dreams. They might be poignant but they are not *dreaming.*

"A warrior, on the other hand, seeks power, and one of the avenues to power is *dreaming.* You may say that the difference between a hunter and a warrior is that a warrior is on his way to power, while a hunter knows nothing or very little about it.

"The decision as to who can be a warrior and who can only be a hunter is not up to us. That decision is in the realm of the powers that guide men. That's why your playing with Mescalito was such an important omen. Those forces guided you to me; they took you to that bus depot, remember? Some clown brought you to me. A perfect omen, a clown pointing you out. So, I taught you how to be a hunter. And then the other perfect omen, Mescalito himself playing with you. See what I mean?"

His weird logic was overwhelming. His words created visions of myself succumbing to something awesome and unknown, something which I had not bargained for, and which I had not conceived existed, even in my wildest fantasies.

"What do you propose I should do?" I asked.

"Become accessible to power; tackle your dreams," he replied. "You call them dreams because you have no power. A warrior, being a man who seeks power, doesn't call them dreams, he calls them real."

"You mean he takes his dreams as being reality?"

"He doesn't take anything as being anything else. What you call dreams are real for a warrior. You must understand that a warrior is not a fool. A warrior is an immaculate hunter who hunts power; he's not drunk, or crazed, and he has neither the time nor the disposition to bluff, or to lie to himself, or to make a wrong move. The stakes are too high for that. The stakes are his trimmed orderly life which he has taken so long to tighten and perfect. He is not going to throw that away by making some stupid miscalculation, by taking something for being something else.

"*Dreaming* is real for a warrior because in it he can act deliberately, he can choose and reject, he can select from a variety of items those which lead to power, and then he can manipulate them and use them, while in an ordinary dream he cannot act deliberately."

"Do you mean then, don Juan, that *dreaming* is real?"

"Of course it is real."

"As real as what we are doing now?"

"If you want to compare things, I can say that it is perhaps more real. In *dreaming* you have power; you can change things; you may find out countless concealed facts; you can control whatever you want."

Don Juan's premises always had appealed to me at a certain level. I could easily understand his liking the idea that one could do anything in dreams, but I could not take him seriously. The jump was too great.

We looked at each other for a moment. His statements were insane and yet he was, to the best of my knowledge, one of the most level-headed men I had ever met.

I told him that I could not believe he took his dreams to be reality. He chuckled as if he knew the magnitude of my untenable position, then he stood up without saying a word and walked inside his house.

I sat for a long time in a state of stupor until he called me to the back of his house. He had made some corn gruel and handed me a bowl.

I asked him about the time when one was awake. I wanted to know if he called it anything in particular. But he did not understand or did not want to answer.

"What do you call this, what we're doing now?" I asked, meaning that what we were doing was reality as opposed to dreams.

"I call it eating," he said and contained his laughter.

"I call it reality," I said. "Because our eating is actually taking place."

"*Dreaming* also takes place," he replied, giggling. "And so does hunting, walking, laughing."

I did not persist in arguing. I could not, however, even if I stretched myself beyond my limits, accept his premise. He seemed to be delighted with my despair.

As soon as we had finished eating he casually stated that we were going to go for a hike, but we were not going to roam in the desert in the manner we had done before.

"It's different this time," he said. "From now on we're going to places of power; you're going to learn how to make yourself accessible to power."

I again expressed my turmoil. I said I was not qualified for that endeavor.

"Come on, you're indulging in silly fears," he said in a low voice, patting me on the back and smiling benevolently. "I've been catering to your hunter's spirit. You like to roam with me in this beautiful desert. It's too late for you to quit."

He began to walk into the desert chaparral. He signaled me with his head to follow him. I could have walked to my car and left, except that I liked to roam in that beautiful desert with him. I liked the sensation, which I experienced only in his company, that this was indeed an awesome, mysterious, yet beautiful world. As he said, I was hooked.

Don Juan led me to the hills towards the east. It was a long hike. It was a hot day; the heat, however, which ordinarily would have been unbearable to me, was somehow unnoticeable.

We walked for quite a distance into a canyon until don Juan came to a halt and sat down in the shade of some boulders. I took some crackers out of my knapsack but he told me not to bother with them.

He said that I should sit in a prominent place. He pointed to a single almost round boulder ten or fifteen feet away and helped me climb to the top. I thought he was also going to sit there, but instead he just climbed part of the way in order to hand me some pieces of dry meat. He told me with a deadly serious expression that it was power meat and should be chewed very slowly and should not be mixed with any other food. He then walked back to the shaded area and sat down with his back against a rock. He seemed relaxed, almost sleepy. He remained in the same position until I had finished eating. Then he sat up straight and tilted his head to the right. He seemed to be listening attentively. He glanced at me two or three times, stood up abruptly, and began to scan the surroundings with his eyes, the way a hunter would do. I automatically froze on the spot and only moved my eyes in order to follow his movements. Very carefully he stepped behind some rocks, as if he were expecting game to come into the area where we were. I realized then that we were in a round covelike bend in the dry water canyon, surrounded by sandstone boulders.

Don Juan suddenly came out from behind the rocks and smiled at me. He stretched his arms, yawned, and walked towards the boulder where I was. I relaxed my tense position and sat down.

"What happened?" I asked in a whisper.

He answered me, yelling, that there was nothing around there to worry about.

I felt an immediate jolt in my stomach. His answer was inappropriate and it was inconceivable to me that he would yell, unless he had a specific reason for it.

I began to slide down from the boulder, but he yelled that I should stay there a while longer.

"What are you doing?" I asked.

He sat down and concealed himself between two rocks at the base of the boulder where I was, and then he said in a very loud voice that he had only been looking around because he thought he had heard something.

I asked if he had heard a large animal. He put his hand to his ear and yelled that he was unable to hear me and that I should shout my words. I felt ill at ease yelling, but he urged me in a loud voice to speak up. I shouted that I wanted to know what was going on, and he shouted back that there was really nothing around there. He yelled, asking if I could see anything unusual from

the top of the boulder. I said no, and he asked me to describe to him the terrain towards the south.

We shouted back and forth for a while and then he
signaled me to come down. I joined him and he whispered in my ear that the yelling was necessary to make
our presence known, because I had to make myself accessible to the power of that specific water hole.

I looked around but could not see the water hole. He
pointed that we were standing on it.

"There's water here," he said in a whisper, "and also
power. There's a spirit here and we have to lure it out;
perhaps it will come after you."

I wanted to know more about the alleged spirit, but he
insisted on total silence. He advised me to stay perfectly
still and not let out a whisper or make the slightest
movement to betray our presence.

Apparently it was easy for him to remain in complete
immobility for hours; for me, however, it was sheer tor-
ture. My legs fell asleep, my back ached, and tension
built up around my neck and shoulders. My entire body
became numb and cold. I was in great discomfort when
don Juan finally stood up. He just sprung to his feet and
extended his hand to me to help me stand up.

As I was trying to stretch my legs I realized the inconceivable easiness with which don Juan had jumped
up after hours of immobility. It took quite some time for
my muscles to regain the elasticity needed for walking.

Don Juan headed back for the house. He walked extremely slowly. He set up a length of three paces as the
distance I should observe in following him. He meandered around the regular route and crossed it four or
five times in different directions; when we finally arrived
at his house it was late afternoon.

I tried to question him about the events of the day.
He explained that talking was unnecessary. For the time
being, I had to refrain from asking questions until we
were in a place of power.

I was dying to know what he meant by that and tried
to whisper a question, but he reminded me, with a cold
severe look, that he meant business.

We sat on the porch for hours. I worked on my notes. From time to time he handed me a piece of dry meat; finally it was too dark to write. I tried to think about the new developments, but some part of myself refused to and I fell asleep.

Saturday, August 19, 1961

Yesterday morning don Juan and I drove to town and ate breakfast at a restaurant. He advised me not to change my eating habits too drastically.

"Your body is not used to power meat," he said. "You'd get sick if you didn't eat your food."

He himself ate heartily. When I joked about it he simply said, "My body likes everything."

Around noon we hiked back to the water canyon. We proceeded to make ourselves noticeable to the spirit by "noisy talk" and by a forced silence which lasted hours.

When we left the place, instead of heading back to the house, don Juan took off in the direction of the mountains. We reached some mild slopes first and then we climbed to the top of some high hills. There, don Juan picked out a spot to rest in the open unshaded area. He told me that we had to wait until dusk and that I should conduct myself in the most natural fashion, which included asking all the questions I wanted.

"I know that the spirit is out there lurking," he said in a very low voice.

"Where?"

"Out there, in the bushes."

"What kind of spirit is it?"

He looked at me with a quizzical expression and retorted. "How many kinds are there?"

We both laughed. I was asking questions out of nervousness.

"It'll come out at dusk," he said. "We just have to wait."

I remained quiet. I had run out of questions.

"This is the time when we must keep on talking," he

said. "The human voice attracts spirits. There's one lurking out there now. We are making ourselves available to it, so keep on talking."

I experienced an idiotic sense of vacuity. I could not think of anything to say. He laughed and patted me on the back.

"You're truly a pill," he said. "When you have to talk, you lose your tongue. Come on, beat your gums."

He made a hilarious gesture of beating his gums together, opening and closing his mouth with great speed.

"There are certain things we will talk about from now on only at places of power," he went on. "I have brought you here, because this is your first trial. This is a place of power, and here we can talk only about power."

"I really don't know what power is," I said.

"Power is something a warrior deals with," he said. "At first it's an incredible, far-fetched affair; it is hard to even think about it. This is what's happening to you know. Then power becomes a serious matter; one may not have it, or one may not even fully realize that it exists, yet one knows that something is there, something which was not noticeable before. Next power is manifested as something uncontrollable that comes to oneself. It is not possible for me to say how it comes or what it really is. It is nothing and yet it makes marvels appear before your very eyes. And finally power is something in oneself, something that controls one's acts and yet obeys one's command."

There was a short pause. Don Juan asked me if I had understood. I felt ludicrous saying I did. He seemed to have noticed my dismay and chuckled.

"I am going to teach you right here the first step to power," he said as if he were dictating a letter to me. "I am going to teach you how to *set up dreaming*."

He looked at me and again asked me if I knew what he meant. I did not. I was hardly following him at all. He explained that to "set up dreaming" meant to have a concise and pragmatic control over the general situation of a dream, comparable to the control one has over any

choice in the desert, such as climbing up a hill or remaining in the shade of a water canyon.

"You must start by doing something very simple," he
said. "Tonight in your dreams you must look at your
hands."

I laughed out loud. His tone was so factual that it was
as if he were telling me to do something commonplace.

"Why do you laugh?" he asked with surprise.

"How can I look at my hands in my dreams?"

"Very simple, focus your eyes on them just like this."

He bent his head forward and stared at his hands with
his mouth open. His gesture was so comical that I had
to laugh.

"Seriously, how can you expect me to do that?" I asked.

"The way I've told you," he snapped. "You can, of
course, look at whatever you goddamn please—your
toes, or your belly, or your pecker, for that matter. I said
your hands because that was the easiest thing for me to
look at. Don't think it's a joke. *Dreaming* is as serious
as *seeing* or dying or any other thing in this awesome,
mysterious world.

"Think of it as something entertaining. Imagine all the
inconceivable things you could accomplish. A man hunting for power has almost no limits in his *dreaming*."

I asked him to give me some pointers.

"There aren't any pointers," he said. "Just look at
your hands."

"There must be more that you could tell me," I insisted.

He shook his head and squinted his eyes, staring at me
in short glances.

"Every one of us is different," he finally said. "What
you call pointers would only be what I myself did when I
was learning. We are not the same; we aren't even
vaguely alike."

"Maybe anything you'd say would help me."

"It would be simpler for you just to start looking at
your hands."

He seemed to be organizing his thoughts and bobbed
his head up and down.

"Every time you look at anything in your dreams it changes shape," he said after a long silence. "The trick in learning to *set up dreaming* is obviously not just to look at things but to sustain the sight of them. *Dreaming* is real when one has succeeded in bringing everything into focus. Then there is no difference between what you do when you sleep and what you do when you are not sleeping. Do you see what I mean?"

I confessed that although I understood what he had said I was incapable of accepting his premise. I brought up the point that in a civilized world there were scores of people who had delusions and could not distinguish what took place in the real world from what took place in their fantasies. I said that such persons were undoubtedly mentally ill, and my uneasiness increased every time he would recommend I should act like a crazy man.

After my long explanation don Juan made a comical gesture of despair by putting his hands to his cheeks and sighing loudly.

"Leave your civilized world alone," he said. "Let it be! Nobody is asking you to behave like a madman. I've already told you, a warrior has to be perfect in order to deal with the powers he hunts; how can you conceive that a warrior would not be able to tell things apart?

"On the other hand, you, my friend, who know what the real world is, would fumble and die in no time at all if you would have to depend on your ability for telling what is real and what is not."

I obviously had not expressed what I really had in mind. Every time I protested I was simply voicing the unbearable frustration of being in an untenable position.

"I am not trying to make you into a sick, crazy man," don Juan went on. "You can do that yourself without my help. But the forces that guide us brought you to me, and I have been endeavoring to teach you to change your stupid ways and live the strong clean life of a hunter. Then the forces guided you again and told me that you should learn to live the impeccable life of a warrior. Apparently you can't. But who can tell? We are as mysterious and as awesome as this unfathomable world, so who can tell what you're capable of?"

There was an underlying tone of sadness in don Juan's voice. I wanted to apologize, but he began to talk again.

"You don't have to look at your hands," he said. "Like I've said, pick anything at all. But pick one thing in advance and find it in your dreams. I said your hands because they'll always be there.

"When they begin to change shape you must move your sight away from them and pick something else, and then look at your hands again. It takes a long time to perfect this technique."

I had become so involved in writing that I had not noticed that it was getting dark. The sun had already disappeared over the horizon. The sky was cloudy and the twilight was imminent. Don Juan stood up and gave furtive glances towards the south.

"Let's go," he said. "We must walk south until the spirit of the water hole shows itself."

We walked for perhaps half an hour. The terrain changed abruptly and we came to a barren area. There was a large round hill where the chaparral had burnt. It looked like a bald head. We walked towards it. I thought that don Juan was going to climb the mild slope, but he stopped instead and remained in a very attentive position. His body seemed to have tensed as a single unit and shivered for an instant. Then he relaxed again and stood limply. I could not figure out how his body could remain erect while his muscles were so relaxed.

At that moment a very strong gust of wind jolted me. Don Juan's body turned in the direction of the wind, towards the west. He did not use his muscles to turn, or at least he did not use them the way I would use mine to turn. Don Juan's body seemed rather to have been pulled from the outside. It was as if someone else had arranged his body to face a new direction.

I kept on staring at him. He looked at me from the corner of his eye. The expression on his face was one of determination, purpose. All of his being was attentive, and I stared at him in wonder. I had never been in any situation that called for such a strange concentration.

Suddenly his body shivered as though he had been splashed by a sudden shower of cold water. He had another jolt and then he started to walk as if nothing had happened.

I followed him. We flanked the naked hills on the east side until we were at the middle part of it; he stopped there, turning to face the west.

From where we stood, the top of the hill was not so round and smooth as it had seemed to be from the distance. There was a cave, or a hole, near the top. I looked at it fixedly because don Juan was doing the same. Another strong gust of wind sent a chill up my spine. Don Juan turned towards the south and scanned the area with his eyes.

"There!" he said in a whisper and pointed to an object on the ground.

I strained my eyes to see. There was something on the ground, perhaps twenty feet away. It was light brown and as I looked at it, it shivered. I focused all my attention on it. The object was almost round and seemed to be curled; in fact, it looked like a curled-up dog.

"What is it?" I whispered to don Juan.

"I don't know," he whispered back as he peered at the object. "What does it look like to you?"

I told him that it seemed to be a dog.

"To large for a dog," he said matter-of-factly.

I took a couple of steps towards it, but don Juan stopped me gently. I stared at it again. It was definitely some animal that was either asleep or dead. I could almost see its head; its ears protruded like the ears of a wolf. By then I was definitely sure that it was a curled-up animal. I thought that it could have been a brown calf. I whispered that to don Juan. He answered that it was too compact to be a calf, besides its ears were pointed.

The animal shivered again and then I noticed that it was alive. I could actually see that it was breathing, yet it did not seem to breathe rhythmically. The breaths that it took were more like irregular shivers. I had a sudden realization at that moment.

"It's an animal that is dying," I whispered to don Juan.

"You're right," he whispered back. "But what kind of an animal?"

I could not make out its specific features. Don Juan took a couple of cautious steps towards it. I followed him. It was quite dark by then and we had to take two more steps in order to keep the animal in view.

"Watch out," don Juan whispered in my ear. "If it is a dying animal it may leap on us with its last strength."

The animal, whatever it was, seemed to be on its last legs; its breathing was irregular, its body shook spasmodically, but it did not change its curled-up position. At a given moment, however, a tremendous spasm actually lifted the animal off the ground. I heard an inhuman shriek and the animal stretched its legs; its claws were more than frightening, they were nauseating. The animal tumbled on its side after stretching its legs and then rolled on its back.

I heard a formidable growl and don Juan's voice shouting, "Run for your life!"

And that was exactly what I did. I scrambled towards the top of the hill with unbelievable speed and agility. When I was halfway to the top I looked back and saw don Juan standing in the same place. He signaled me to come down. I ran down the hill.

"What happened?" I asked, completely out of breath.

"I think the animal is dead," he said.

We advanced cautiously towards the animal. It was sprawled on its back. As I came closer to it I nearly yelled with fright. I realized that it was not quite dead yet. Its body was still trembling. Its legs, which were sticking up in the air, shook wildly. The animal was definitely in its last gasps.

I walked in front of don Juan. A new jolt moved the animal's body and I could see its head. I turned to don Juan, horrified. Judging by its body the animal was obviously a mammal, yet it had a beak, like a bird.

I stared at it in complete and absolute horror. My

mind refused to believe it. I was dumbfounded. I could not even articulate a word. Never in my whole existence had I witnessed anything of that nature. Something inconceivable was there in front of my very eyes. I wanted don Juan to explain that incredible animal but I could only mumble to him. He was staring at me. I glanced at him and glanced at the animal, and then something in me arranged the world and I knew at once what the animal was. I walked over to it and picked it up. It was a large branch of a bush. It had been burnt, and possibly the wind had blown some burnt debris which got caught in the dry branch and thus gave the appearance of a large bulging round animal. The color of the burnt debris made it look light brown in contrast with the green vegetation.

I laughed at my idiocy and excitedly explained to don Juan that the wind blowing through it had made it look like a live animal. I thought he would be pleased with the way I had resolved the mystery, but he turned around and began walking to the top of the hill. I followed him. He crawled inside the depression that looked like a cave. It was not a hole but a shallow dent in the sandstone.

Don Juan took some small branches and used them to scoop up the dirt that had accumulated in the bottom of the depression.

"We have to get rid of the ticks," he said.

He signaled me to sit down and told me to make myself comfortable because we were going to spend the night there.

I began to talk about the branch, but he hushed me up.

"What you've done is no triumph," he said. "You've wasted a beautiful power, a power that blew life into that dry twig."

He said that a real triumph would have been for me to let go and follow the power until the world had ceased to exist. He did not seem to be angry with me or disappointed with my performance. He repeatedly stated that this was only the beginning, that it took time to handle power. He patted me on the shoulder and joked that earlier that day I was the person who knew what was real and what was not.

I felt embarrassed. I began to apologize for my tendency of always being so sure of my ways.

"It doesn't matter," he said. "That branch was a real animal and it was alive at the moment the power touched it. Since what kept it alive was power, the trick was, like in *dreaming,* to sustain the sight of it. See what I mean?"

I wanted to ask something else, but he hushed me up and said that I should remain completely silent but awake all night and that he alone was going to talk for a while.

He said that the spirit, which knew his voice, might become subdued with the sound of it and leave us alone. He explained that the idea of making oneself accessible to power had serious overtones. Power was a devastating force that could easily lead to one's death and had to be treated with great care. Becoming available to power had to be done systematically, but always with great caution.

It involved making one's presence obvious by a contained display of loud talk or any other type of noisy activity, and then it was mandatory to observe a prolonged and total silence. A controlled outburst and a controlled quietness were the mark of a warrior. He said that properly I should have sustained the sight of the live monster for a while longer. In a controlled fashion, without losing my mind or becoming deranged with excitation or fear, I should have striven to "stop the world." He pointed out that after I had run up the hill for dear life I was in a perfect state for "stopping the world." Combined in that state were fear, awe, power and death; he said that such a state would be pretty hard to repeat.

I whispered in his ear, "What do you mean by 'stopping the world'?"

He gave me a ferocious look before he answered that it was a technique practiced by those who were hunting for power, a technique by virtue of which the world as we know it was made to collapse.

11

THE MOOD OF A WARRIOR

I drove up to don Juan's house on Thursday, August 31, 1961, and before I even had a chance to greet him he stuck his head through the window of my car, smiled at me, and said, "We must drive quite a distance to a place of power and it's almost noon."

He opened the door of my car, sat down next to me in the front seat, and directed me to drive south for about seventy miles; we then turned east onto a dirt road and followed it until we had reached the slopes of the mountains. I parked my car off the road in a depression don Juan picked because it was deep enough to hide the car from view. From there we went directly to the top of the low hills, crossing a vast flat desolate area.

When it got dark don Juan selected a place to sleep. He demanded complete silence.

The next day we ate frugally annd continued our journey in an easterly direction. The vegetation was no longer desert shrubbery but thick green mountain bushes and trees.

Around mid-afternoon we climbed to the top of a gigantic bluff of conglomerate rock which looked like a wall. Don Juan sat down and signaled me to sit down also.

"This is a place of power," he said after a moment's pause. "This is the place where warriors were buried a long time ago."

At that instant a crow flew right above us, cawing. Don Juan followed its flight with a fixed gaze.

I examined the rock and was wondering how and where the warriors had been buried when he tapped me on the shoulder.

"Not here, you fool," he said, smiling. "Down there."

He pointed to the field right below us at the bottom of the bluff, towards the east; he explained that the field in question was surrounded by a natural corral of boulders. From where I was sitting I saw an area which was perhaps a hundred yards in diameter and which looked like a perfect circle. Thick bushes covered its surface, camouflaging the boulders. I would not have noticed its perfect roundness if don Juan had not pointed it out to me.

He said that there were scores of such places scattered in the old world of the Indians. They were not exactly places of power, like certain hills or land formations which were the abode of spirits, but rather places of enlightenment where one could be taught, where one could find solutions to dilemmas.

"All you have to do is come here," he said. "Or spend the night on this rock in order to rearrange your feelings."

"Are we going to spend the night here?"

"I thought so, but a little crow just told me not to do that."

I tried to find out more about the crow but he hushed me up with an impatient movement of his hand.

"Look at that circle of boulders," he said. "Fix it in your memory and then someday a crow will lead you to another one of these places. The more perfect its roundness is, the greater its power."

"Are the warriors' bones still buried here?"

Don Juan made a comical gesture of puzzlement and then smiled broadly.

"This is not a cemetery," he said. "Nobody is buried here. I said warriors were once buried here. I meant they used to come here to bury themselves for a night, or for two days, or for whatever length of time they needed to. I did not mean dead people's bones are buried here. I'm not concerned with cemeteries. There is no power in them. There is power in the bones of a warrior, though, but they are never in cemeteries. And there is even more power in the bones of a man of knowledge, yet it would be practically impossible to find them."

"Who is a man of knowledge, don Juan?"

"Any warrior could become a man of knowledge. As I told you, a warrior is an impeccable hunter that hunts power. If he succeeds in his hunting he can be a man of knowledge."

"What do you . . ."

He stopped my question with a movement of his hand. He stood up, signaled me to follow, and began descending on the steep east side of the bluff. There was a definite trail in the almost perpendicular face, leading to the round area.

We slowly worked our way down the perilous path, and when we reached the bottom floor don Juan, without stopping at all, led me through the thick chaparral to the middle of the circle. There he used some thick dry branches to sweep a clean spot for us to sit. The spot was also perfectly round.

"I intended to bury you here all night," he said. "But I know now that it is not time yet. You don't have power. I'm going to bury you only for a short while."

I became very nervous with the idea of being enclosed and asked how he was planning to bury me. He giggled like a child and began collecting dry branches. He did not let me help him and said I should sit down and wait.

He threw the branches he was collecting inside the clean circle. Then he made me lie down with my head towards the east, put my jacket under my head, and made a cage around my body. He constructed it by sticking pieces of branches about two and a half feet in length in the soft dirt; the branches, which ended in forks, served as supports for some long sticks that gave the cage a frame and the appearance of an open coffin. He closed the box-like cage by placing small branches and leaves over the long sticks, encasing me from the shoulders down. He let my head stick out with my jacket as a pillow.

He then took a thick piece of dry wood and, using it as a digging stick, he loosened the dirt around me and covered the cage with it.

The frame was so solid and the leaves were so well placed that no dirt came inside. I could move my legs freely and could actually slide in and out.

Don Juan said that ordinarily a warrior would construct the cage and then slip into it and seal it from the inside.

"How about the animals?" I asked. "Can they scratch the surface dirt and sneak into the cage and hurt the man?"

"No, that's not a worry for a warrior. It's a worry for you because you have no power. A warrior, on the other hand, is guided by his unbending purpose and can fend off anything. No rat, or snake, or mountain lion could bother him."

"What do they bury themselves for, don Juan?"

"For enlightenment and for power."

I experienced an extremely pleasant feeling of peace and satisfaction; the world at that moment seemed at ease. The quietness was exquisite and at the same time unnerving. I was not accustomed to that kind of silence. I tried to talk but he hushed me. After a while the tranquility of the place affected my mood. I began to think of my life and my personal history and experienced a familiar sensation of sadness and remorse. I told him that I did not deserve to be there, that his world was strong and fair and I was weak, and that my spirit had been distorted by the circumstances of my life.

He laughed and threatened to cover my head with dirt if I kept on talking in that vein. He said that I was a man. And like any man I deserved everything that was a man's lot—joy, pain, sadness and struggle—and that the nature of one's acts was unimportant as long as one acted as a warrior.

Lowering his voice to almost a whisper, he said that if I really felt that my spirit was distorted I should simply fix it—purge it, make it perfect—because there was no other task in our entire lives which was more worthwhile. Not to fix the spirit was to seek death, and that was the same as to seek nothing, since death was going to overtake us regardless of anything.

He paused for a long time and then he said with a

tone of profound conviction, "To seek the perfection of the warrior's spirit is the only task worthy of our manhood."

His words acted as a catalyst. I felt the weight of my past actions as an unbearable and hindering load. I admitted that there was no hope for me. I began to weep, talking about my life. I said that I had been roaming for such a long time that I had become callous to pain and sadness, except on certain occasions when I would realize my aloneness and my helplessness.

He did not say anything. He grabbed me by the armpits and pulled me out of the cage. I sat up when he let go of me. He also sat down. An uneasy silence set in between us. I thought he was giving me time to compose myself. I took my notebook and scribbled out of nervousness.

"You feel like a leaf at the mercy of the wind, don't you?" he finally said, staring at me.

That was exactly the way I felt. He seemed to empathize with me. He said that my mood reminded him of a song and began to sing in a low tone; his singing voice was very pleasing and the lyrics carried me away: "I'm so far away from the sky where I was born. Immense nostalgia invades my thoughts. Now that I am so alone and sad like a leaf in the wind, sometimes I want to weep, sometimes I want to laugh with longing." (Que lejos estoy del cielo donde he nacido. Immensa nostalgia invade mi pensamiento. Ahora que estoy tan solo y triste cual hoja al viento, quisiera llorar, quisiera reir de sentimiento.)

We did not speak for a long while. He finally broke the silence.

"Since the day you were born, one way or another, someone has been doing something to you," he said.

"That's correct," I said.

"And they have been doing something to you against your will."

"True."

"And by now you're helpless, like a leaf in the wind."

"That's correct. That's the way it is."

I said that the circumstances of my life had sometimes

been devastating. He listened attentively but I could not figure out whether he was just being agreeable or genuinely concerned until I noticed that he was trying to hide a smile.

"No matter how much you like to feel sorry for yourself, you have to change that," he said in a soft tone. "It doesn't jibe with the life of a warrior."

He laughed and sang the song again but contorted the intonation of certain words; the result was a ludicrous lament. He pointed out that the reason I had liked the song was because in my own life I had done nothing else but find flaws with everything and lament. I could not argue with him. He was correct. Yet I believed I had sufficient reasons to justify my feeling of being like a leaf in the wind.

"The hardest thing in the world is to assume the mood of a warrior," he said. "It is of no use to be sad and complain and feel justified in doing so, believing that someone is always doing something to us. Nobody is doing anything to anybody, much less to a warrior.

"You are here, with me, because you want to be here. You should have assumed full responsibility by now, so the idea that you are at the mercy of the wind would be inadmissible."

He stood up and began to disassemble the cage. He scooped the dirt back to where he had gotten it from and carefully scattered all the sticks in the chaparral. Then he covered the clean circle with debris, leaving the area as if nothing had ever touched it.

I commented on his proficiency. He said that a good hunter would know that we had been there no matter how careful he had been, because the tracks of men could not be completely erased.

He sat cross-legged and told me to sit down as comfortably as possible, facing the spot where he had buried me, and stay put until my mood of sadness had dissipated.

"A warrior buries himself in order to find power, not to weep with self-pity," he said.

I attempted to explain but he made me stop with an impatient movement of his head. He said that he had to pull me out of the cage in a hurry because my mood was intolerable and he was afraid that the place would resent my softness and injure me.

"Self-pity doesn't jibe with power," he said. "The mood of a warrior calls for control over himself and at the same time it calls for abandoning himself."

"How can that be?" I asked. "How can he control and abandon himself at the same time?"

"It is a difficult technique," he said.

He seemed to deliberate whether or not to continue talking. Twice he was on the verge of saying something but he checked himself and smiled.

"You're not over your sadness yet," he said. "You still feel weak and there is no point in talking about the mood of a warrior now."

Almost an hour went by in complete silence. Then he abruptly asked me if I had succeeded in learning the "dreaming" techniques he had taught me. I had been practicing assiduously and had been able, after a monumental effort, to obtain a degree of control over my dreams. Don Juan was very right in saying that one could interpret the exercises as being entertainment. For the first time in my life I had been looking forward to going to sleep.

I gave him a detailed report of my progress.

It had been relatively easy for me to learn to sustain the image of my hands after I had learned to command myself to look at them. My visions, although not always of my own hands, would last a seemingly long time, until I would finally lose control and would become immersed in ordinary unpredictable dreams. I had no volition whatsoever over when I would give myself the command to look at my hands, or to look at other items of the dreams. It would just happen. At a given moment I would remember that I had to look at my hands and then at the surroundings. There were nights, however, when I could not recall having done it at all.

He seemed to be satisfied and wanted to know what were the usual items I had been finding in my visions. I could not think of anything in particular and started elaborating on a nightmarish dream I had had the night before.

"Don't get so fancy," he said dryly.

I told him that I had been recording all the details of my dreams. Since I had begun to practice looking at my hands my dreams had become very compelling and my sense of recall had increased to the point that I could remember minute details. He said that to follow them was a waste of time, because details and vividness were in no way important.

"Ordinary dreams get very vivid as soon as you begin to *set up dreaming*," he said. "That vividness and clarity is a formidable barrier and you are worse off than anyone I have ever met in my life. You have the worst mania. You write down everything you can."

In all fairness, I believed what I was doing was appropriate. Keeping a meticulous record of my dreams was giving me a degree of clarity about the nature of the visions I had while sleeping.

"Drop it!" he said imperatively. "It's not helping anything. All you're doing is distracting yourself from the purpose of *dreaming,* which is control and power."

He lay down and covered his eyes with his hat and talked without looking at me.

"I'm going to remind you of all the techniques you must practice." he said. "First you must focus your gaze on your hands as the starting point. Then shift your gaze to other items and look at them in brief glances. Focus your gaze on as many things as you can. Remember that if you only glance briefly the images do not shift. Then go back to your hands.

"Every time you look at your hands you renew the power needed for dreaming, so in the beginning don't look at too many things. Four items will suffice every time. Later on. you may enlarge the scope until you can cover all you want, but as soon as the images begin to shift and you feel you are losing control go back to your hands.

"When you feel you can gaze at things indefinitely you will be ready for a new technique. I'm going to teach you this new technique now, but I expect you to put it to use only when you are ready."

He was quiet for about fifteen minutes. Finally he sat up and looked at me.

"The next step in *setting up dreaming* is to learn to travel," he said. "The same way you have learned to look at your hands you can will yourself to move, to go places. First you have to establish a place you want to go to. Pick a well-known spot—perhaps your school, or a park, a friend's house—then, will yourself to go there.

"This technique is very difficult. You must perform two tasks: You must will yourself to go to the specific locale; and then, when you have mastered that technique, you have to learn to control the exact time of your traveling."

As I wrote down his statements I had the feeling that I was really nuts. I was actually taking down insane instructions, knocking myself out in order to follow them. I experienced a surge of remorse and embarrassment.

"What are you doing to me, don Juan?" I asked, not really meaning it.

He seemed surprised. He stared at me for an instant and then smiled.

"You've been asking me the same question over and over. I'm not doing anything to you. You are making yourself accessible to power; you're hunting it and I'm just guiding you."

He tilted his head to the side and studied me. He held my chin with one hand and the back of my head with the other and then moved my head back and forth. The muscles of my neck were very tense and moving my head reduced the tension.

Don Juan looked up to the sky for a moment and seemed to examine something in it.

"It's time to leave," he said dryly and stood up.

We walked in an easterly direction until we came upon a patch of small trees in a valley between two large hills. It was almost five P.M. by then. He casually said that we might have to spend the night in that place. He pointed to the trees and said that there was water around there.

He tensed his body and began sniffing the air like an

animal. I could see the muscles of his stomach contracting in very fast short spasms as he blew and inhaled through his nose in rapid succession. He urged me to do the same and find out by myself where the water was. I reluctantly tried to imitate him. After five or six minutes of fast breathing I was dizzy, but my nostrils had cleared out in an extraordinary way and I could actually detect the smell of river willows. I could not tell where they were, however.

Don Juan told me to rest for a few minutes and then he started me sniffing again. The second round was more intense. I could actually distinguish a whiff of river willow coming from my right. We headed in that direction and found, a good quarter of a mile away, a swamplike spot with stagnant water. We walked around it to a slightly higher flat mesa. Above and around the mesa the chaparral was very thick.

"This place is crawling with mountain lions and other smaller cats," don Juan said casually, as if it were a commonplace observation.

I ran to his side and he broke out laughing.

"Usually I wouldn't come here at all," he said. "But the crow pointed out this direction. There must be something special about it."

"Do we really have to be here, don Juan?"

"We do. Otherwise I would avoid this place."

I had become extremely nervous. He told me to listen attentively to what he had to say.

"The only thing one can do in this place is hunt lions," he said. "So I'm going to teach you how to do that.

"There is a special way of constructing a trap for water rats that live around water holes. They serve as bait. The sides of the cage are made to collapse and very sharp spikes are put along the sides. The spikes are hidden when the trap is up and they do not affect anything unless something falls on the cage, in which case the sides collapse and the spikes pierce whatever hits the trap."

I could not understand what he meant but he made a diagram on the ground and showed me that if the side sticks of the cage were placed on pivotlike hollow spots on the frame, the cage would collapse onto either side if something pushed its top.

The spikes were pointed sharp slivers of hard wood, which were placed all around the frame and fixed to it.

Don Juan said that usually a heavy load of rocks was placed over a net of sticks, which were connected to the cage and hung way above it. When the mountain lion came upon the trap baited with the water rats, it would usually try to break it by pawing it with all its might; then the slivers would go through its paws and the cat, in a frenzy, would jump up, unleashing an avalanche of rocks on top of him.

"Someday you might need to catch a mountain lion," he said. "They have special powers. They are terribly smart and the only way to catch them is by fooling them with pain and with the smell of river willows."

With astounding speed and skill he assembled a trap and after a long wait he caught three chubby squirrel-like rodents.

He told me to pick a handful of willows from the edge of the swamp and made me rub my clothes with them. He did the same. Then, quickly and skillfully, he wove two simple carrying nets out of reeds, scooped up a large clump of green plants and mud from the swamp, and carried it back to the mesa, where he concealed himself.

In the meantime the squirrel-like rodents had begun to squeak very loudly.

Don Juan spoke to me from his hiding place and told me to use the other carrying net, gather a good chunk of mud and plants, and climb to the lower branches of a tree near the trap where the rodents were.

Don Juan said that he did not want to hurt the cat or the rodents, so he was going to hurl the mud at the lion if it came to the trap. He told me to be on the alert and hit the cat with my bundle after he had, in order to scare it away. He recommended I should be extremely careful not to fall out of the tree. His final instructions were to be so still that I would merge with the branches.

I could not see where don Juan was. The squealing of the rodents became extremely loud and finally it was so dark that I could hardly distinguish the general features of the terrain. I heard a sudden and close sound of soft steps and a muffled catlike exhalation, then a very soft growl and the squirrel-like rodents ceased to squeak. It was right then that I saw the dark mass of an animal right under the tree where I was. Before I could even be sure that it was a mountain lion it charged against the trap, but before it reached it something hit it and made it recoil. I hurled my bundle, as don Juan had told me to do. I missed, yet it made a very loud noise. At that instant don Juan let out a series of penetrating yells that sent chills through my spine, and the cat, with extraordinary agility, leaped to the mesa and disappeared.

Don Juan kept on making the penetrating noises a while longer and then he told me to come down from the tree, pick up the cage with the squirrels, run up to the mesa, and get to where he was as fast as I could.

In an incredibly short period of time I was standing next to don Juan. He told me to imitate his yelling as close as possible in order to keep the lion off while he dismantled the cage and let the rodents free.

I began to yell but could not produce the same effect. My voice was raspy because of the excitation.

He said I had to abandon myself and yell with real feeling, because the lion was still around. Suddenly I fully realized the situation. The lion was real. I let out a magnificent series of piercing yells.

Don Juan roared with laughter.

He let me yell for a moment and then he said we had to leave the place as quietly as possible, because the lion was no fool and was probably retracing its steps back to where we were.

"He'll follow us for sure," he said. "No matter how careful we are we'll leave a trail as wide as the Pan American highway."

I walked very close to don Juan. From time to time he would stop for an instant and listen. At one moment he

began to run in the dark and I followed him with my
hands extended in front of my eyes to protect myself
from the branches.

We finally got to the base of the bluff where we had
been earlier. Don Juan said that if we succeeded in
climbing to the top without being mauled by the lion
we were safe. He went up first to show me the way. We
started to climb in the dark. I did not know how, but I
followed him with dead sure steps. When we were near
the top I heard a peculiar animal cry. It was almost like
the mooing of a cow, except that it was a bit longer
and coarser.

"Up! Up!" don Juan yelled.

I scrambled to the top in total darkness ahead of don
Juan. When he reached the flat top of the bluff I was already sitting catching my breath.

He rolled on the ground. I thought for a second that
the exertion had been too great for him, but he was laughing at my speedy climb.

We sat in complete silence for a couple of hours and
then we started back to my car.

Sunday, September 3, 1961

Don Juan was not in the house when I woke up. I worked
over my notes and had time to get some firewood from
the surrounding chaparral before he returned. I was eating when he walked into the house. He began to laugh at
what he called my routine of eating at noon, but he
helped himself to my sandwiches.

I told him that what had happened with the mountain
lion was baffling to me. In retrospect, it all seemed unreal.
It was as if everything had been staged for my benefit.
The succession of events had been so rapid that I really
had not had time to be afraid. I had had enough time to
act, but not to deliberate upon my circumstances. In writing my notes the question of whether I had really seen
the mountain lion came to mind. The dry branch was still
fresh in my memory.

"It was a mountain lion," don Juan said imperatively.

"Was it a real flesh and blood animal?"

"Of course."

I told him that my suspicions had been roused because of the easiness of the total event. It was as if the lion had been waiting out there and had been trained to do exactly what don Juan had planned.

He was unruffled by my barrage of skeptical remarks. He laughed at me.

"You're a funny fellow," he said. "You saw and heard the cat. It was right under the tree where you were. He didn't smell you and jump at you because of the river willows. They kill any other smell, even for cats. You had a batch of them in your lap."

I said that it was not that I doubted him, but that everything that had happened that night was extremely foreign to the events of my everyday life. For a while, as I was writing my notes, I even had had the feeling that don Juan may have been playing the role of the lion. However, I had to discard the idea because I had really seen the dark shape of a four-legged animal charging at the cage and then leaping to the mesa.

"Why do you make such a fuss?" he said. "It was just a big cat. There must be thousands of cats in those mountains. Big deal. As usual, you are focusing your attention on the wrong item. It makes no difference whatsoever whether it was a lion or my pants. Your feelings at that moment were what counted."

In my entire life I had never seen or heard a big wildcat on the prowl. When I thought of it, I could not get over the fact that I had been only a few feet away from one.

Don Juan listened patiently while I went over the entire experience.

"Why the awe for the big cat?" he asked with an inquisitive expression. "You've been close to most of the animals that live around here and you've never been so awed by them. Do you like cats?"

"No, I don't."

"Well, forget about it then. The lesson was not on how to hunt lions, anyway."

"What was it about?"

"The little crow pointed out that specific spot to me, and at that spot I *saw* the opportunity of making you understand how one acts while one is in the mood of a warrior.

"Everything you did last night was done within a proper mood. You were controlled and at the same time abandoned when you jumped down from the tree to pick up the cage and run up to me. You were not paralyzed with fear. And then, near the top of the bluff, when the lion let out a scream, you moved very well. I'm sure you wouldn't believe what you did if you looked at the bluff during the daytime. You had a degree of abandon, and at the same time you had a degree of control over yourself. You did not let go and wet your pants, and yet you let go and climbed that wall in complete darkness. You could have missed the trail and killed yourself. To climb that wall in darkness required that you had to hold on to yourself and let go of yourself at the same time. That's what I call the mood of a warrior."

I said that whatever I had done that night was the product of my fear and not the result of any mood of control and abandon.

"I know that," he said, smiling. "And I wanted to show you that you can spur yourself beyond your limits if you are in the proper mood. A warrior makes his own mood. You didn't know that. Fear got you into the mood of a warrior, but now that you know about it, anything can serve to get you into it."

I wanted to argue with him, but my reasons were not clear. I felt an inexplicable sense of annoyance.

"It's convenient to always act in such a mood," he continued. "It cuts through the crap and leaves one purified. It was a great feeling when you reached the top of the bluff. Wasn't it?"

I told him that I understood what he meant, yet I felt it would be idiotic to try to apply what he was teaching me to everyday life.

"One needs the mood of a warrior for every single act," he said. "Otherwise one becomes distorted and ugly.

There is no power in a life that lacks this mood. Look at yourself. Everything offends and upsets you. You whine and complain and feel that everyone is making you dance to their tune. You are a leaf at the mercy of the wind. There is no power in your life. What an ugly feeling that must be!

"A warrior, on the other hand, is a hunter. He calculates everything. That's control. But once his calculations are over, he acts. He lets go. That's abandon. A warrior is not a leaf at the mercy of the wind. No one can push him; no one can make him do things against himself or against his better judgment. A warrior is tuned to survive, and he survives in the best of all possible fashions."

I liked his stance although I thought it was unrealistic. It seemed too simplistic for the complex world in which I lived.

He laughed at my arguments and I insisted that the mood of a warrior could not possibly help me overcome the feeling of being offended or actually being injured by the actions of my fellow men, as in the hypothetical case of being physically harassed by a cruel and malicious person placed in a position of authority.

He roared with laughter and admitted the example was apropos.

"A warrior could be injured but not offended," he said. "For a warrior there is nothing offensive about the acts of his fellow men as long as he himself is acting within the proper mood.

"The other night you were not offended by the lion. The fact that it chased us did not anger you. I did not hear you cursing it, nor did I hear you say that he had no right to follow us. It could have been a cruel and malicious lion for all you know. But that was not a consideration while you struggled to avoid it. The only thing that was pertinent was to survive. And that you did very well.

"If you would have been alone and the lion had caught up with you and mauled you to death, you would have never even considered complaining or feeling offended by its acts.

"The mood of a warrior is not so far-fetched for yours

or anybody's world. You need it in order to cut through all the guff."

I explained my way of reasoning. The lion and my fellow men were not on a par, because I knew the intimate quirks of men while I knew nothing about the lion. What offended me about my fellow men was that they acted maliciously and knowingly.

"I know, I know," don Juan said patiently. "To achieve the mood of a warrior is not a simple matter. It is a revolution. To regard the lion and the water rats and our fellow men as equals is a magnificent act of the warrior's spirit. It takes power to do that."

12

A BATTLE OF POWER

Thursday, December 28, 1961

We started on a journey very early in the morning. We drove south and then east to the mountains. Don Juan had brought gourds with food and water. We ate in my car before we started walking.

"Stick close to me," he said. "This is an unknown region to you and there is no need to take chances. You are going in search of power and everything you do counts. Watch the wind, especially towards the end of the day. Watch when it changes directions, and shift your position so that I always shield you from it."

"What are we going to do in these mountains, don Juan?"

"You're hunting power."

"I mean what are we going to do in particular?"

"There's no plan when it comes to hunting power. Hunting power or hunting game is the same. A hunter hunts whatever presents itself to him. Thus he must always be in a state of readiness.

"You know about the wind, and now you may hunt power in the wind by yourself. But there are other things you don't know about which are, like the wind, the center of power at certain times and at certain places.

"Power is a very peculiar affair," he said. "It is impossible to pin it down and say what it really is. It is a feeling that one has about certain things. Power is personal. It belongs to oneself alone. My benefactor, for instance, could make a person mortally ill by merely looking at him. Women would wane away after he had set eyes on them. Yet he did not make people sick all the time but only when his personal power was involved."

"How did he choose who to make sick?"

"I don't know that. He didn't know it himself. Power is like that. It commands you and yet it obeys you.

"A hunter of power entraps it and then stores it away as his personal finding. Thus, personal power grows, and you may have the case of a warrior who has so much personal power that he becomes a man of knowledge."

"How does one store power, don Juan?"

"That again is another feeling. It depends on what kind of a person the warrior is. My benefactor was a man of violent nature. He stored power through that feeling. Everything he did was strong and direct. He left me a memory of something crushing through things. And everything that happened to him took place in that manner."

I told him that I could not understand how power was stored through a feeling.

"There's no way to explain it," he said after a long pause. "You have to do it yourself."

He picked up the gourds with food and fastened them to his back. He handed me a string with eight pieces of dry meat strung on it and made me hang it from my neck.

"This is power food," he said.

"What makes it power food, don Juan?"

"It is the meat of an animal that had power. A deer, a unique deer. My personal power brought it to me. This meat will sustain us for weeks, months if need be. Chew little bits of it at a time, and chew it thoroughly. Let the power sink slowly into your body."

We began to walk. It was almost eleven A.M. Don Juan reminded me once more of the procedure to follow.

"Watch the wind," he said. "Don't let it trip you. And don't let it make you tired. Chew your power food and hide from the wind behind my body. The wind won't hurt me; we know each other very well."

He led me to a trail that went straight to the high mountains. The day was cloudy and it was about to rain. I could see low rain clouds and fog up above in the mountains descending into the area where we were.

We hiked in complete silence until about three o'clock in the afternoon. Chewing the dry meat was indeed invigorating. And watching for sudden changes in the direction of the wind became a mysterious affair, to the point that my entire body seemed to sense changes before they actually happened. I had the feeling that I could detect waves of wind as a sort of pressure on my upper chest, on my bronchial tubes. Every time I was about to feel a gust of wind my chest and throat would itch.

Don Juan stopped for a moment and looked around. He appeared to be orienting himself and then he turned to the right. I noticed that he was also chewing dry meat. I felt very fresh and was not tired at all. The task of being aware of shifts in the wind had been so consuming that I had not been aware of time.

We walked into a deep ravine and then up one side to a small plateau on the sheer side of an enormous mountain. We were quite high, almost to the top of the mountain.

Don Juan climbed a huge rock at the end of the plateau and helped me up to it. The rock was placed in such a way as to look like a dome on top of preciptous walls. We slowly walked around it. Finally I had to move around the rock on my seat, holding on to the surface with my heels and hands. I was soaked in perspiration and had to dry my hands repeatedly.

From the other side I could see a very large shallow cave near the top of the mountain. It looked like a hall that had been carved out of the rock. It was sandstone which had been weathered into a sort of balcony with two pillars.

Don Juan said that we were going to camp there, that it was a very safe place because it was too shallow to be a den for lions or any other predators, too open to be a nest for rats, and too windy for insects. He laughed and said that it was an ideal place for men, since no other living creatures could stand it.

He climbed up to it like a mountain goat. I marveled at his stupendous agility.

I slowly dragged myself down the rock on my seat and then tried to run up the side of the mountain in order to reach the ledge. The last few yards completely exhausted me. I kiddingly asked don Juan how old he really was. I thought that in order to reach the ledge the way he had done it one had to be extremely fit and young.

"I'm as young as I want to be," he said. "This again is a matter of personal power. If you store power your body can perform unbelievable feats. On the other hand, if you dissipate power you'll be a fat old man in no time at all."

The length of the ledge was oriented along an east-west line. The open side of the balcony-like formation was to the south. I walked to the west end. The view was superb. The rain had circumvented us. It looked like a sheet of transparent material hung over the low land.

Don Juan said that we had enough time to build a shelter. He told me to make a pile of as many rocks as I could carry onto the ledge while he gathered some branches for a roof.

In an hour he had built a wall about a foot thick on the east end of the ledge. It was about two feet long and three feet high. He wove and tied some bundles of branches he had collected and made a roof, securing it onto two long poles that ended in forks. There was another pole of the same length that was affixed to the roof itself and which supported it on the opposite side of the wall. The structure looked like a high table with three legs.

Don Juan sat cross-legged under it, on the very edge of the balcony. He told me to sit next to him, to his right. We remained quiet for a while.

Don Juan broke the silence. He said in a whisper that we had to act as if nothing was out of the ordinary. I asked if there was something in particular that I should do. He said that I should get busy writing and do it in such a way that it would be as if I were at my desk with no worries in the world except writing. At a given moment he was going to nudge me and then I should look where he was pointing with his eyes. He warned me that no matter what I saw I should not utter a single word. Only he could talk with impunity because he was known to all the powers in those mountains.

I followed his instructions and wrote for over an hour. I became immersed in my task. Suddenly I felt a soft tap on my arm and saw don Juan's eyes and head move to point out a bank of fog about two hundred yards away which was descending from the top of the mountain. Don Juan whispered in my ear with a tone barely audible even at that close range.

"Move your eyes back and forth along the bank of fog, he said. "But don't look at it directly. Blink your eyes and don't focus them on the fog. When you see a green spot on the bank of fog, point it out to me with your eyes."

I moved my eyes from left to right along the bank of fog that was slowly coming down to us. Perhaps half an hour went by. It was getting dark. The fog moved extremely slowly. At one moment I had the sudden feeling that I had detected a faint glow to my right. At first I thought that I had seen a patch of green shrubbery through the fog. When I looked at it directly I did not notice anything, but when I looked without focusing I could detect a vague greenish area.

I pointed it out to don Juan. He squinted his eyes and stared at it.

"Focus your eyes on that spot," he whispered in my ear. "Look without blinking until you *see*."

I wanted to ask what I was supposed to see but he
glared at me as if to remind me that I should not talk.

I stared again. The bit of fog that had come down from
above hung as if it were a piece of solid matter. It was
lined up right at the spot where I had noticed the green
tint. As my eyes became tired again and I squinted, I saw
at first the bit of fog superimposed on the fog bank, and
then I saw a thin strip of fog in between that looked like
a thin unsupported structure, a bridge joining the mountain above me and the bank of fog in front of me. For a
moment I thought I could see the transparent fog, which
was being blown down from the top of the mountain, going by the bridge without disturbing it. It was as if the
bridge were actually solid. At one instant the mirage became so complete that I could actually distinguish the
darkness of the part under the bridge proper, as opposed
to the light sandstone color of its side.

I stared at the bridge, dumbfounded. And then I either
lifted myself to its level, or the bridge lowered itself to
mine. Suddenly I was looking at a straight beam in front
of me. It was an immensely long, solid beam, narrow and
without railings, but wide enough to walk on.

Don Juan shook me by the arm vigorously. I felt my
head bobbing up and down and then I noticed that my
eyes itched terribly. I rubbed them quite unconsciously.
Don Juan kept on shaking me until I opened my eyes
again. He poured some water from his gourd into the hollow of his hand and sprinkled my face with it. The sensation was very unpleasant. The coldness of the water was
so extreme that the drops felt like sores on my skin. I
noticed then that my body was very warm. I was feverish.

Don Juan hurriedly gave me some water to drink and
then splashed water on my ears and neck.

I heard a very loud, eerie and prolonged bird cry. Don
Juan listened attentively for an instant and then pushed
the rocks of the wall with his foot and collapsed the roof.
He threw the roof into the shrubs and tossed all the
rocks, one by one, over the side.

He whispered in my ear, "Drink some water and chew

your dry meat. We cannot stay here. That cry was not a bird."

We climbed down the ledge and began to walk in an easterly direction. In no time at all it was so dark that it was as if there were a curtain in front of my eyes. The fog was like an impenetrable barrier. I had never realized how crippling the fog was at night. I could not conceive how don Juan walked. I held on to his arm as if I were blind.

Somehow I had the feeling I was walking on the edge of a precipice. My legs refused to move on. My reason trusted don Juan and I was rationally willing to go on, but my body was not, and don Juan had to drag me in total darkness.

He must have known the terrain to ultimate perfection. He stopped at a certain point and made me sit down. I did not dare let go of his arm. My body felt, beyond the shadow of a doubt, that I was sitting on a barren dome-like mountain and if I moved an inch to my right I would fall beyond the tolerance point into an abysm. I was absolutely sure I was sitting on a curved mountainside, because my body moved unconsciously to the right. I thought it did so in order to keep its verticality, so I tried to compensate by leaning to the left against don Juan, as far as I could.

Don Juan suddenly moved away from me and without the support of his body I fell on the ground. Touching the ground restored my sense of equilibrium. I was lying on a flat area. I began to reconnoiter my immediate surroundings by touch. I recognized dry leaves annd twigs.

There was a sudden flash of lightning that illuminated the whole area and tremendous thunder. I saw don Juan standing to my left. I saw huge trees and a cave a few feet behind him.

Don Juan told me to get into the hole. I crawled into it and sat down with my back against the rock.

I felt don Juan leaning over to whisper that I had to be totally silent.

There were three flashes of lightning, one after the other. In a glance I saw don Juan sitting cross-legged to my left. The cave was a concave formation big enough for two or three persons to sit in. The hole seemed to have been carved at the bottom of a boulder. I felt that it had indeed been wise of me to have crawled into it, because if I had been walking I would have knocked my head against the rock.

The brilliancy of the lightning gave me an idea of how thick the bank of fog was. I noticed the trunks of enormous trees as dark silhouettes against the opaque light gray mass of the fog.

Don Juan whispered that the fog and the lightning were in cahoots with each other and I had to keep an exhausting vigil because I was engaged in a battle of power. At that moment a stupendous flash of lightning rendered the whole scenery phantasmagorical. The fog was like a white filter that frosted the light of the electrical discharge and diffused it uniformly; the fog was like a dense whitish substance hanging between the tall trees, but right in front of me at the ground level the fog was thinning out. I plainly distinguished the features of the terrain. We were in a pine forest. Very tall trees surrounded us. They were so extremely big that I could have sworn we were in the redwoods if I had not previously known our whereabouts.

There was a barrage of lightning that lasted several minutes. Each flash made the features I had already observed more discernible. Right in front of me I saw a definite trail. There was no vegetation on it. It seemed to end in an area clear of trees.

There were so many flashes of lightning that I could not keep track of where they were coming from. The scenery, however, had been so profusely illuminated that I felt much more at ease. My fears and uncertainties had vanished as soon as there had been enough light to lift the heavy curtain of darkness. So when there was a long pause between the flashes of lightning I was no longer disoriented by the blackness around me.

Don Juan whispered that I had probably done enough watching, and that I had to focus my attention on the sound of thunder. I realized to my amazement that I had not paid any attention to thunder at all, in spite of the fact that it had really been tremendous. Don Juan added that I should follow the sound and look in the direction where I thought it came from.

There were no longer barrages of lightning and thunder but only sporadic flashes of intense light and sound. The thunder seemed to always come from my right. The fog was lifting and I, already being accustomed to the pitch black, could distinguish masses of vegetation. The lightning and thunder continued and suddenly the whole right side opened up and I could see the sky.

The electrical storm seemed to be moving towards my right. There was another flash of lightning and I saw a distant mountain to my extreme right. The light illuminated the background, silhouetting the bulky mass of the mountain. I saw trees on top of it; they looked like neat black cutouts superimposed on the brilliantly white sky. I even saw cumulus clouds over the mountains.

The fog had cleared completely around us. There was a steady wind and I could hear the rustling of leaves in the big trees to my left. The electrical storm was too distant to illuminate the trees, but their dark masses remained discernible. The light of the storm allowed me to establish, however, that there was a range of distant mountains to my right and that the forest was limited to the left side. It seemed that I was looking down into a dark valley, which I could not see at all. The range over which the electrical storm was taking place was on the opposite side of the valley.

Then it began to rain. I pressed back against the rock as far as I could. My hat served as a good protection. I was sitting with my knees to my chest and only my calves and shoes got wet.

It rained for a long time. The rain was lukewarm. I felt it on my feet. And then I fell asleep.

The noises of birds woke me up. I looked around for don Juan. He was not there; ordinarily I would have wondered whether he had left me there alone, but the shock of seeing the surroundings nearly paralyzed me.

I stood up. My legs were soaking wet, the brim of my

hat was soggy and there was still some water in it that spilled over me. I was not in a cave at all, but under some thick bushes. I experienced a moment of unparalleled confusion. I was standing on a flat piece of land between two small dirt hills covered with bushes. There were no trees to my left and no valley to my right. Right in front of me, where I had seen the path in the forest, there was a gigantic bush.

I refused to believe what I was witnessing. The incongruency of my two versions of reality made me grapple for any kind of explanation. It occurred to me that it was perfectly possible that I had slept so soundly that don Juan might have carried me on his back to another place without waking me.

I examined the spot where I had been sleeping. The ground there was dry, and so was the ground on the spot next to it, where don Juan had been.

I called him a couple of times and then had an attack of anxiety and bellowed his name as loud as I could. He came out from behind some bushes. I immediately became aware that he knew what was going on. His smile was so mischievous that I ended up smiling myself.

I did not want to waste any time in playing games with him. I blurted out what was the matter with me. I explained as carefully as possible every detail of my night-long hallucinations. He listened without interrupting. He could not, however, keep a serious face and started to laugh a couple of times, but he regained his composure right away.

I asked for his comments three or four times; he only shook his head as if the whole affair was also incomprehensible to him.

When I ended my account he looked at me and said, "You look awful. Maybe you need to go to the bushes."

He cackled for a moment and then added that I should take off my clothes and wring them out so they would dry.

The sunlight was brilliant. There were very few clouds. It was a windy brisk day.

Don Juan walked away, telling me that he was going to

look for some plants and that I should compose myself and eat something and not call him until I was calm and strong.

My clothes were really wet. I sat down in the sun to dry. I felt that the only way for me to relax was to get out my notebook and write. I ate while I worked on my notes.

After a couple of hours I was more relaxed and I called don Juan. He answered from a place near the top of the mountain. He told me to gather the gourds and climb up to where he was. When I reached the spot, I found him sitting on a smooth rock. He opened the gourds and served himself some food. He handed me two big pieces of meat.

I did not know where to begin. There were so many things I wanted to ask. He seemed to be aware of my mood and laughed with sheer delight.

"How do you feel?" he asked in a facetious tone.

I did not want to say anything. I was still upset.

Don Juan urged me to sit down on the flat slab. He said that the stone was a power object and that I would be renewed after being there for a while.

"Sit down," he commanded me dryly.

He did not smile. His eyes were piercing. I automatically sat down.

He said that I was being careless with power by acting morosely, and that I had to put an end to it or power would turn against both of us and we would never leave those desolate hills alive.

After a moment's pause he casually asked, "How is your *dreaming?*"

I explained to him how difficult it had become for me to give myself the command to look at my hands. At first it had been relatively easy, perhaps because of the newness of the concept. I had had no trouble at all in reminding myself that I had to look at my hands. But the excitation had worn off and some nights I could not do it at all.

"You must wear a headband to sleep," he said. "Getting a headband is a tricky maneuver. I cannot give you one, because you yourself have to make it from scratch. But you cannot make one until you have had a vision of it in *dreaming*. See what I mean? The headband has to be made according to the specific vision. And it must have a strip across it that fits tightly on top of the head. Or it may very well be like a tight cap. *Dreaming* is easier when one wears a power object on top of the head. You could wear your hat or put on a cowl, like a friar, and go to sleep, but those items would only cause intense dreams, not *dreaming*."

He was silent for a moment and then proceeded to tell me in a fast barrage of words that the vision of the headband did not have to occur only in "dreaming" but could happen in states of wakefulness and as a result of any far-fetched and totally unrelated event, such as watching the flight of birds, the movement of water, the clouds, and so on.

"A hunter of power watches everything," he went on. "And everything tells him some secret."

"But how can one be sure that things are telling secrets?" I asked.

I thought he may have had a specific formula that allowed him to make "correct" interpretations.

"The only way to be sure is by following all the instructions I have been giving you, starting from the first day you came to see me," he said. "In order to have power one must live with power."

He smiled benevolently. He seemed to have lost his fierceness; he even nudged me lightly on the arm.

"Eat your power food," he urged me.

I began to chew some dry meat and at that moment I had the sudden realization that perhaps the dry meat contained a psychotropic substance, hence the hallucinations. For a moment I felt almost relieved. If he had put something in the meat my mirages were perfectly understandable. I asked him to tell me if there was anything at all in the "power meat."

He laughed but did not answer me directly. I insisted, assuring him that I was not angry or even annoyed, but that I had to know so I could explain the events of the previous night to my own satisfaction. I urged him, coaxed him, and finally begged him to tell me the truth.

"You are quite cracked," he said, shaking his head in a gesture of disbelief. "You have an insidious tendency. You persist in trying to explain everything to your satisfaction. There is nothing in the meat except power. The power was not put there by me or by any other man but by power itself. It is the dry meat of a deer and that deer was a gift to me in the same way a certain rabbit was a gift to you not too long ago. Neither you nor I put anything in the rabbit. I didn't ask you to dry the rabbit's meat, because that act required more power than you had. However, I did tell you to eat the meat. You didn't eat much of it, because of your own stupidity.

"What happened to you last night was neither a joke nor a prank. You had an encounter with power. The fog, the darkness, the lightning, the thunder and the rain were all part of a great battle of power. You had the luck of a fool. A warrior would give anything to have such a battle."

My argument was that the whole event could not be a battle of power because it had not been real.

"And what is real?" don Juan asked me very calmly.

"This, what we're looking at is real," I said, pointing to the surroundings.

"But so was the bridge you saw last night, and so was the forest and everything else."

"But if they were real where are they now?"

"They are here. If you had enough power you could call them back. Right now you cannot do that because you think it is very helpful to keep on doubting and nagging. It isn't, my friend. It isn't. There are worlds upon worlds, right here in front of us. And they are nothing to laugh at. Last night if I hadn't grabbed your arm you would have walked on that bridge whether you wanted to or not. And earlier I had to protect you from the wind that was seeking you out."

"What would have happened if you hadn't protected me?"

"Since you don't have enough power, the wind would

have made you lose your way and perhaps even killed you by pushing you into a ravine. But the fog was the real thing last night. Two things could have happened to you in the fog. You could have walked across the bridge to the other side, or you could have fallen to your death. Either would have depended on power. One thing, however, would have been for sure. If I had not protected you, you would have had to walk on that bridge regardless of anything. That is the nature of power. As I told you before, it commands you and yet it is at your command. Last night, for instance, the power would have forced you to walk across the bridge and then it would have been at your command to sustain you while you were walking. I stopped you because I know you don't have the means to use power, and without power the bridge would have collapsed."

"Did you see the bridge yourself, don Juan?"

"No. I just *saw* power. It may have been anything. Power for you, this time, was a bridge. I don't know why a bridge. We are most mysterious creatures."

"Have you ever seen a bridge in the fog, don Juan?"

"Never. But that's because I'm not like you. I saw other things. My battles of power are very different than yours."

"What did you see, don Juan? Can you tell me?"

"I saw my enemies during my first battle of power in the fog. You have no enemies. You don't hate people. I did at that time. I indulged in hating people. I don't do that any more. I have vanquished my hate, but at that time my hate nearly destroyed me.

"Your battle of power, on the other hand, was neat. It didn't consume you. You are consuming yourself now with your own crappy thoughts and doubts. That's your way of indulging yourself.

"The fog was impeccable with you. You have an affinity with it. It gave you a stupendous bridge, and that bridge will be there in the fog from now on. It will reveal itself to you over and over, until someday you will have to cross it.

"I strongly recommend that from this day on you don't

walk into foggy areas by yourself until you know what you're doing.

"Power is a very weird affair. In order to have it and command it one must have power to begin with. It's possible, however, to store it, little by little, until one has enough to sustain oneself in a battle of power."

"What is a battle of power?"

"What happened to you last night was the beginning of a battle of power. The scenes that you beheld were the seat of power. Someday they will make sense to you; those scenes are most meaningful."

"Can you tell me their meaning yourself, don Juan?"

"No. Those scenes are your own personal conquest which you cannot share with anyone. But what happened last night was only the beginning, a skirmish. The real battle will take place when you cross that bridge. What's on the other side? Only you will know that. And only you will know what's at the end of that trail through the forest. But all that is something that may or may not happen to you. In order to journey through those unknown trails and bridges one must have enough power of one's own."

"What happens if one doesn't have enough power?"

"Death is always waiting, and when the warrior's power wanes death simply taps him. Thus, to venture into the unknown without any power is stupid. One will only find death."

I was not really listening. I kept on playing with the idea that the dry meat may have been the agent that had caused the hallucinations. It appeased me to indulge in that thought.

"Don't tax yourself trying to figure it out," he said as if he were reading my thoughts. "The world is a mystery. This, what you're looking at, is not all there is to it. There is much more to the world, so much more, in fact, that it is endless. So when you're trying to figure it out, all you're really doing is trying to make the world familiar. You and I are right here, in the world that you call real, simply because we both know it. You don't know the world of power, therefore you cannot make it into a familiar scene."

"You know that I really can't argue your point," I said. "But my mind can't accept it either."

He laughed and touched my head lightly.

"You're really crazy," he said. "But that's all right. I know how difficult it is to live like a warrior. If you would have followed my instructions and performed all the acts I have taught you, you would by now have enough power to cross the bridge. Enough power to *see* and to *stop the world*."

"But why should I want power, don Juan?"

"You can't think of a reason now. However, if you would store enough power, the power itself will find you a good reason. Sounds crazy, doesn't it?"

"Why did you want power yourself, don Juan?"

"I'm like you. I didn't want it. I couldn't find a reason to have it. I had all the doubts that you have and never followed the instructions I was given, or I never thought I did; yet in spite of my stupidity I stored enough power, and one day my personal power made the world collapse."

"But why would anyone wish to *stop the world?*"

"Nobody does, that's the point. It just happens. And once you know what it is like to *stop the world* you realize there is a reason for it. You see, one of the arts of the warrior is to collapse the world for a specific reason and then restore it again in order to keep on living."

I told him that perhaps the surest way to help me would be to give me an example of a specific reason for collapsing the world.

He remained silent for some time. He seemed to be thinking what to say.

"I can't tell you that," he said. "It takes too much power to know that. Someday you will live like a warrior, in spite of yourself; then perhaps you will have stored enough personal power to answer that question yourself.

"I have taught you nearly everything a warrior needs to know in order to start off in the world, storing power by himself. Yet I know that you can't do that and I have to be patient with you. I know for a fact that it takes a lifelong struggle to be by oneself in the world of power."

Don Juan looked at the sky and the mountains. The sun was already on its descent towards the west and rain clouds were rapidly forming on the mountains. I did not know the time; I had forgotten to wind my watch. I asked if he could tell the time of the day and he had such an attack of laughter that he rolled off the slab into the bushes.

He stood up and stretched his arms, yawning.

"It is early," he said. "We must wait until the fog gathers on top of the mountain and then you must stand alone on this slab and thank the fog for its favors. Let it come and envelop you. I'll be nearby to assist, if need be."

Somehow the prospect of staying alone in the fog terrified me. I felt idiotic for reacting in such an irrational manner.

"You cannot leave these desolate mountains without saying your thanks," he said in a firm tone. "A warrior never turns his back to power without atoning for the favors received."

He lay down on his back with his hands behind his head and covered his face with his hat.

"How should I wait for the fog?" I asked. "What should I do?"

"Write!" he said through his hat. "But don't close your eyes or turn your back to it."

I tried to write but I could not concentrate. I stood up and moved around restlessly. Don Juan lifted his hat and looked at me with an air of annoyance.

"Sit down!" he ordered me.

He said that the battle of power had not yet ended, and that I had to teach my spirit to be impassive. Nothing of what I did should betray my feelings, unless I wanted to remain trapped in those mountains.

He sat up and moved his hand in a gesture of urgency. He said that I had to act as if nothing was out of the ordinary, because places of power, such as the one in which we were, had the potential of draining people who were disturbed. And thus one could develop strange and injurious ties with a locale.

"Those ties anchor a man to a place of power, sometimes for a lifetime," he said. "And this is not the place for you. You did not find it yourself. So tighten your belt and don't lose your pants."

His admonitions worked like a spell on me. I wrote for hours without interruption.

Don Juan went back to sleep and did not wake up until the fog was perhaps a hundred yards away, descending from the top of the mountain. He stood up and examined the surroundings. I looked around without turning my back. The fog had already invaded the lowlands, descending from the mountains to my right. On my left side the scenery was clear; the wind, however, seemed to be coming from my right and was pushing the fog into the lowlands as if to surround us.

Don Juan whispered that I should remain impassive, standing where I was without closing my eyes, and that I should not turn around until I was completely surrounded by the fog; only then was it possible to start our descent.

He took cover at the foot of some rocks a few feet behind me.

The silence in those mountains was something magnificent and at the same time awesome. The soft wind that was carrying the fog gave me the sensation that the fog was hissing in my ears. Big chunks of fog came downhill like solid clumps of whitish matter rolling down on me. I smelled the fog. It was a peculiar mixture of a pungent and fragrant smell. And then I was enveloped in it.

I had the impression the fog was working on my eyelids. They felt heavy and I wanted to close my eyes. I was cold. My throat itched and I wanted to cough but I did not dare. I lifted my chin up and stretched my neck to ease the cough, and as I looked up I had the sensation I could actually see the thickness of the fog bank. It was as if my eyes could assess the thickness by going through it. My eyes began to close and I could not fight off the desire to fall asleep. I felt I was going to collapse on the ground any moment. At that instant don Juan jumped up and grabbed me by the arms and shook me. The jolt was enough to restore my lucidity.

He whispered in my ear that I had to run downhill as fast as I could. He was going to follow behind because he did not want to get smashed by the rocks that I might turn over in my path. He said that I was the leader, since it was my battle of power, and that I had to be clearheaded and abandoned in order to guide us safely out of there.

"This is it," he said in a loud voice. "If you don't have the mood of a warrior, we may never leave the fog."

I hesitated for a moment. I was not sure I could find my way down from those mountains.

"Run, rabbit, run!" don Juan yelled and shoved me gently down the slope.

13

A WARRIOR'S LAST STAND

Sunday, January 28, 1962

Around ten A.M. don Juan walked into his house. He had left at the crack of dawn. I greeted him. He chuckled and in a clowning mood he shook hands with me and greeted me ceremoniously.

"We're going to go on a little trip," he said. "You're going to drive us to a very special place in search of power."

He unfolded two carrying nets and placed two gourds filled with food in each of them, tied them with a thin rope, and handed me a net.

We leisurely drove north some four hundred miles

and then we left the Pan American highway and took a gravel road towards the west. My car seemed to have been the only car on the road for hours. As we kept on driving I noticed that I could not see through my windshield. I strained desperately to look at the surroundings but it was too dark and my windshield was overlaid with crushed insects and dust.

I told don Juan that I had to stop to clean my windshield. He ordered me to go on driving even if I had to crawl at two miles an hour, sticking my head out of the window to see ahead. He said that we could not stop until we had reached our destination.

At a certain place he told me to turn to the right. It was so dark and dusty that even the headlights did not help much. I drove off the road with great trepidation. I was afraid of the soft shoulders, but the dirt was packed.

I drove for about one hundred yards at the lowest possible speed, holding the door open to look out. Finally don Juan told me to stop. He said that I had parked right behind a huge rock that would shield my car from view.

I got out of the car and walked around, guided by the headlights. I wanted to examine the surroundings because I had no idea where I was. But don Juan turned off the lights. He said loudly that there was no time to waste, that I should lock my car so we could start on our way.

He handed me my net with gourds. It was so dark that I stumbled and nearly dropped them. Don Juan ordered me in a soft firm tone to sit down until my eyes were accustomed to the darkness. But my eyes were not the problem. Once I got out of my car I could see fairly well. What was wrong was a peculiar nervousness that made me act as if I were absentminded. I was glossing over everything.

"Where are we going?" I asked.

"We're going to hike in total darkness to a special place," he said.

"What for?"

"To find out for sure whether or not you're capable of continuing to hunt power."

I asked him if what he was proposing was a test, and if I failed the test would he still talk to me and tell me about his knowledge.

He listened without interrupting. He said that what we were doing was not a test, that we were waiting for an omen, and if the omen did not come the conclusion would be that I had not succeeded in hunting power, in which case I would be free from any further imposition, free to be as stupid as I wanted. He said that no matter what happened he was my friend and he would always talk to me.

Somehow I knew I was going to fail.

"The omen will not come," I said jokingly. "I know it. I have a little power."

He laughed and patted me on the back gently.

"Don't you worry," he retorted. "The omen will come. I know it. I have more power than you."

He found his statement hilarious. He slapped his thighs and clapped his hands and roared with laughter.

Don Juan tied my carrying net to my back and said that I should walk one step behind him and step in his tracks as much as possible.

In a very dramatic tone he whispered, "This is a walk for power, so everything counts."

He said that if I would walk in his footsteps the power that he was dissipating as he walked would be transmitted to me.

I looked at my watch; it was eleven P.M.

He made me line up like a soldier at attention. Then he pushed my right leg to the front and made me stand as if I had just taken a step forward. He lined up in front of me in the same position and then began to walk, after repeating the instructions that I should try to match his footsteps to perfection. He said in a clear whisper that I should not concern myself with anything else except stepping in his tracks. I should not look ahead or to the side but at the ground where he was walking.

He started off at a very relaxed pace. I had no trouble at all following him; we were walking on relatively hard ground. For about thirty yards I maintained his pace and

I matched his steps perfectly; then I glanced to the side
for an instant and the next thing I knew I had bumped
into him.

He giggled and assured me that I had not injured his
ankle at all when I had stepped on it with my big shoes,
but if I were going to keep on blundering one of us
would be a cripple by morning. He said, laughing, in a
very low but firm voice, that he did not intend to get
hurt by my stupidity and lack of concentration and that
if I stepped on him again I would have to walk barefoot.

"I can't walk without shoes," I said in a loud raspy
voice.

Don Juan doubled up with laughter and we had to
wait until he had stopped.

He assured me again that he had meant what he said.
We were journeying to tap power and things had to be
perfect.

The prospect of walking in the desert without shoes
scared me beyond belief. Don Juan joked that my family
were probably the type of farmers that did not take off
their shoes even to go to bed. He was right, of course. I
had never walked barefoot and to walk in the desert without shoes would have been suicidal for me.

"This desert is oozing power," don Juan whispered in
my ear. "There is no time for being timid."

We started walking again. Don Juan kept an easy
pace. After a while I noticed that we had left the hard
ground and were walking on soft sand. Don Juan's feet
sank into it and left deep tracks.

We walked for hours before don Juan came to a halt.
He did not stop suddenly but warned me ahead of time
that he was going to stop so I would not bump into him.
The terrain had become hard again and it seemed that
we were going up an incline.

Don Juan said that if I needed to go to the bushes I
should do it, because from then on we had a solid stretch
without a single pause. I looked at my watch; it was
one A.M.

After a ten- or fifteen-minute rest don Juan made me
line up and we began to walk again. He was right, it was

a dreadful stretch. I had never done anything that de-
minded so much concentration. Don Juan's pace was so
fast and the tension of watching every step mounted to
such heights that at a given moment I could not feel
that I was walking any more. I could not feel my feet or
my legs. It was as if I were walking on air and some force
were carrying me on and on. My concentration had been
so total that I did not notice the gradual change in light.
Suddenly I became aware that I could see don Juan
in front of me. I could see his feet and his tracks instead
of half guessing as I had done most of the night.

At a given moment he unexpectedly jumped to the side
and my momentum carried me for about twenty yards
further. As I slowed down my legs became weak and
started to shake until finally I collapsed on the ground.

I looked up at don Juan, who was calmly examining me.
He did not seem to be tired. I was panting for breath and
soaked in cold perspiration.

Don Juan twirled me around in my lying position by
pulling me by the arm. He said that if I wanted to regain
my strength I had to lie with my head towards the east.
Little by little I relaxed and rested my aching body. Finally I had enough energy to stand up. I wanted to look
at my watch, but he prevented me by putting his hand
over my wrist. He very gently turned me around to face
the east and said that there was no need for my confounded timepiece, that we were on magical time, and
that we were going to find out for sure whether or not I
was capable of pursuing power.

I looked around. We were on top of a very large high
hill. I wanted to walk towards something that looked like
an edge or a crevice in the rock, but don Juan jumped
and held me down.

He ordered me imperatively to stay on the place I had
fallen until the sun had come out from behind some black
mountain peaks a short distance away.

He pointed to the east and called my attention to a
heavy bank of clouds over the horizon. He said that it
would be a proper omen if the wind blew the clouds

away in time for the first rays of the sun to hit my body on the hilltop.

He told me to stand still with my right leg in front, as if I were walking, and not to look directly at the horizon but look without focusing.

My legs became very stiff and my calves hurt. It was an agonizing position and my leg muscles were too sore to support me. I held on as long as I could. I was about to collapse. My legs were shivering uncontrollably when don Juan called the whole thing off. He helped me to sit down.

The bank of clouds had not moved and we had not seen the sun rising over the horizon.

Don Juan's only comment was, "Too bad."

I did not want to ask right off what the real implications of my failure were, but knowing don Juan, I was sure he had to follow the dictum of his omens. And there had been no omen that morning. The pain in my calves vanished and I felt a wave of well-being. I began to trot in order to loosen up my muscles. Don Juan told me very softly to run up an adjacent hill and gather some leaves from a specific bush and rub my legs in order to alleviate the muscular pain.

From where I stood I could very plainly see a large lush green bush. The leaves seemed to be very moist. I had used them before. I never felt that they had helped me, but don Juan had always maintained that the effect of really friendly plants was so subtle that one could hardly notice it, yet they always produced the results they were supposed to.

I ran down the hill and up the other. When I got to the top I realized that the exertion had almost been too much for me. I had a hard time catching my breath and my stomach was upset. I squatted and then crouched over for a moment until I felt relaxed. Then I stood up and reached over to pick the leaves he had asked me to. But I could not find the bush. I looked around. I was sure I was on the right spot, but there was nothing in that area of the hilltop that even vaguely resembled that particular plant. Yet that had to be the spot where I had seen it. Any other place would have been out of range for anyone looking from where don Juan was standing.

I gave up the search and walked to the other hill. Don Juan smiled benevolently as I explained my mistake.

"Why do you call it a mistake?" he asked.

"Obviously the bush is not there," I said.

"But you saw it, didn't you?"

"I thought I did."

"What do you see in its place now?"

"Nothing."

There was absolutely no vegetation on the spot where I thought I had seen the plant. I attempted to explain what I had seen as a visual distortion, a sort of mirage. I had really been exhausted, and because of my exhaustion I may have easily believed I was seeing something that I expected to be there but which was not there at all.

Don Juan chuckled softly and stared at me for a brief moment.

"I see no mistake," he said. "The plant is there on that hilltop."

It was my turn to laugh. I scanned the whole area carefully. There were no such plants in view and what I had experienced was, to the best of my knowledge, a hallucination.

Don Juan very calmly began to descend the hill and signaled me to follow. We climbed together to the other hilltop and stood right where I thought I had seen the bush.

I chuckled with the absolute certainty I was right. Don Juan also chuckled.

"Walk to the other side of the hill," don Juan said. "You'll find the plant there."

I brought up the point that the other side of the hill had been outside my field of vision, that a plant may be there, but that that did not mean anything.

Don Juan signaled me with a movement of his head to follow him. He walked around the top of the hill instead of going directly across, and dramatically stood by a green bush without looking at it.

He turned and looked at me. It was a peculiarly piercing glance.

"There must be hundreds of such plants around here," I said.

Don Juan very patiently descended the other side of the hill, with me trailing along. We looked everywhere for a similar bush. But there was none in sight. We covered about a quarter of a mile before we came upon another plant.

Without saying a word, don Juan led me back to the first hilltop. We stood there for a moment and then he guided me on another excursion to look for the plant but in the opposite direction. We combed the area and found two more bushes, perhaps a mile away. They had grown together and stuck out as a patch of intense rich green, more lush than all the other surrounding bushes.

Don Juan looked at me with a serious expression. I did not know what to think of it.

"This is a very strange omen," he said.

We returned to the first hilltop, making a wide detour in order to approach it from a new direction. He seemed to be going out of his way to prove to me that there were very few such plants around there. We did not find any of them on our way. When we reached the hilltop we sat down in complete silence. Don Juan untied his gourds.

"You'll feel better after eating," he said.

He could not hide his delight. He had a beaming grin as he patted me on the head. I felt disoriented. The new developments were disturbing, but I was too hungry and tired to really ponder upon them.

After eating I felt very sleepy. Don Juan urged me to use the technique of looking without focusing in order to find a suitable spot to sleep on the hilltop where I had seen the bush.

I selected one. He picked up the debris from the spot and made a circle with it the size of my body. Very gently he pulled some fresh branches from the bushes and swept the area inside the circle. He only went through the motions of sweeping, he did not really touch the ground with the branches. He then removed all the surface rocks from the area inside the circle and placed them in the center after meticulously sorting them by size into two piles of equal number.

"What are you doing with those rocks?" I asked.

"They are not rocks," he said. "They are strings. They will hold your spot suspended."

He took the smaller rocks and marked the circumference of the circle with them. He spaced them evenly and with the aid of a stick he secured each rock firmly in the ground as if he were a mason.

He did not let me come inside the circle but told me to walk around and watch what he did. He counted eighteen rocks, following a counterclockwise direction.

"Now run down to the bottom of the hill and wait," he said. "And I will come to the edge and see if you are standing in the appropriate spot."

"What are you going to do?"

"I'm going to toss each of these strings to you," he said, pointing to the pile of bigger rocks. "And you have to place them in the ground at the spot I will indicate in the same manner I have placed the other ones.

"You must be infinitely careful. When one is dealing with power, one has to be perfect. Mistakes are deadly here. Each of these is a string, a string that could kill us if we leave it around loose; so you simply can't make any mistakes. You must fix your gaze on the spot where I will throw the string. If you get distracted by anything at all, the string will become an ordinary rock and you won't be able to tell it apart from the other rocks lying around."

I suggested that it would be easier if I carried the "strings" downhill one at a time.

Don Juan laughed and shook his head negatively.

"These are strings," he insisted. "And they have to be tossed by me and have to be picked up by you."

It took hours to fulfill the task. The degree of concentration needed was excruciating. Don Juan reminded me every time to be attentive and focus my gaze. He was right in doing so. To pick out a specific rock that came hurtling downhill, displacing other rocks in its way, was indeed a maddening affair.

When I had completely closed the circle and walked to

the top, I thought I was about to drop dead. Don Juan
had picked some small branches and had matted the circle.
He handed me some leaves and told me to put them inside my pants, against the skin of my umbilical region. He
said that they would keep me warm and I would not need
a blanket to sleep. I tumbled down inside the circle. The
branches made a fairly soft bed and I fell asleep instantly.

It was late afternoon when I woke up. It was windy
and cloudy. The clouds overhead were compact cumulus
clouds, but towards the west they were thin cirrus clouds
and the sun shone on the land from time to time.

Sleeping had renewed me. I felt invigorated and happy.
The wind did not bother me. I was not cold. I propped
my head up with my arms and looked around. I had not
noticed before but the hilltop was quite high. The view
towards the west was impressive. I could see a vast area
of low hills and then the desert. There was a range of
dark brown mountain peaks towards the north and east,
and towards the south an endless expanse of land and hills
and distant blue mountains.

I sat up. Don Juan was not anywhere in sight. I had a
sudden attack of fear. I thought he may have left me
there alone, and I did not know the way back to my car.
I lay down again on the mat of branches and strangely
enough my apprehension vanished. I again experienced a
sense of quietness, an exquisite sense of well-being. It was
an extremely new sensation to me; my thoughts seemed
to have been turned off. I was happy. I felt healthy. A
very quiet ebullience filled me. A soft wind was blowing
from the west and swept over my entire body without
making me cold. I felt it on my face and around my ears,
like a gentle wave of warm water that bathed me and
then receded and bathed me again. It was a strange state
of being that had no parallel in my busy and dislocated
life. I began to weep, not out of sadness or self-pity but
out of some ineffable, inexplicable joy.

I wanted to stay in that spot forever and I may have,
had don Juan not come and yanked me out of the place.

"You've had enough rest," he said as he pulled me up.

He led me very calmly on a walk around the periphery of the hilltop. We walked slowly and in complete silence. He seemed to be interested in making me observe the scenery all around us. He pointed to clouds and mountains with a movement of his eyes or with a movement of his chin.

The scenery in the late afternoon was superb. It evoked sensations of awe and despair in me. It reminded me of sights in my childhood.

We climbed to the highest point of the hilltop, a peak of igneous rock, and sat down comfortably with our backs against the rock, facing the south. The endless expanse of land towards the south was truly majestic.

"Fix all this in your memory," don Juan whispered in my ear. "This spot is yours. This morning you *saw*, and that was the omen. You found this spot by *seeing*. The omen was unexpected, but it happened. You are going to hunt power whether you like it or not. It is not a human decision, not yours or mine.

"Now, properly speaking, this hilltop is your place, your beloved place; all that is around you is under your care. You must look after everything here and everything will in turn look after you."

In a joking way I asked if everything was mine. He said yes in a very serious tone. I laughed and told him that what we were doing reminded me of the story of how the Spaniards that conquered the New World had divided the land in the name of their king. They used to climb to the top of a mountain and claim all the land they could see in any specific direction.

"That's a good idea," he said. "I'm going to give you all the land you can see, not in one direction but all around you."

He stood up and pointed with his extended hand, turning his body around to cover a complete circle.

"All this land is yours," he said.

I laughed out loud.

He giggled and asked me, "Why not? Why can't I give you this land?"

"You don't own this land," I said.

"So what? The Spaniards didn't own it either and yet they divided it and gave it away. So why can't you take possession of it in the same vein?"

I scrutinized him to see if I could detect the real mood behind his smile. He had an explosion of laughter and nearly fell off the rock.

"All this land, as far as you can see, is yours," he went on, still smiling. "Not to use but to remember. This hilltop, however, is yours to use for the rest of your life. I am giving it to you because you have found it yourself. It is yours. Accept it."

I laughed, but don Juan seemed to be very serious. Except for his funny smile, he appeared to actually believe that he could give me that hilltop.

"Why not?" he asked as if he were reading my thoughts.

"I accept it," I said half in jest.

His smile disappeared. He squinted his eyes as he looked at me.

"Every rock and pebble and bush on this hill, especially on the top, is under your care," he said. "Every worm that lives here is your friend. You can use them and they can use you."

We remained silent for a few minutes. My thoughts were unusually scarce. I vaguely felt that his sudden change of mood was foreboding to me, but I was not afraid or apprehensive. I just did not want to talk any more. Somehow, words seemed to be inaccurate and their meanings difficult to pinpoint. I had never felt that way about talking, and upon realizing my unusual mood I hurriedly began to talk.

"But what can I do with this hill, don Juan?"

"Fix every feature of it in your memory. This is the place where you will come in *dreaming*. This is the place where you will meet with powers, where secrets will someday be revealed to you.

"You are hunting power and this is your place, the place where you will store your resources.

"It doesn't make sense to you now. So let it be a piece of nonsense for the time being."

We climbed down the rock and he led me to a small

bowl-like depression on the west side of the hilltop. We sat down and ate there.

Undoubtedly there was something indescribably pleasant for me on that hilltop. Eating, like resting, was an unknown exquisite sensation.

The light of the setting sun had a rich, almost copperish, glow, and everything in the surroundings seemed to be dabbed with a golden hue. I was given totally to observing the scenery; I did not even want to think.

Don Juan spoke to me almost in a whisper. He told me to watch every detail of the surroundings, no matter how small or seemingly trivial. Especially the features of the scenery that were most prominent in a westerly direction. He said that I should look at the sun without focusing on it until it had disappeared over the horizon.

The last minutes of light, right before the sun hit a blanket of low clouds or fog, were, in a total sense, magnificent. It was as if the sun were inflaming the earth, kindling it like a bonfire. I felt a sensation of redness in my face.

"Stand up!" don Juan shouted as he pulled me up.

He jumped away from me and ordered me in an imperative but urging voice to trot on the spot where I was standing.

As I jogged on the same spot, I began to feel a warmth invading my body. It was a copperish warmth. I felt it in my palate and in the "roof" of my eyes. It was as if the top part of my head were burning with a cool fire that radiated a copperish glow.

Something in myself made me trot faster and faster as the sun began to disappear. At a given moment I truly felt I was so light that I could have flown away. Don Juan very firmly grabbed my right wrist. The sensation caused by the pressure of his hand brought back a sense of sobriety and composure. I plunked down on the ground and he sat down by me.

After a few minutes' rest he quietly stood up, tapped me on the shoulder, and signaled me to follow him. We climbed back again to the peak of igneous rock where we had sat before. The rock shielded us from the cold wind. Don Juan broke the silence.

"It was a fine omen," he said. "How strange! It happened at the end of the day. You and I are so different. You are more a creature of the night. I prefer the young brilliancy of the morning. Or rather the brilliancy of the morning sun seeks me, but it shies away from you. On the other hand, the dying sun bathed you. Its flames scorched you without burning you. How strange!"

"Why is it strange?"

"I've never seen it happen. The omen, when it happens, has always been in the realm of the young sun."

"Why is it that way, don Juan?"

"This is not the time to talk about it," he said cuttingly. "Knowledge is power. It takes a long time to harness enough power to even talk about it."

I tried to insist, but he changed the topic abruptly. He asked me about my progress in "dreaming."

I had begun to dream about specific places, such as the school and the houses of a few friends.

"Were you at those places during the day or during the night?" he asked.

My dreams corresponded to the time of the day when I ordinarily was accustomed to being at those places—in the school during the day, at my friends' houses at night.

He suggested that I should try "dreaming" while I took a nap during the daytime and find out if I could actually visualize the chosen place as it was at the time I was "dreaming." If I were "dreaming" at night, my visions of the locale should be of nighttime. He said that what one experiences in "dreaming" has to be congruous with the time of the day when "dreaming" was taking place; otherwise the visions one might have were not "dreaming" but ordinary dreams.

"In order to help yourself you should pick a specific object that belongs to the place you want to go and focus your attention on it," he went on. "On this hilltop here, for instance, you now have a specific bush that you must observe until it has a place in your memory. You can come back here while *dreaming* simply by recalling that bush, or by recalling this rock where we are sitting, or by recalling any other thing here. It is easier to travel in *dreaming* when you can focus on a place of power, such as this one. But if you don't want to come here you may use any other place. Perhaps the school where you go is a place of power for you. Use it. Focus your attention on any object there and then find it in *dreaming*.

"From the specific object you recall, you must go back to your hands and then to another object and so on.

"But now you must focus your attention on everything that exists on this hilltop, because this is the most important place in your life."

He looked at me as if judging the effect of his words.

"This is the place where you will die," he said in a soft voice.

I fidgeted nervously, changing sitting positions, and he smiled.

"I will have to come with you over and over to this hilltop," he said. "And then you will have to come by yourself until you're saturated with it, until the hilltop is oozing you. You will know the time when you are filled with it. This hilltop, as it is now, will then be the place of your last dance."

"What do you mean by my last dance, don Juan?"

"This is the site of your last stand," he said. "You will die here no matter where you are. Every warrior has a place to die. A place of his predilection which is soaked with unforgettable memories, where powerful events left their mark, a place where he has witnessed marvels, where secrets have been revealed to him, a place where he has stored his personal power.

"A warrior has the obligation to go back to that place of his predilection every time he taps power in order to store it there. He either goes there by means of walking or by means of *dreaming*.

"And finally, one day when his time on earth is up and he feels the tap of his death on his left shoulder, his spirit, which is always ready, flies to the place of his predilection and there the warrior dances to his death.

"Every warrior has a specific form, a specific posture

of power, which he develops throughout his life. It is a
sort of dance. A movement that he does under the influence of his personal power.

"If a dying warrior has limited power, his dance is
short; if his power is grandiose, his dance is magnificent.
But regardless of whether his power is small or magnificent, death must stop to witness his last stand on earth.
Death cannot overtake the warrior who is recounting
the toil of his life for the last time until he has finished
his dance."

Don Juan's words made me shiver. The quietness, the
twilight, the magnificent scenery, all seemed to have
been placed there as props for the image of a warrior's
last dance of power.

"Can you teach me that dance even though I am not
a warrior?" I asked.

"Any man that hunts power has to learn that dance,"
he said. "Yet I cannot teach you now. Soon you may
have a worthy opponent and I will show you then the first
movement of power. You must add the other movements
yourself as you go on living. Every new one must be ob-
tained during a struggle of power. So, properly speaking, the posture, the form of a warrior, is the story of his
life, a dance that grows as he grows in personal power."

"Does death really stop to see a warrior dance?"

"A warrior is only a man. A humble man. He cannot
change the designs of his death. But his impeccable spiri-
it, which has stored power after stupendous hardships,
can certainly hold his death for a moment, a moment
long enough to let him rejoice for the last time in recalling his power. We may say that that is a gesture which
death has with those who have an impeccable spirit."

I experienced an overwhelming anxiety and I talked
just to alleviate it. I asked him if he had known warriors
that had died, and in what way their last dance had affected their dying.

"Cut it out," he said dryly. "Dying is a monumental
affair. It is more than kicking your legs and becoming
stiff."

"Will I too dance to my death, don Juan?"

"Certainly. You are hunting personal power even though you don't live like a warrior yet. Today the sun gave you an omen. Your best production in your life's work will be done towards the end of the day. Obviously you don't like the youthful brilliancy of early light. Journeying in the morning doesn't appeal to you. But your cup of tea is the dying sun, old yellowish, and mellow. You don't like the heat, you like the glow.

"And thus you will dance to your death here, on this hilltop, at the end of the day. And in your last dance you will tell of your struggle, of the battles you have won and of those you have lost; you will tell of your joys and bewilderments upon encountering personal power. Your dance will tell about the secrets and about the marvels you have stored. And your death will sit here and watch you.

"The dying sun will glow on you without burning, as it has done today. The wind will be soft and mellow and your hilltop will tremble. As you reach the end of your dance you will look at the sun, for you will never see it again in waking or in *dreaming,* and then your death will point to the south. To the vastness."

14

THE GAIT OF POWER

Saturday, April 8, 1962

"Is death a personage, don Juan?" I asked as I sat down on the porch.

There was an air of bewilderment in don Juan's look. He was holding a bag of groceries I had brought him. He carefully placed them on the ground and sat down in front of me. I felt encouraged and explained that I wanted to know if death was a person, or like a person, when it watched a warrior's last dance.

"What difference does it make?" don Juan asked.

I told him that the image was fascinating to me and I wanted to know how he had arrived at it. How he knew that that was so.

"It's all very simple," he said. "A man of knowledge knows that death is the last witness because he *sees.*"

"Do you mean that you have witnessed a warrior's last dance yourself?"

"No. One cannot be such a witness. Only death can do that. But I have *seen* my own death watching me and I have danced to it as though I were dying. At the end of my dance death did not point in any direction, and my place of predilection did not shiver saying goodbye to me. So my time on earth was not up yet and I did not die. When all that took place, I had limited power and I did not understand the designs of my own death, thus I believed I was dying."

"Was your death like a person?"

"You're a funny bird. You think you are going to understand by asking questions. I don't think you will, but who am I to say?

"Death is not like a person. It is rather a presence. But one may also choose to say that it is nothing and yet it is everything. One will be right on every count. Death is whatever one wishes.

"I am at ease with people, so death is a person for me. I am also given to mysteries, so death has hollow eyes for me. I can look through them. They are like two windows and yet they move, like eyes move. And so I can say that death with its hollow eyes looks at a warrior while he dances for the last time on earth."

"But is that so only for you, don Juan, or is it the same for other warriors?"

"It is the same for every warrior that has a dance of power, and yet it is not. Death witnesses a warrior's last dance, but the manner in which a warrior sees his death is a personal matter. It could be anything—a bird, a light, a person, a bush, a pebble, a piece of fog, or an unknown presence."

Don Juan's images of death disturbed me. I could not find adequate words to voice my questions and I stammered. He stared at me, smiling, and coaxed me to speak up.

I asked him if the manner in which a warrior saw his death depended on the way he had been brought up. I used the Yuma and Yaqui Indians as examples. My own idea was that culture determined the way in which one would envision death.

"It doesn't matter how one was brought up," he said. "What determines the way one does anything is personal power. A man is only the sum of his personal power, and that sum determines how he lives and how he dies."

"What is personal power?"

"Personal power is a feeling," he said. "Something like being lucky. Or one may call it a mood. Personal power is something that one acquires regardless of one's origin. I already have told you that a warrior is a hunter of power, and that I am teaching you how to hunt and store it. The difficulty with you, which is the difficulty with all of us, is to be convinced. You need to believe that personal power can be used and that it is possible to store it, but you haven't been convinced so far."

I told him that he had made his point and that I was as convinced as I would ever be. He laughed.

"That is not the type of conviction I am talking about," he said.

He tapped my shoulder with two or three soft punches and added with a cackle, "I don't need to be humored, you know."

I felt obliged to assure him that I was serious.

"I don't doubt it," he said. "But to be convinced means that you can act by yourself. It will still take you a great deal of effort to do that. Much more has to be done. You have just begun."

He was quiet for a moment. His face acquired a placid expression.

"It's funny the way you sometimes remind me of myself," he went on. "I too did not want to take the path of a warrior. I believed that all that work was for nothing, and since we are all going to die what difference would it make to be a warrior? I was wrong. But I had to find that out for myself. Whenever you do realize that you are wrong, and that it certainly makes a world of difference, you can say that you are convinced. And then you can proceed by yourself. And by yourself you may even become a man of knowledge."

I asked him to explain what he meant by a man of knowledge.

"A man of knowledge is one who has followed truthfully the hardships of learning," he said. "A man who has, without rushing or faltering, gone as far as he can in unraveling the secrets of personal power."

He discussed the concept in brief terms and then discarded it as a topic of conversation, saying that I should only be concerned with the idea of storing personal power.

"That's incomprehensible," I protested. "I can't really figure out what you are driving at."

"Hunting power is a peculiar event," he said. "It first has to be an idea, then it has to be set up, step by step, and then, bingo! It happens."

"How does it happen?"

Don Juan stood up. He began stretching his arms and arching his back like a cat. His bones, as usual, made a series of cracking sounds.

"Let's go," he said. "We have a long journey ahead of us."

"But there are so many things I want to ask you," I said.

"We are going to a place of power," he said as he stepped inside his house. "Why don't you save your questions for the time we are there? We may have an opportunity to talk."

I thought we were going to drive, so I stood up and walked to my car, but don Juan called me from the house and told me to pick up my net with gourds. He was waiting for me at the edge of the desert chaparral behind his house.

"We have to hurry up," he said.

We reached the lower slopes of the western Sierra Madre mountains around three P.M. It had been a warm day but towards the late afternoon the wind became cold. Don Juan sat down on a rock and signaled me to do likewise.

"What are we going to do here this time, don Juan?"

"You know very well that we're here to hunt power."

"I know that. But what are we going to do here in particular?"

"You know that I don't have the slightest idea."

"Do you mean that you never follow a plan?"

"Hunting power is a very strange affair," he said. "There is no way to plan it ahead of time. That's what's exciting about it. A warrior proceeds as if he had a plan though, because he trusts his personal power. He knows for a fact that it will make him act in the most appropriate fashion."

I pointed out that his statements were somehow contradictory. If a warrior already had personal power, why was he hunting for it?

Don Juan raised his brows and made a gesture of feigned disgust.

"You're the one who is hunting personal power," he said. "And I am the warrior who already has it. You asked me if I had a plan and I said that I trust my personal power to guide me and that I don't need to have a plan."

We remained quiet for a moment and then began walking again. The slopes were very steep and climbing them was very difficult and extremely tiring for me. On the other hand, there seemed to be no end to don Juan's stamina. He did not run or hurry. His walking was steady and tireless. I noticed that he was not even perspiring, even after having climbed an enormous and almost vertical slope. When I reached the top of it, don Juan was already there, waiting for me. As I sat down next to him I felt that my heart was about to burst out of my chest. I lay on my back and perspiration literally poured from my brows.

Don Juan laughed out loud and rolled me back and forth for a while. The motion helped me catch my breath.

I told him that I was simply awed by his physical prowess.

"I've been trying to draw your attention to it all along," he said.

"You're not old at all, don Juan!"

"Of course not. I've been trying to make you notice it."

"How do you do it?"

"I don't do anything. My body feels fine, that's all. I treat myself very well, therefore, I have no reason to feel tired or ill at ease. The secret is not in what you do to yourself but rather in what you don't do."

I waited for an explanation. He seemed to be aware of my incapacity to understand. He smiled knowingly and stood up.

"This is a place of power," he said. "Find a place for us to camp here on this hilltop."

I began to protest. I wanted him to explain what I should not do to my body. He made an imperative gesture.

"Cut the guff," he said softly. "This time just act for a change. It doesn't matter how long it takes you to find a suitable place to rest. It might take you all night. It is not important that you find the spot either; the important issue is that you try to find it."

I put away my writing pad and stood up. Don Juan reminded me, as he had done countless times, whenever he had asked me to find a resting place, that I had to look without focusing on any particular spot, squinting my eyes until my view was blurred.

I began to walk, scanning the ground with my half-closed eyes. Don Juan walked a few feet to my right and a couple of steps behind me.

I covered the periphery of the hilltop first. My intention was to work my way in a spiral to the center. But once I had covered the circumference of the hilltop, don Juan made me stop.

He said I was letting my preference for routines take over. In a sarcastic tone he added that I was certainly covering the whole area systematically, but in such a stagnant way that I would not be able to perceive the suitable place. He added that he himself knew where it was, so there was no chance for improvisations on my part.

"What should I be doing instead?" I asked.

Don Juan made me sit down. He then plucked a single leaf from a number of bushes and gave them to me. He ordered me to lie down on my back and loosen my belt and place the leaves against the skin of my umbilical region. He supervised my movements and instructed me to press the leaves against my body with both hands. He then ordered me to close my eyes and warned me that if I wanted perfect results I should not lose hold of the leaves, or open my eyes, or try to sit up when he shifted my body to a position of power.

He grabbed me by the right armpit and swirled me around. I had an invincible desire to peek through my half-closed eyelids, but don Juan put his hand over my eyes. He commanded me to concern myself only with the feeling of warmth that was going to come from the leaves.

I lay motionless for a moment and then I began to feel a strange heat emanating from the leaves. I first sensed it with the palms of my hands, then the warmth extended to my abdomen, and finally it literally invaded my entire body. In a matter of minutes my feet were burning up with a heat that reminded me of times when I had had a high temperature.

I told don Juan about the unpleasant sensation and my desire to take off my shoes. He said that he was going to help me stand up, that I should not open my eyes until he told me to, and that I should keep pressing the leaves to my stomach until I had found the suitable spot to rest.

When I was on my feet he whispered in my ear that I should open my eyes, and that I should walk without a plan, letting the power of the leaves pull me and guide me.

I began to walk aimlessly. The heat of my body was uncomfortable. I believed I was running a high temperature, and I became absorbed in trying to conceive by what means don Juan had produced it.

Don Juan walked behind me. He suddenly let out a scream that nearly paralyzed me. He explained, laughing, that abrupt noises scare away unpleasant spirits. I squinted my eyes and walked back and forth for about half an hour. In that time the uncomfortable heat of my body turned into a pleasurable warmth. I experienced a sensation of lightness as I paced up and down the hilltop. I felt disappointed, however; I had somehow expected to detect some kind of visual phenomenon, but there were no changes whatsoever in the periphery of my field of vision, no unusual colors, or glare, or dark masses.

I finally became tired of squinting my eyes and opened them. I was standing in front of a small ledge of sandstone, which was one of the few barren rocky places on the hilltop; the rest was dirt with widely spaced small bushes. It seemed that the vegetation had burned sometime before and the new growth was not fully mature yet. For some unknown reason I thought that the sandstone ledge was beautiful. I stood in front of it for a long time. And then I simply sat down on it.

"Good! Good!" don Juan said and patted me on the back.

He then told me to carefully pull the leaves from under my clothes and place them on the rock.

As soon as I had taken the leaves away from my skin I began to cool off. I took my pulse. It seemed to be normal

Don Juan laughed and called me "doctor Carlos" and asked me if I could also take his pulse. He said that what I had felt was the power of the leaves, and that that power had cleared me and had enabled me to fulfill my task.

I asserted in all sincerity that I had done nothing in particular, and that I sat down on that place because I was tired and because I found the color of the sandstone very appealing.

Don Juan did not say anything. He was standing a few feet away from me. Suddenly he jumped back and with incredible agility ran and leaped over some bushes to a high crest of rocks some distance away.

"What's the matter?" I asked, alarmed.

"Watch the direction in which the wind will blow your leaves," he said. "Count them quickly. The wind is coming. Keep half of them and put them back against your belly."

I counted twenty leaves. I stuck ten under my shirt and then a strong gust of wind scattered the other ten in a westerly direction. I had the eerie feeling as I saw the leaves being blown off that a real entity was deliberately sweeping them into the amorphous mass of green shrubbery.

Don Juan walked back to where I was and sat down next to me, to my left, facing the south.

We did not speak a word for a long time. I did not know what to say. I was exhausted. I wanted to close my eyes, but I did not dare. Don Juan must have noticed my state and said that it was all right to fall asleep. He told me to place my hands on my abdomen, over the leaves, and try to feel that I was lying suspended on the bed of "strings" that he had made for me on the "place of my predilection." I closed my eyes and a memory of the peace and plenitude I had experienced while sleeping on that other hilltop invaded me. I wanted to find out if I could actually feel I was suspended but I fell asleep.

I woke up just before the sunset. Sleeping had refreshed and invigorated me. Don Juan had also fallen alleep. He opened his eyes at the same time I did. It was windy but I did not feel cold. The leaves on my stomach seemed to have acted as a furnace, a heater of some sort.

I examined the surroundings. The place I had selected to rest was like a small basin. One could actually sit on it as on a long couch; there was enough of a rock wall to serve as a backrest. I also found out that don Juan had brought my writing pads and placed them underneath my head.

"You found the right place," he said, smiling. "And the whole operation took place as I had told you it would. Power guided you here without any plan on your part."

"What kind of leaves did you give me?" I asked.

The warmth that had radiated from the leaves and had kept me in such a comfortable state, without any blankets or extra thick clothing, was indeed an absorbing phenomenon for me.

"They were just leaves," don Juan said.

"Do you mean that I could grab leaves from any bush and they would produce the same effect on me?"

"No. I don't mean that you yourself can do that. You have no personal power. I mean that any kind of leaves would help you, providing that the person who gives them to you has power. What helped you today was not the leaves but power."

"Your power, don Juan?"

"I suppose you could say that it was my power, although that is not really accurate. Power does not belong to anyone. Some of us may gather it and then it could be given directly to someone else. You see, the key to stored power is that it can be used only to help someone else store power."

I asked him if that meant that his power was limited only to helping others. Don Juan patiently explained that he could use his personal power however he pleased, in anything he himself wanted, but when it came to giving it directly to another person, it was useless unless that person utilized it for his own search of personal power.

"Everything a man does hinges on his personal power," don Juan went on. "Therefore, for one who doesn't have any, the deeds of a powerful man are incredible. It takes power to even conceive what power is. This is what I have been trying to tell you all along. But I know you don't understand, not because you don't want to but because you have very little personal power."

"What should I do, don Juan?"

"Nothing. Just proceed as you are now. Power will find a way."

He stood up and turned around in a complete circle, staring at everything in the surroundings. His body moved at the same time his eyes moved; the total effect was that of a hieratic mechanical toy that turned in a complete circle in a precise and unaltered movement.

I looked at him with my mouth open. He hid a smile, cognizant of my surprise.

"Today you are going to hunt power in the darkness of the day," he said and sat down.

"I beg your pardon?"

"Tonight you'll venture into those unknown hills. In the darkness they are not hills."

"What are they?"

"They are something else. Something unthinkable for you, since you have never witnessed their existence."

"What do you mean, don Juan? You always scare me with that spooky talk."

He laughed and kicked my calf softly.

"The world is a mystery," he said. "And it is not at all as you picture it."

He seemed to reflect for a moment. His head bobbed up and down with a rhythmical shake, then he smiled and added, "Well, it is also as you picture it, but that's not all there is to the world; there is much more to it. You have been finding that out all along, and perhaps tonight you will add one more piece."

His tone sent a chill through my body.

"What are you planning to do?" I asked.

"I don't plan anything. All is decided by the same power that allowed you to find this spot."

Don Juan got up and pointed to something in the distance. I assumed that he wanted me to stand up and look. I tried to jump to my feet, but before I had fully stood up, don Juan pushed me down with great force.

"I didn't ask you to follow me," he said in a severe voice. Then he softened his tone and added, "You're going to have a difficult time tonight, and you will need all the personal power you can muster. Stay where you are and save yourself for later."

He explained that he was not pointing at anything but just making sure that certain things were out there. He assured me that everything was all right and said that I should sit quietly and get busy, because I had a lot of time to write before total darkness had set in the land. His smile was contagious and very comforting.

"But what are we going to do, don Juan?"

He shook his head from side to side in an exaggerated gesture of disbelief.

"Write!" he commanded me and turned his back to me.

There was nothing else for me to do. I worked on my notes until it was too dark to write.

Don Juan maintained the same position all the time I was working. He seemed to be absorbed in staring into the distance towards the west. But as soon as I stopped he turned to me and said in a joking tone that the only ways to shut me up were to give me something to eat, or make me write, or put me to sleep.

He took a small bundle from his knapsack and ceremoniously opened it. It contained pieces of dry meat. He handed me a piece and took another for himself and began to chew on it. He casually informed me that it was power food, which both of us needed on that occasion. I was too hungry to think about the possibility that the dry meat may have contained a psychotropic substance. We ate in complete silence until there was no more meat, and by that time it was quite dark.

Don Juan stood up and stretched his arms and back. He suggested I should do the same. He said it was a good practice to stretch the entire body after sleeping, sitting, or walking.

I followed his advice and some of the leaves I had kept under my shirt slid through the legs of my pants. I wondered if I should try to pick them up, but he said to forget about it, that there was no longer any need for them and that I should let them fall as they might.

Then don Juan came very close to me and whispered in my right ear that I was supposed to follow him at very close range and imitate everything he did. He said that we were safe on the spot where we stood, because we were, so to speak, at the edge of the night.

"This is not the night," he whispered, stomping on the rock where we were standing. "The night is out there."

He pointed to the darkness all around us.

He then checked my carrying net to see if the food gourds and my writing pads were secured and in a soft voice said that a warrior always made sure that everything was in proper order, not because he believed that he was going to survive the ordeal he was about to undertake, but because that was part of his impeccable behavior.

Instead of making me feel relieved, his admonitions created the complete certainty that my doom was approaching. I wanted to weep. Don Juan was, I was sure, completely aware of the effect of his words.

"Trust your personal power," he said in my ear. "That's all one has in this whole mysterious world."

He pulled me gently and we started to walk. He took the lead a couple of steps ahead of me. I followed him with my eyes fixed on the ground. Somehow I did not dare to look around, and focusing my sight on the ground made me feel strangely calm; it almost mesmerized me.

After a short walk don Juan stopped. He whispered that total darkness was near and that he was going to get ahead of me, but was going to give me his position by imitating the cry of a specific small owl. He reminded me that I already knew that his particular imitation was raspy at the beginning and then it became as mellow as the cry of a real owl. He warned me to be deadly aware of other owl cries which did not bear that mark.

By the time don Juan finished giving me all those instructions I was practically panic-stricken. I grabbed him by the arm and would not let go. It took two or three minutes for me to calm myself enough so I could articulate my words. A nervous ripple ran along my stomach and abdomen and kept me from talking coherently.

In a calm soft voice he urged me to get hold of myself, because the darkness was like the wind, an unknown entity at large that could trick me if I was not careful. And I had to be perfectly calm in order to deal with it.

"You must let yourself go so your personal power will merge with the power of the night," he said in my ear.

He said he was going to move ahead of me and I had another attack of irrational fear.

"This is insane," I protested.

Don Juan did not get angry or impatient. He laughed quietly and said something in my ear which I did not quite understand.

"What did you say?" I said loudly through chattering teeth.

Don Juan put his hand over my mouth and whispered that a warrior acted as if he knew what he was doing, when in effect he knew nothing. He repeated one statement three or four times, as if he wanted me to memorize it. He said, "A warrior is impeccable when he trusts his personal power regardless of whether it is small or enormous."

After a short wait he asked me if I was all right. I nodded and he went swiftly out of sight with hardly a sound.

I tried to look around. I seemed to be standing in an area of thick vegetation. All I could distinguish was the dark mass of shrubs, or perhaps small trees. I concentrated my attention on sounds, but nothing was outstanding. The whizzing of the wind muffled every other sound except the sporadic piercing cries of large owls and the whistling of other birds.

I waited for a while in a state of utmost attention. And then came the raspy prolonged cry of a small owl. I had no doubt it was don Juan. It came from a place behind me. I turned around and began to walk in that direction. I moved slowly because I felt inextricably encumbered by the darkness.

I walked for perhaps ten minutes. Suddenly some dark mass jumped in front of me. I screamed and fell backward on my seat. My ears began buzzing. The fright was so great that it cut my wind. I had to open my mouth to breathe.

"Stand up," don Juan said softly. "I didn't mean to scare you. I just came to meet you."

He said that he had been watching my crappy way of walking and that when I moved in the darkness I looked like a crippled old lady trying to tiptoe between mud puddles. He found this image funny and laughed out loud.

He then proceeded to demonstrate a special way of walking in the darkness, a way which he called "the gait of power." He stooped over in front of me and made me run my hands over his back and knees, in order to get an idea of the position of his body. Don Juan's trunk was slightly bent forward, but his spine was straight. His knees were also slightly bent.

He walked slowly in front of me so I could take notice that he raised his knees almost to his chest every time he took a step. And then he actually ran out of sight and came back again. I could not conceive how he could run in total darkness.

"The gait of power is for running at night," he whispered in my ear.

He urged me to try it myself. I told him that I was sure I would break my legs falling into a crevice or a rock. Don Juan very calmly said that the "gait of power" was completely safe.

I pointed out that the only way I could understand his acts was by assuming he knew those hills to perfection and thus could avoid the pitfalls.

Don Juan took my head in his hands and whispered forcefully, "This is the night! And it is power!"

He let go of my head and then added in a soft voice that at night the world was different, and that his ability to run in the darkness had nothing to do with his knowledge of those hills. He said that the key to it was to let one's personal power flow out freely, so it could merge with the power of the night, and that once that power took over there was no chance for a slip-up. He added, in a tone of utmost seriousness, that if I doubted it I should consider for a moment what was taking place. For a man of his age to run in those hills at that hour would be suicidal if the power of the night was not guiding him.

"Look!" he said and ran swiftly out into the darkness and came back again.

The way his body moved was so extraordinary that I could not believe what I was seeing. He sort of jogged on the same spot for a moment. The manner in which he lifted his legs reminded me of a sprinter doing preliminary warm-up exercises.

He then told me to follow him. I did it with utter constraint and uneasiness. With extreme care I tried to look where I was stepping but it was impossible to judge distance. Don Juan came back and jogged by my side. He whispered that I had to abandon myself to the power of the night and trust the little bit of personal power that I had, or I would never be able to move with freedom, and that the darkness was encumbering only because I relied on my sight for everything I did, not knowing that another way to move was to let power be the guide.

I tried various times without any success. I simply could not let go. The fear of injuring my legs was overpowering. Don Juan ordered me to keep on moving in the same spot and to try to feel as if I were actually using the "gait of power."

He then said that he was going to run ahead and that I should wait for his owl's cry. He disappeared in the darkness before I could say anything. I closed my eyes at times and jogged on the same spot with my knees and trunk bent for perhaps an hour. Little by little my tension began to ease up until I was fairly comfortable. Then I heard don Juan's cry.

I ran five or six yards in the direction where the cry came from, trying to "abandon myself," as don Juan had suggested. But stumbling into a bush immediately brought back my feelings of insecurity.

Don Juan was waiting for me and corrected my posture. He insisted I should first curl my fingers against my palms, stretching out the thumb and index of each hand. Then he said that in his opinion I was just indulging myself in my feelings of inadequacy, since I knew for a fact

I could always see fairly well, no matter how dark the night was, if I did not focus on anything but kept scanning the ground right in front of me. The "gait of power" was similar to finding a place to rest. Both entailed a sense of abandon, and a sense of trust. The "gait of power" required that one keep the eyes on the ground directly in front, because even a glance to either side would produce an alteration in the flow of movement. He explained that bending the trunk forward was necessary in order to lower the eyes, and the reason for lifting the knees up to the chest was because the steps had to be very short and safe. He warned me that I was going to stumble a great deal at first but he assured me that with practice I could run as swiftly and as safely as I could in the daytime.

For hours I tried to imitate his movements and get into the mood he recommended. He would very patiently jog on the same spot in front of me, or he would take off in a short run and return to where I was, so I could see how he moved. He would even push me and make me run a few yards.

Then he took off and called me with a series of owl cries. In some inexplicable way I moved with an unexpected degree of self-confidence. To my knowledge I had done nothing to warrant that feeling, but my body seemed to be cognizant of things without thinking about them. For example, I could not really see the jagged rocks in my way, but my body always mannaged to step on the edges and never in the crevices, except for a few mishaps when I lost my balance because I became distracted. The degree of concentration needed to keep scanning the area directly in front had to be total. As don Juan had warned me, any slight glance to the side or too far ahead altered the flow.

I located don Juan after a long search. He was sitting by some dark shapes that seemed to be trees. He came towards me and said that I was doing very well, but it was time to quit because he had been using his whistle long enough and was sure that by then it could be imitated by others.

I agreed that it was time to stop. I was nearly exhausted by my attempts. I felt relieved and asked him who would imitate his cry.

"Powers, allies, spirits, who knows?" he said in a whisper.

He explained that those "entities of the night" usually made very melodious sounds but were at a great disadvantage in reproducing the raspiness of human cries or bird whistlings. He cautioned me to always stop moving if I ever heard such a sound and to keep in mind all he had said, because at some other time I might need to make the proper identification. In a reassuring tone he said that I had a very good idea what the "gait of power" was like, and that in order to master it I needed only a slight push, which I could get on another occasion when we ventured again into the night. He patted me on the shoulder and announced that he was ready to leave.

"Let's get out of here," he said and began running.

"Wait! Wait!" I screamed frantically. "Let's walk."

Don Juan stopped and took off his hat.

"Golly!" he said in a tone of perplexity. "We're in a fix. You know that I cannot walk in the dark. I can only run. I'll break my legs if I walk."

I had the feeling he was grinning when he said that, although I could not see his face.

He added in a confidential tone that he was too old to walk and the little bit of the "gait of power" that I had learned that night had to be stretched to meet the occasion.

"If we don't use the 'gait of power' we will be mowed down like grass," he whispered in my ear.

"By whom?"

"There are things in the night that act on people," he whispered in a tone that sent chills through my body.

He said that it was not important that I keep up with him, because he was going to give repeated signals of four owl cries at a time so I could follow him.

I suggested that we should stay in those hills until dawn and then leave. He retorted in a very dramatic tone that to stay there would be suicidal; and even if we came out alive, the night would have drained our personal power to the point that we could not avoid being the victims of the first hazard of the day.

"Let's not waste any more time," he said with a note or urgency in his voice. "Let's get out of here."

He reassured me that he would try to go as slowly as possible. His final instructions were that I should try not to utter a sound, not even a gasp, no matter what happened. He gave me the general direction we were going to go in and began running at a markedly slower pace. I followed him, but no matter how slow he moved I could not keep up with him, and he soon disappeared in the darkness ahead of me.

After I was alone I became aware that I had adopted a fairly fast walk without realizing it. And that came as a shock to me. I tried to maintain that pace for a long while and then I heard don Juan's call a little bit to my right. He whistled four times in succession.

After a very short while I again heard his owl cry, this time to my far right. In order to follow it I had to make a forty-five-degree turn. I began to move in the new direction, expecting that the other three cries of the set would give me a better orientation.

I heard a new whistle, which placed don Juan almost in the direction where we had started. I stopped and listened. I heard a very sharp noise a short distance away. Something like the sound of two rocks being struck against each other. I strained to listen and detected a series of soft noises, as if two rocks were being struck gently. There was another owl's cry and then I knew what don Juan had meant. There was something truly melodious about it. It was definitely longer and even more mellow than a real owl's.

I felt a strange sensation of fright. My stomach contracted as if something were pulling me down from the middle part of my body. I turned around and started to semi-jog in the opposite direction.

I heard a faint owl cry in the distance. There was a rapid succession of three more cries. They were don Juan's. I ran in their direction. I felt that he must have been a good quarter of a mile away and if he kept up that pace I would soon be incxtricably alone in those hills. I could not understand why don Juan would run ahead, when he could have run around me, if he needed to keep that pace.

I noticed then that there seemed to be something moving with me to my left. I could almost see it in the extreme periphery of my visual field. I was about to panic, but a sobering thought crossed my mind. I could not possibly see anything in the dark. I wanted to stare in that direction but I was afraid to lose my momentum.

Another owl cry jolted me out of my deliberations. It came from my left. I did not follow it because it was without a doubt the most sweet and melodious cry I had ever heard. It did not frighten me though. There was something very appealing, or perhaps haunting, or even sad about it.

Then a very swift dark mass crossed from left to right ahead of me. The suddenness of its movements made me look ahead, I lost my balance and crashed noisily against some shrubs. I fell down on my side and then I heard the melodious cry a few steps to my left. I stood up, but before I could start moving forward again there was another cry, more demanding and compelling than the first. It was as if something there wanted me to stop and listen. The sound of the owl cry was so prolonged and gentle that it eased my fears. I would have actually stopped had I not heard at that precise moment don Juan's four raspy cries. They seemed to be nearer. I jumped and took off in that direction.

After a moment I noticed again a certain flicker or a wave in the darkness to my left. It was not a sight proper, but rather a feeling, and yet I was almost sure I was perceiving it with my eyes. It moved faster than I did, and again it crossed from left to right, making me lose my balance. This time I did not fall down, and strangely enough not falling down annoyed me. I suddenly became angry and the incongruency of my feelings threw me into true panic. I tried to accelerate my pace. I wanted to give out an owl cry myself to let don Juan know where I was, but I did not dare to disobey his instructions.

At that moment some gruesome thing came to my attention. There was actually something like an animal to my left, almost touching me. I jumped involuntarily and veered to my right. The fright almost suffocated me. I was so intensely gripped by fear that there were no thoughts in my mind as I moved in the darkness as fast as I could. My fear seemed to be a bodily sensation that had nothing to do with my thoughts. I found that condition very unusual. In the course of my life, my fears had always been mounted on an intellectual matrix and had been engendered by threatening social situations, or by people behaving towards me in dangerous ways. This time, however, my fear was a true novelty. It came from an unknown part of the world and hit me in an unknown part of myself.

I heard an owl cry very close and slightly to my left. I could not catch the details of its pitch, but it seemed to be don Juan's. It was not melodious. I slowed down. Another cry followed. The raspiness of don Juan's whistles was there, so I moved faster. A third whistle came from a very short distance away. I could distinguish a dark mass of rocks or perhaps trees. I heard another owl's cry and I thought that don Juan was waiting for me because we were out of the field of danger. I was almost at the edge of the darker area when a fifth cry froze me on the spot. I strained to see ahead into the dark area, but a sudden rustling sound to my left made me turn around in time to notice a black object, blacker than the surroundings, rolling or sliding by my side. I gasped and jumped away. I heard a clicking sound, as if someone were smacking his lips, and then a very large dark mass lurched out of the darker area. It was square, like a door, perhaps eight to ten feet high.

The suddenness of its appearance made me scream. For a moment my fright was all out of proportion, but a second later I found myself awesomely calm, staring at the dark shape.

My reactions were, as far as I was concerned, another total novelty. Some part of myself seemed to pull me towards the dark area with an eerie insistence, while another part of me resisted. It was as if I wanted to find out for sure on the one hand, and on the other I wanted to run hysterically out of there.

I barely heard don Juan's owl cries. They seemed to be very close by and they seemed to be frantic; they were longer and raspier, as though he was whistling while he ran towards me.

Suddenly I seemed to regain control of myself and was able to turn around and for a moment I ran just as don Juan had been wanting me to.

"Don Juan!" I shouted when I found him.

He put his hand on my mouth and signaled me to follow and we both jogged at a very comfortable pace until we came to the sandstone ledge where we had been before.

We sat in absolute silence on the ledge for about an hour, until dawn. Then we ate food from the gourds. Don Juan said that we had to remain on the ledge until midday, and that we were not going to sleep at all but were going to talk as if nothing was out of the ordinary.

He asked me to relate in detail everything that had happened to me from the moment he had left me. When I concluded my narration he stayed quiet for a long time. He seemed to be immersed in deep thought.

"It doesn't look too good," he finally said. "What happened to you last night was very serious, so serious that you cannot venture into the night alone any more. From now on the entities of the night won't leave you alone."

"What happened to me last night, don Juan?"

"You stumbled on some entities which are in the world, and which act on people. You know nothing about them because you have never encountered them. Perhaps it would be more proper to call them entities of the mountains; they don't really belong to the night. I call them entities of the night because one can perceive them in the darkness with greater ease. They are here, around us at all times. In daylight, however, it is more difficult to perceive them, simply because the world is familiar to us, and that which is familiar takes precedence. In the darkness, on the other hand, everything is equally strange and very few things take precedence, so we are more susceptible to those entities at night."

"But are they real, don Juan?"

"Of course! They are so real that ordinarily they kill people, especially those who stray into the wilderness and have no personal power."

"If you knew they were so dangerous, why did you leave me alone there?"

"There is only one way to learn, and that way is to get down to business. To only talk about power is useless. If you want to know what power is, and if you want to stress it you must tackle everything yourself.

"The road to knowledge and power is very difficult and very long. You may have noticed that I have not let you venture into the darkness by yourself until last night. You did not have enough power to do that. Now you do have enough to wage a good battle, but not enough to stay in the dark by yourself."

"What would happen if I did?"

"You'll die. The entities of the night will crush you like a bug."

"Does that mean that I cannot spend a night by myself?"

"You can spend the night by yourself in your bed, but not in the mountains."

"What about the flatlands?"

"It applies only to the wilderness, where there are no people around, especially the wilderness in high mountains. Since the natural abodes of the entities of the night are rocks and crevices, you cannot go to the mountains from now on unless you have stored enough personal power."

"But how can I store personal power?"

"You are doing it by living the way I have recommended. Little by little you are plugging up all your points of drainage. You don't have to be deliberate about it, because power always finds a way. Take me as an example. I didn't know I was storing power when I first began to learn the ways of a warrior. Just like you, I thought I wasn't doing anything in particular, but that was not so.

Power has the peculiarity of being unnoticeable when it is being stored."

I asked him to explain how he had arrived at the conclusion that it was dangerous for me to stay by myself in the darkness.

"The entities of the night moved along your left," he said. "They were trying to merge with your death. Especially the door that you saw. It was an opening, you know, and it would have pulled you until you had been forced to cross it. And that would have been your end."

I mentioned, in the best way I could, that I thought it was very strange that things always happened when he was around, and that it was as if he had been concocting all the events himself. The times I had been alone in the wilderness at night had always been perfectly normal and uneventful. I had never experienced shadows or strange noises. In fact, I had never been frightened by anything.

Don Juan chuckled softly and said that everything was proof he had enough personal power to call a myriad of things to his aid.

I had the feeling he perhaps was hinting that he actually had called on some people as his confederates.

Don Juan seemed to have read my thoughts and laughed out loud.

"Don't tax yourself with explanations," he said. "What I said makes no sense to you, simply because you still don't have enough personal power. Yet you have more than when you started, so things have begun to happen to you. You already had a powerful encounter with the fog and lightning. It is not important that you understand what happened to you that night. What's important is that you have acquired the memory of it. The bridge and everything else you saw that night will be repeated some day when you have enough personal power."

"For what purpose would all that be repeated, don Juan?"

"I don't know. I am not you. Only you can answer that. We are all different. That's why I had to leave you by yourself last night, although I knew it was mortally dangerous; you had to test yourself against those entities. The reason I chose the owl's cry was because owls are the entities' messengers. To imitate the cry of an owl brings them out. They became dangerous to you not because they are naturally malevolent but because you were not impeccable. There is something in you that is very chintzy and I know what it is. You are just humoring me. You have been humoring everybody all along and, of course, that places you automatically above everyone and everything. But you know yourself that that cannot be so. You are only a man, and your life is too brief to encompass all the wonders and all the horrors of this marvelous world. Therefore, your humoring is chintzy; it cuts you down to a crappy size."

I wanted to protest. Don Juan had nailed me, as he had done dozens of times before. For a moment I became angry. But, as it had happened before, writing detached me enough so I could remain impassive.

"I think I have a cure for it," don Juan went on after a long interval. "Even you would agree with me if you could remember what you did last night. You ran as fast as any sorcerer only when your opponent became unbearable. We both know that and I believe I have already found a worthy opponent for you."

"What are you going to do, don Juan?"

He did not answer. He stood up and stretched his body. He seemed to contract every muscle. He ordered me to do the same.

"You must stretch your body many times during the day," he said. "The more times the better, but only after a long period of work or a long period of rest."

"What kind of opponent are you going to find for me?" I asked.

"Unfortunately only our fellow men are our worthy opponents," he said. "Other entities have no volition of their own and one must go to meet them and lure them out. Our fellow men, on the contrary, are relentless.

"We have talked long enough," don Juan said in an abrupt tone and turned to me. "Before we leave you must do one more thing, the most important of all. I am going to tell you something right now to set your mind at ease about why you are here. The reason you keep on coming to see me is very simple; every time you have seen me your body has learned certain things, even against your desire. And finally your body now needs to come back to me to learn more. Let's say that your body knows that it is going to die, even though you never think about it. So I've been telling your body that I too am going to die and before I do I would like to show your body certain things, things which you cannot give to your body yourself. For example, your body needs fright. It likes it. Your body needs the darkness and the wind. Your body now knows the gait of power and can't wait to try it. So let's say then that your body returns to see me because I am its friend."

Don Juan remained silent for a long while. He seemed to be struggling with his thoughts.

"I've told you that the secret of a strong body is not in what you do to it but what you don't do," he finally said. "Now it is time for you not to do what you always do. Sit here until we leave and *not-do*."

"I don't follow you, don Juan."

He put his hands over my notes and took them away from me. He carefully closed the pages of my notebook, secured it with a rubber band, and then threw it like a disk far into the chaparral.

I was shocked and began to protest but he put his hand over my mouth. He pointed to a large bush and told me to fix my attention not on the leaves but on the shadows of the leaves. He said that running in the darkness did not have to be spurred by fear but could be a very natural reaction of a jubilant body that knew how "to not do." He repeated over and over in a whisper in my right ear that "to not do what I knew how to do" was the key to power. In the case of looking at a tree, what I knew how to do was to focus immediately on the foliage. The shadows of the leaves or the spaces in between the leaves were never my concern. His last admonitions were to start focusing on the shadows of the leaves on one single branch and then eventually work my way to the whole

tree, and not to let my eyes go back to the leaves, because the first deliberate step to storing personal power
was to allow the body to "not-do."

Perhaps it was because of my fatigue or my nervous
excitation, but I became so immersed in the shadows of
the leaves that by the time don Juan stood up I could
almost group the dark masses of shadows as effectively
as I normally grouped the foliage. The total effect was
startling. I told don Juan that I would like to stay longer.
He laughed and patted me on my hat.

"I've told you," he said. "The body likes things like
this."

He then said that I should let my stored power guide
me through the bushes to my notebook. He gently
pushed me into the chaparral. I walked aimlessly for a
moment and then I came upon it. I thought that I must
have unconsciously memorized the direction in which don
Juan had thrown it. He explained the event, saying that
I went directly to the notebook because my body had
been soaked for hours in "not-doing."

15

NOT-DOING

Wednesday, April 11, 1962

Upon returning to his house, don Juan recommended that
I work on my notes as if nothing had happened to me,
and not to mention or even be concerned with any of
the events I had experienced.

After a day's rest he announced that we had to leave
the area for a few days because it was advisable to put
distance between us and those "entities." He said that

they had affected me deeply, although I was not noticing their effect yet because my body was not sensitive enough. In a short while, however, I would fall seriously ill if I did not go to my "place of predilection" to be cleansed and restored.

We left before dawn and drove north, and after an exhausting drive and a fast hike we arrived at the hilltop in the late afternoon.

Don Juan, as he had done before, covered the spot where I had once slept with small branches and leaves. Then he gave me a handful of leaves to put against the skin of my abdomen and told me to lie down and rest. He fixed another place for himself slightly to my left, about five feet away from my head, and also lay down.

In a matter of minutes I began to feel an exquisite warmth and a sense of supreme well-being. It was a sense of physical comfort, a sensation of being suspended in mid-air. I could fully agree with don Juan's statement that the "bed of strings" would keep me floating. I commented on the unbelievable quality of my sensory experience. Don Juan said in a factual tone that the "bed" was made for that purpose.

"I can't believe that this is possible!" I exclaimed.

Don Juan took my statement literally and scolded me. He said he was tired of my acting as an ultimately important being that has to be given proof over and over that the world is unknown and marvelous.

I tried to explain that a rhetorical exclamation had no significance. He retorted that if that were so I could have chosen another statement. It seemed that he was seriously annoyed with me. I sat up halfway and began to apologize, but he laughed and, imitating my manner of speaking, suggested a series of hilarious rhetorical exclamations I could have used instead. I ended up laughing at the calculated absurdity of some of his proposed alternatives.

He giggled and in a soft tone reminded me that I should abandon myself to the sensation of floating.

The soothing feeling of peace and plenitude that I experienced in that mysterious place aroused some deeply buried emotions in me. I began to talk about my life. I confessed that I had never respected or liked anybody, not even myself, and that I had always felt I was inherently evil, and thus my attitude towards others was always veiled with a certain bravado and daring.

"True," don Juan said. "You don't like yourself at all."

He cackled and told me that he had been "seeing" while I talked. His recommendation was that I should not have remorse for anything I had done, because to isolate one's acts as being mean, or ugly, or evil was to place an unwarranted importance on the self.

I moved nervously and the bed of leaves made a rustling sound. Don Juan said that if I wanted to rest I should not make my leaves feel agitated, and that I should imitate him and lie without making a single movement. He added that in his "seeing" he had come across one of my moods. He struggled for a moment, seemingly to find a proper word, and said that the mood in question was a frame of mind I continually lapsed into. He described it as a sort of trap door that opened at unexpected times and swallowed me.

I asked him to be more specific. He replied that it was impossible to be specific about "seeing."

Before I could say anything else he told me I should relax, but not fall asleep, and be in a state of awareness for as long as I could. He said that the "bed of strings" was made exclusively to allow a warrior to arrive at a certain state of peace and well-being.

In a dramatic tone don Juan stated that well-being was a condition one had to groom, a condition one had to become acquainted with in order to seek it.

"You don't know what well-being is, because you have never experienced it," he said.

I disagreed with him. But he continued arguing that well-being was an achievement one had to deliberately seek. He said that the only thing I knew how to seek was a sense of disorientation, ill-being, and confusion.

He laughed mockingly and assured me that in order to accomplish the feat of making myself miserable I had to work in a most intense fashion, and that it was absurd I had never realized I could work just the same in making myself complete and strong.

"The trick is in what one emphasizes," he said. "We either make ourselves miserable, or we make ourselves strong. The amount of work is the same."

I closed my eyes and relaxed again and began to feel I was floating; for a short while it was as if I were actually moving through space, like a leaf. Although it was utterly pleasurable, the feeling somehow reminded me of times when I had become sick and dizzy and would experience a sensation of spinning. I thought perhaps I had eaten something bad.

I heard don Juan talking to me but I did not really make an effort to listen. I was trying to make a mental inventory of all the things I had eaten that day, but I could not become interested in it. It did not seem to matter.

"Watch the way the sunlight changes," he said.

His voice was clear. I thought it was like water, fluid and warm.

The sky was totally free of clouds towards the west and the sunlight was spectacular. Perhaps the fact that don Juan was cuing me made the yellowish glow of the afternoon sun truly magnificent.

"Let that glow kindle you," don Juan said. "Before the sun goes down today you must be perfectly calm and restored, because tomorrow or the day after, you are going to learn *not-doing*."

"Learn not doing what?" I asked.

"Never mind now," he said. "Wait until we are in those lava mountains."

He pointed to some distant jagged, dark, menacing-looking peaks towards the north.

Thursday, April 12, 1962

We reached the high desert around the lava mountains in the late afternoon. In the distance the dark brown lava mountains looked almost sinister. The sun was very low on the horizon and shone on the western face of the solidified lava, tinting its dark brownness with a dazzling array of yellow reflections.

I could not keep my eyes away. Those peaks were truly mesmerizing.

By the end of the day the bottom slopes of the mountains were in sight. There was very little vegetation on the high desert; all I could see were cacti and a kind of tall grass that grew in tufts.

Don Juan stopped to rest. He sat down, carefully propped his food gourds against a rock, and said that we were going to camp on that spot for the night. He had picked a relatively high place. From where I stood I could see quite a distance away, all around us.

It was a cloudy day and the twilight quickly enveloped the area. I became involved in watching the speed with which the crimson clouds on the west faded into a uniform thick dark gray.

Don Juan got up and went to the bushes. By the time he came back the silhouette of the lava mountains was a dark mass. He sat down next to me and called my attention to what seemed to be a natural formation on the mountains towards the northeast. It was a spot which had a color much lighter than its surroundings. While the whole range of lava mountains looked uniformly dark brown in the twilight, the spot he was pointing at was actually yellowish or dark beige. I could not figure out what it could be. I stared at it for a long time. It seemed to be moving; I fancied it to be pulsating. When I squinted my eyes it actually rippled as if the wind were moving it.

"Look at it fixedly!" don Juan commanded me.

At one moment, after I had maintained my stare for quite a while, I felt that the whole range of mountains was moving towards me. That feeling was accompanied by an unusual agitation in the pit of my stomach. The discomfort became so acute that I stood up.

"Sit down!" don Juan yelled, but I was already on my feet.

From my new point of view the yellowish formation

was lower on the side of the mountains. I sat down again, without taking my eyes away, and the formation shifted to a higher place. I stared at it for an instant and suddenly I arranged everything into the correct perspective. I realized that what I had been looking at was not in the mountains at all but was really a piece of yellowish green cloth hanging from a tall cactus in front of me.

I laughed out loud and explained to don Juan that the twilight had helped to create an optical illusion.

He got up and walked to the place where the piece of cloth was hanging, took it down, folded it, and put it inside his pouch.

"What are you doing that for?" I asked.

"Because this piece of cloth has power," he said casually. "For a moment you were doing fine with it and there is no way of knowing what may have happened if you had remained seated."

Friday, April 13, 1962

At the crack of dawn we headed for the mountains. They were surprisingly far away. By midday we walked into one of the canyons. There was some water in shallow pools. We sat to rest in the shade of a hanging cliff.

The mountains were clumps of a monumental lava flow. The solidified lava had weathered over the millennia into a porous dark brown rock. Only a few sturdy weeds grew between the rocks and in the cracks.

Looking up at the almost perpendicular walls of the canyon, I had a weird sensation in the pit of my stomach. The walls were hundreds of feet high and gave me the feeling that they were closing in on me. The sun was almost overhead, slightly towards the southwest.

"Stand up here," don Juan said and maneuvered my body until I was looking towards the sun.

He told me to look fixedly at the mountain walls above me.

The sight was stupendous. The magnificent height of

the lava flow staggered my imagination. I began to wonder what a volcanic upheaval it must have been. I looked up and down the sides of the canyon various times. I became immersed in the richness of color in the rock wall. There were specks of every conceivable hue. There were patches of light gray moss or lichen in every rock. I looked right above my head and noticed that the sunlight was producing the most exquisite reflections when it hit the brilliant specks of the solidified lava.

I stared at an area in the mountains where the sunlight was being reflected. As the sun moved, the intensity diminished, then it faded completely.

I looked across the canyon and saw another area of the same exquisite light refractions. I told don Juan what was happening, and then I spotted another area of light, and then another in a different place, and another, until the whole canyon was blotched with big patches of light.

I felt dizzy; even if I closed my eyes I could still see the brilliant lights. I held my head in my hands and tried to crawl under the hanging cliff, but don Juan grabbed my arm firmly and imperatively told me to look at the walls of the mountains and try to figure out spots of heavy darkness in the midst of the fields of light.

I did not want to look, because the glare bothered my eyes. I said that what was happening to me was similar to staring into a sunny street through a window and then seeing the window frame as a dark silhouette everywhere else.

Don Juan shook his head from side to side and began to chuckle. He let go of my arm and we sat down again under the hanging cliff.

I was jotting down my impressions of the surroundings when don Juan, after a long silence, suddenly spoke in a dramatic tone.

"I have brought you here to teach you one thing," he said and paused. "You are going to learn *not-doing*. We might as well talk about it because there is no other way for you to proceed. I thought you might catch on to *not-doing* without my having to say anything. I was wrong."

"I don't know what you're talking about, don Juan."

"It doesn't matter," he said. "I am going to tell you about something that is very simple but very difficult to perform; I am going to talk to you about *not-doing,* in spite of the fact that there is no way to talk about it, because it is the body that does it."

He stared at me in glances and then said that I had to pay the utmost attention to what he was going to say.

I closed my notebook, but to my amazement he insisted that I should keep on writing.

"*Not-doing* is so difficult and so powerful that you should not mention it," he went on. "Not until you have *stopped the world*; only then can you talk about it freely, if that's what you'd want to do."

Don Juan looked around and then pointed to a large rock.

"That rock over there is a rock because of *doing,*" he said.

We looked at each other and he smiled. I waited for an explanation but he remained silent. Finally I had to say that I had not understood what he meant.

"That's *doing!*" he exclaimed.

"Pardon me?"

"That's also *doing.*"

"What are you talking about, don Juan?"

"*Doing* is what makes that rock a rock and that bush a bush. *Doing* is what makes you yourself and me myself."

I told him that his explanation did not explain anything. He laughed and scratched his temples.

"That's the problem with talking," he said. "It always makes one confuse the issues. If one starts talking about *doing,* one always ends up talking about something else. It is better to just act.

"Take that rock for instance. To look at it is *doing,* but to *see* it is *not-doing.*"

I had to confess that his words were not making sense to me.

"Oh yes they do!" he exclaimed. "But you are convinced that they don't because that is your *doing*. That is the way you act towards me and the world."

He again pointed to the rock.

"That rock is a rock because of all the things you know how to do to it," he said. "I call that *doing*. A man of knowledge, for instance, knows that the rock is a rock only because of *doing*, so if he doesn't want the rock to be a rock all he has to do is *not-doing*. See what I mean?"

I did not understand him at all. He laughed and made another attempt at explaining.

"The world is the world because you know the *doing* involved in making it so," he said. "If you didn't know its *doing*, the world would be different."

He examined me with curiosity. I stopped writing. I just wanted to listen to him. He went on explaining that without that certain "doing" there would be nothing familiar in the surroundings.

He leaned over and picked up a small rock between the thumb and index of his left hand and held it in front of my eyes.

"This is a pebble because you know the *doing* involved in making it into a pebble," he said.

"What are you saying?" I asked with a feeling of bona fide confusion.

Don Juan smiled. He seemed to be trying to hide a mischievous delight.

"I don't know why you are so confused," he said. "Words are your predilection. You should be in heaven."

He gave me a mysterious look and raised his brows two or three times. Then he pointed again to the small rock he was holding in front of my eyes.

"I say that you are making this into a pebble because you know the *doing* involved in it," he said. "Now, in order to *stop the world* you must stop *doing*."

He seemed to know that I still had not understood and smiled, shaking his head. He then took a twig and pointed to the uneven edge of the pebble.

"In the case of this little rock," he went on, "the first thing which *doing* does to it is to shrink it to this size. So the proper thing to do, which a warrior does if he wants to *stop the world,* is to enlarge a little rock, or any other thing, by *not-doing."*

He stood up and placed the pebble on the boulder and then asked me to come closer and examine it. He told me to look at the holes and depressions in the pebble and try to pick out the minute detail in them. He said that if I could pick out the detail, the holes and depressions would disappear and I would understand what "not-doing" meant.

"This damn pebble is going to drive you crazy today," he said.

I must have had a look of bewilderment on my face. He looked at me and laughed uproariously. Then he pretended to get angry with the pebble and hit it two or three times with his hat.

I urged him to clarify his point. I argued that it was possible for him to explain anything he wanted to if he made an effort.

He gave me a sly glance and shook his head as if the situation were hopeless.

"Sure I can explain anything," he said, laughing. "But could you understand it?"

I was taken aback by his insinuation.

"Doing makes you separate the pebble from the larger boulder," he continued. "If you want to learn *not-doing,* let's say that you have to join them."

He pointed to the small shadow that the pebble cast on the boulder and said that it was not a shadow but a glue which bound them together. He then turned around and walked away, saying that he was coming back to check on me later.

I stared at the pebble for a long time. I could not focus my attention on the minute detail in the holes and depressions, but the tiny shadow that the pebble cast on the boulder became a most interesting point. Don Juan was right; it was like a glue. It moved and shifted. I had the impression it was being squeezed from underneath the pebble.

When don Juan returned I related to him what I had observed about the shadow.

"That's a good beginning," he said. "A warrior can tell all kinds of things from the shadows."

He then suggested that I should take the pebble and bury it somewhere.

"Why?" I asked.

"You've been watching it for a long time," he said. "It has something of you now. A warrior always tries to affect the force of *doing* by changing it into *not-doing*. *Doing* would be to leave the pebble lying around because it is merely a small rock. *Not-doing* would be to proceed with that pebble as if it were something far beyond a mere rock. In this case, that pebble has soaked in you for a long time and now it is you, and as such, you cannot leave it lying around but must bury it. If you would have personal power, however, *not-doing* would be to change that pebble into a power object."

"Can I do that now?"

"Your life is not tight enough to do that. If you would *see*, you would know that your heavy concern has changed that pebble into something quite unappealing, therefore the best thing you can do is to dig a hole and bury it and let the earth absorb its heaviness."

"Is all this true, don Juan?"

"To say yes or no to your question is *doing*. But since you are learning *not-doing* I have to tell you that it really doesn't matter whether or not all this is true. It is here that a warrior has a point of advantage over the average man. An average man cares that things are either true or false, but a warrior doesn't. An average man proceeds in a specific way with things that he knows are true, and in a different way with things that he knows are not true. If things are said to be true, he acts and believes in what he does. But if things are said to be untrue, he doesn't care to act, or he doesn't believe in what he does. A warrior, on the other hand, acts in both instances. If things are said to be true, he would act in order to do *doing*. If things are said to be untrue, he still would act in order to do *not-doing*. See what I mean?"

"No, I don't see what you mean at all," I said.

Don Juan's statements put me in a belligerent mood.

I could not make sense of what he was saying. I told him it was gibberish, and he mocked me and said that I did not even have an impeccable spirit in what I liked to do the most, talking. He actually made fun of my verbal command and found it faulty and inadequate.

"If you are going to be all mouth, be a mouth warrior," he said and roared with laughter.

I felt dejected. My ears were buzzing. I experienced an uncomfortable heat in my head. I was actually embarrassed and presumably red in the face.

I stood up and went into the chaparral and buried the pebble.

"I was teasing you a little bit," don Juan said when I returned and sat down again. "And yet I know that if you don't talk you don't understand. Talking is *doing* for you, but talking is not appropriate and if you want to know what I mean by *not-doing* you have to do a simple exercise. Since we are concerned with *not-doing* it doesn't matter whether you do the exercise now or ten years from now."

He made me lie down and took my right arm and bent it at my elbow. Then he turned my hand until the palm was facing the front; he curved my fingers so my hand looked as if I were holding a doorknob, and then he began to move my arm back and forth with a circular motion that resembled the act of pushing and pulling a lever attached to a wheel.

Don Juan said that a warrior executed that movement every time he wanted to push something out of his body, something like a disease or an unwelcoming feeling. The idea was to push and pull an imaginary opposing force until one felt a heavy object, a solid body, stopping the free movements of the hand. In the case of the exercise, "not-doing" consisted in repeating it until one felt the heavy body with the hand, in spite of the fact that one could never believe it was possible to feel it.

I began moving my arm and in a short while my hand became ice cold. I had begun to feel a sort of mushiness around my hand. It was as if I were paddling through some heavy viscous liquid matter.

Don Juan made a sudden movement and grabbed my arm to stop the motion. My whole body shivered as though stirred by some unseen force. He scrutinized me as I sat up, and then walked around me before he sat back down on the place where he had been.

"You've done enough," he said. "You may do this exercise some other time, when you have more personal power."

"Did I do something wrong?"

"No. *Not-doing* is only for very strong warriors and you don't have the power to deal with it yet. Now you will only trap horrendous things with your hand. So do it little by little, until your hand doesn't get cold any more. Whenever your hand remains warm you can actually feel the lines of the world with it."

He paused as if to give me time to ask about the lines. But before I had a chance to, he started explaining that there were infinite numbers of lines that joined us to things. He said that the exercise of "not-doing" that he had just described would help anyone to feel a line that came out from the moving hand, a line that one could place or cast wherever one wanted to. Don Juan said that this was only an exercise, because the lines formed by the hand were not durable enough to be of real value in a practical situation.

"A man of knowledge uses other parts of his body to produce durable lines," he said.

"What parts of the body, don Juan?"

"The most durable lines that a man of knowledge produces come from the middle of the body," he said, "But he can also make them with his eyes."

"Are they real lines?"

"Surely."

"Can you see them and touch them?"

"Let's say that you can feel them. The most difficult part about the warrior's way is to realize that the world is a feeling. When one is *not-doing*, one is feeling the world, and one feels the world through its lines."

He paused and examined me with curiosity. He raised his brows and opened his eyes and then blinked. The effect was like the eyes of a bird blinking. Almost immediately I felt a sensation of discomfort and queasiness. It was actually as if something was applying pressure to my stomach.

"See what I mean?" don Juan asked and moved his eyes away.

I mentioned that I felt nauseated and he replied in a matter-of-fact tone that he knew it, and that he was trying to make me feel the lines of the world with his eyes. I could not accept the claim that he himself was making me feel that way. I voiced my doubts. I could hardly conceive the idea that he was causing my feeling of nausea, since he had not, in any physical way, impinged on me.

"*Not-doing* is very simple but very difficult," he said. "It is not a matter of understanding but of mastering it. *Seeing,* of course, is the final accomplishment of a man of knowledge, and *seeing* is attained only when one has *stopped the world* through the technique of *not-doing.*"

I smiled involuntarily. I had not understood what he meant.

"When one does something with people," he said, "the concern should be only with presenting the case to their bodies. That's what I've been doing with you so far, letting your body know. Who cares whether or not you understand?"

"But that's unfair, don Juan. I want to understand everything, otherwise coming here would be a waste of my time."

"A waste of your time!" he exclaimed parodying my tone of voice. "You certainly are conceited."

He stood up and told me that we were going to hike to the top of the lava peak to our right.

The ascent to the top was an excruciating affair. It was actual mountain climbing, except that there were no ropes to aid and protect us. Don Juan repeatedly told me not to look down; and he had to actually pull me up bodily a couple of times, after I had begun to slide down the rock. I felt terribly embarrassed that don Juan, being so old, had to help me. I told him that I was in poor physical condition because I was too lazy to do any exercise. He replied that once one had arrived at a certain level of personal power, exercise or any training of that sort was unnecessary, since all one needed, to be in an impeccable form, was to engage oneself in "not-doing."

When we arrived at the top I lay down. I was about to be sick. He rolled me back and forth with his foot as he had done once before. Little by little the motion restored my balance. But I felt nervous. It was as if I were somehow waiting for the sudden appearance of something. I involuntarily looked two or three times to each side. Don Juan did not say a word but he also looked in the direction I was looking.

"Shadows are peculiar affairs," he said all of a sudden. "You must have noticed that there is one following us."

"I haven't noticed anything of the sort," I protested in a loud voice.

Don Juan said that my body had noticed our pursuer, in spite of my stubborn opposition, and assured me in a confident tone that there was nothing unusual about being followed by a shadow.

"It is just a power," he said. "These mountains are filled with them. It is just like one of those entities that scared you the other night."

I wanted to know if I could actually perceive it myself. He asserted that in the daytime I could only feel its presence.

I wanted an explanation of why he called it a shadow when obviously it was not like the shadow of a boulder. He replied that both had the same lines, therefore both were shadows.

He pointed to a long boulder standing directly in front of us.

"Look at the shadow of that boulder," he said. "The shadow is the boulder, and yet it isn't. To observe the boulder in order to know what the boulder is, is *doing,* but to observe its shadow is *not-doing.*

"Shadows are like doors, the doors of *not-doing.* A man of knowledge, for example, can tell the innermost feelings of men by watching their shadows."

"Is there movement in them?" I asked.

"You may say that there is movement in them, or
you may say that the lines of the world are shown in
them, or you may say that feelings come from them."

"But how could feelings come out of shadows, don
Juan?"

"To believe that shadows are just shadows is *doing*,"
he explained. "That belief is somehow stupid. Think
about it this way: There is so much more to everything in
the world that obviously there must be more to shadows
too. After all, what makes them shadows is merely our
doing."

There was a long silence. I did not know what else to
say.

"The end of the day is approaching," don Juan said,
looking at the sky. "You have to use this brilliant sunlight to perform one last exercise."

He led me to a place where there were two peaks the
size of a man standing parallel to each other, about four or
five feet apart. Don Juan stopped ten yards away from
them, facing the west. He marked a spot for me to stand
on and told me to look at the shadows of the peaks. He
said that I should watch them and cross my eyes in the
same manner I ordinarily crossed them when scanning
the ground for a place to rest. He clarified his directions
by saying that when searching for a resting place one
had to look without focusing but in observing shadows
one had to cross the eyes and yet keep a sharp image in
focus. The idea was to let one shadow be superimposed
on the other by crossing the eyes. He explained that
through that process one could ascertain a certain feeling which emanated from shadows. I commented on his
vagueness, but he maintained that there was really no
way of describing what he meant.

My attempt to carry out the exercise was futile. I
struggled until I got a headache. Don Juan was not at all
concerned with my failure. He climbed to a domelike
peak and yelled from the top, telling me to look for two
small long and narrow pieces of rock. He showed with
his hands the size rock he wanted.

I found two pieces and handed them to him. Don

Juan placed each rock about a foot apart in two crevices, made me stand above them facing the west, and told me to do the same exercise with their shadows.

This time it was an altogether different affair. Almost immediately I was capable of crossing my eyes and perceiving their individual shadows as if they had merged into one. I noticed that the act of looking without converging the images gave the single shadow I had formed an unbelievable depth and a sort of transparency. I stared at it, bewildered. Every hole in the rock, on the area where my eyes were focused, was neatly discernible; and the composite shadow, which was superimposed on them, was like a film of indescribable transparency.

I did not want to blink, for fear of losing the image I was so precariously holding. Finally my sore eyes forced me to blink, but I did not lose the view of the detail at all. In fact, by remoistening my cornea the image became even clearer. I noticed at that point that it was as if I were looking from an immeasurable height at a world I had never seen before. I also noticed that I could scan the surroundings of the shadow without losing the focus of my visual perception. Then, for an instant, I lost the notion that I was looking at a rock. I felt that I was landing in a world, vast beyond anything I had ever conceived. This extraordinary perception lasted for a second and then everything was turned off. I automatically looked up and saw don Juan standing directly above the rocks, facing me. He had blocked the sunlight with his body.

I described the unusual sensation I had had, and he explained that he had been forced to interrupt it because he "saw" that I was about to get lost in it. He added that it was a natural tendency for all of us to indulge ourselves when feelings of that nature occur, and that by indulging myself in it I had almost turned "not-doing" into my old familiar "doing." He said that what I should have done was to maintain the view without succumbing to it, because in a way "doing" was a manner of succumbing.

I complained that he should have told me beforehand what to expect and what to do, but he pointed out that he had no way of knowing whether or not I would succeed in merging the shadows.

I had to confess I was more mystified than ever about "not-doing." Don Juan's comments were that I should be satisfied with what I had done, because for once I had proceeded correctly, that by reducing the world I had enlarged it, and that, although I had been far from feeling the lines of the world, I had correctly used the shadow of the rocks as a door into "not-doing."

The statement that I had enlarged the world by reducing it intrigued me to no end. The detail of the porous rock, in the small area where my eyes were focused, was so vivid and so precisely defined that the top of the round peak became a vast world for me; and yet it was really a reduced vision of the rock. When don Juan blocked the light and I found myself looking as I normally would do, the precise detail became dull, the tiny holes in the porous rock became bigger, the brown color of the dried lava became opaque, and everything lost the shiny transparency that made the rock into a real world.

Don Juan then took the two rocks, laid them gently into a deep crevice, and sat down cross-legged facing the west, on the spot where the rocks had been. He patted a spot next to him to his left and told me to sit down.

We did not speak for a long time. Then we ate, also in silence. It was only after the sun had set that he suddenly turned and asked me about my progress in "dreaming."

I told him that it had been easy in the beginning, but that at the moment I had ceased altogether to find my hands in my dreams.

"When you first started dreaming you were using my personal power, that's why it was easier," he said. "Now you are empty. But you must keep on trying until you have enough power of your own. You see, *dreaming* is the *not-doing* of dreams, and as you progress in your *not-doing* you will also progress in *dreaming*. The trick is not to stop looking for your hands, even if you don't believe that what you are doing has any meaning. In fact, as I

have told you before, a warrior doesn't need to believe,
because as long as he keeps on acting without believing
he is *not-doing*."

We looked at each other for a moment.

"There is nothing else I can tell you about *dreaming*,"
he continued. "Everything I may say would only be *not-doing*. But if you tackle *not-doing* directly, you yourself
would know what to do in *dreaming*. To find your
hands is essential, though, at this time, and I am sure
you will."

"I don't know, don Juan. I don't trust myself."

"This is not a matter of trusting anybody. This whole
affair is a matter of a warrior's struggle; and you will keep
on struggling, if not under your own power, then perhaps under the impact of a worthy opponent, or with the
help of some allies, like the one which is already following
you."

I made a jerky involuntary movement with my right
arm. Don Juan said that my body knew much more than
I suspected, because the force that had been pursuing us
was to my right. He confided in a low voice that twice
that day the ally had come so close to me that he had
had to step in and stop it.

"During the day shadows are the doors of *not-doing*,"
he said. "But at night, since very little *doing* prevails in
the dark, everything is a shadow, including the allies.
I've already told you about this when I taught you the
gait of power."

I laughed out loud and my own laughter scared me.

"Everything I have taught you so far has been an as-
pect of *not-doing*," he went on. "A warrior applies *not-doing* to everything in the world, and yet I can't tell you
more about it than what I have said today. You must
let your own body discover the power and the feeling of
not-doing."

I had another fit of nervous cackling.

"It is stupid for you to scorn the mysteries of the world
simply because you know the *doing* of scorn," he said
with a serious face.

I assured him that I was not scorning anything or any-

one, but that I was more nervous and incompetent than
he thought.

"I've always been that way," I said. "And yet I want
to change, but I don't know how. I am so inadequate."

"I already know that you think you are rotten," he
said. "That's your *doing*. Now in order to affect that *doing* I am going to recommend that you learn another *doing*. From now on, and for a period of eight days, I want
you to lie to yourself. Instead of telling yourself the
truth, that you are ugly and rotten and inadequate, you
will tell yourself that you are the complete opposite, knowing that you are lying and that you are absolutely beyond hope."

"But what would be the point of lying like that, don
Juan?"

"It may hook you to another *doing* and then you may
realize that both *doings* are lies, unreal, and that to hinge
yourself to either one is a waste of time, because the
only thing that is real is the being in you that is going
to die. To arrive at that being is the *not-doing* of the
self."

16

THE RING OF POWER

Saturday, April 14, 1962

Don Juan felt the weight of our gourds and concluded
that we had exhausted our food supply and that it was
time to return home. I casually mentioned that it was
going to take us at least a couple of days to get to his
house. He said he was not going back to Sonora but to a

border town where he had some business to take care of.

I thought we were going to start our descent through a water canyon but don Juan headed towards the northwest on the high plateaus of the lava mountains. After about an hour of walking he led me into a deep ravine, which ended at a point where two peaks almost joined. There was a slope there, going almost to the top of the range, a strange slope which looked like a slanted concave bridge between the two peaks.

Don Juan pointed to an area on the face of the slope. "Look there fixedly," he said. "The sun is almost right."

He explained that at midday the light of the sun could help me with "not-doing." He then gave me a series of commands: to loosen all the tight garments I had on, to sit in a cross-legged position, and to look intently at the spot he had specified.

There were very few clouds in the sky and none towards the west. It was a hot day and the sunlight beamed on the solidified lava. I kept a very close watch over the area in question.

After a long vigil I asked what, specifically, I was supposed to look for. He made me be quiet with an impatient gesture of his hand.

I was tired. I wanted to go to sleep. I half closed my eyes; they were itching and I rubbed them, but my hands were clammy and the sweat made my eyes sting. I looked at the lava peaks through half-closed eyelids and suddenly the whole mountain was lit up.

I told don Juan that if I squinted my eyes I could see the whole range of mountains as an intricate array of light fibers.

He told me to breathe as little as possible in order to maintain the view of the light fibers, and not to stare intently into it but to look casually at a point on the horizon right above the slope. I followed his instructions and was able to hold the view of an interminable extension covered with a web of light.

Don Juan said in a very soft voice that I should try to

isolate areas of darkness within the field of light fibers, and that right after finding a dark spot I should open my eyes and check where that spot was on the face of the slope.

I was incapable of perceiving any dark areas. I squinted my eyes and then opened them up various times. Don Juan drew closer to me and pointed to an area to my right, and then to another one right in front of me. I tried to change the position of my body; I thought that perhaps if I shifted my perspective I would be able to perceive the supposed area of darkness he was pointing to, but don Juan shook my arm and told me in a severe tone to keep still and be patient.

I again squinted my eyes and once more saw the web of light fibers. I looked at it for a moment and then I opened my eyes wider. At that instant I heard a faint rumble—it could have easily been explained as the distant sound of a jet plane—and then, with my eyes wide open, I saw the whole range of mountains in front of me as an enormous field of tiny dots of light. It was as if for a brief moment some metallic specks in the solidified lava were reflecting the sunlight in unison. Then the sunlight grew dim and was suddenly turned off and the mountains became a mass of dull dark brown rock and at the same time it also became windy and cold.

I wanted to turn around to see if the sun had disappeared behind a cloud but don Juan held my head and did not let me move. He said that if I turned I might catch a glimpse of an entity of the mountains, the ally that was following us. He assured me that I did not have the necessary strength to stand a sight of that nature, and then he added in a calculated tone that the rumble I had heard was the peculiar way in which an ally heralded its presence.

He then stood up and announced that we were going to start climbing up the side of the slope.

"Where are we going?" I asked.

He pointed to one of the areas he had isolated as being a spot of darkness. He explained that "not-doing" had allowed him to single out that spot as a possible center of power, or perhaps as a place where power objects might be found.

We reached the spot he had in mind after a painful climb. He stood motionless for a moment a few feet in front of me. I tried to come closer to him but he signaled me with his hand to stop. He seemed to be orienting himself. I could see the back of his head moving as if he were sweeping his eyes up and down the mountain, then with sure steps he led the way to a ledge. He sat down and began to wipe some loose dirt off the ledge with his hand. He dug with his fingers around a small piece of rock that was sticking out, cleaning the dirt around it. Then he ordered me to dig it out.

Once I had dislodged the piece of rock, he told me to immediately put it inside my shirt because it was a power object that belonged to me. He said that he was giving it to me to keep, and that I should polish and care for it.

Right after that we began our descent into a water canyon, and a couple of hours later we were in the high desert at the foot of the lava mountains. Don Juan walked about ten feet ahead of me and kept up a very good pace. We went south until just before sunset. A heavy bank of clouds in the west prevented us from seeing the sun but we paused until it had presumably disappeared over the horizon.

Don Juan changed directions then and headed towards the southeast. We went over a hill and as we got to the top I spotted four men coming towards us from the south.

I looked at don Juan. We had never encountered people in our excursions and I did not know what to do in a case like that. But he did not seem to be concerned. He kept on walking as if nothing had happened.

The men moved as if they were not in a hurry; they meandered towards where we were in a leisurely way. When they were closer to us I noticed that they were four young Indians. They seemed to recognize don Juan. He talked to them in Spanish. They were very soft-spoken and treated him with great deference. Only one of them spoke to me. I asked don Juan in a whisper if I could also talk to them and he nodded his head affirmatively.

Once I engaged them in conversation they were very friendly and communicative, especially the one who had first spoken to me. They told me they were there in search of power quartz crystals. They said that they had been wandering around the lava mountains for several days but they had not had any luck.

Don Juan looked around and pointed to a rocky area about two hundred yards away.

"That's a good place to camp for a while," he said.

He began to walk towards the rocks and we all followed him.

The area he had selected was very rugged. There were no bushes on it. We sat down on the rocks. Don Juan announced that he was going to go back into the chaparral to gather dry branches for a fire. I wanted to help him, but he whispered to me that this was a special fire for those brave young men and he did not need my help.

The young men sat down around me in a close cluster. One of them sat with his back against mine. I felt a bit embarrassed.

When don Juan returned with a pile of sticks, he commended them for their carefulness and told me that the young men were a sorcerer's apprentices, and that it was the rule to make a circle and have two people back to back in the center when going on hunting parties for power objects.

One of the young men asked me if I had ever found any crystals myself. I told him that don Juan had never taken me to look for them.

Don Juan selected a place close to a big boulder and started to make a fire. None of the young men moved to help him but watched him attentively. When all the sticks were burning, don Juan sat with his back against the boulder. The fire was to his right.

The young men apparently knew what was going on, but I did not have the faintest idea about the procedure to follow when one was dealing with sorcerer's apprentices.

I watched the young men. They sat facing don Juan, making a perfect half circle. I noticed then that don Juan was directly facing me and two of the young men had sat to my left and the other two to my right.

Don Juan began telling them that I was in the lava mountains to learn "not-doing" and that an ally had been following us. I thought that that was a very dramatic beginning and I was right. The young men changed positions and sat with their left legs tucked under their seats. I had not observed how they were sitting before. I had assumed that they were sitting the same way I was, cross-legged. A casual glance at don Juan revealed to me that he was also sitting with his left leg tucked in. He made a barely perceptible gesture with his chin to point at my sitting position. I casually tucked in my left leg.

Don Juan had once told me that that was the posture that a sorcerer used when things were uncertain. It had always proved, however, to be a very tiring position for me. I felt it was going to be a terrible imposition on me to remain seated in that fashion for the duration of his talk. Don Juan seemed to be thoroughly aware of my handicap and in a succinct manner explained to the young men that quartz crystals could be found in certain specific spots in that area, and that once they were found they had to be coaxed to leave their abode by means of special techniques. The crystals then became the man himself, and their power went beyond our understanding.

He said that ordinarily quartz crystals were found in clusters, and that it was up to the man who had found them to choose five of the longest and best-looking blades of quartz and sever them from their matrix. The finder was responsible for carving and polishing them in order to make them pointed and to make them fit perfectly to the size and shape of the fingers of his right hand.

Then he told us that the quartz crystals were weapons used for sorcery, that they were usually hurled to kill, and that they penetrated the enemy's body and then returned to their owner's hand as though they had never left it.

Next he talked about the search for the spirit that would turn the ordinary crystals into weapons and said that the first thing one had to do was to find a propitious place to lure out the spirit. That place had to be on a hilltop and was found by sweeping the hand, with the palm turned towards the earth. until a certain heat was detected with the palm of the hand. A fire had to be made on that spot. Don Juan explained that the ally was attracted by the flames and manifested itself through a series of consistent noises. The person searching for an ally had to follow the direction of the noises until the ally revealed itself, and then wrestle it to the ground in order to overpower it. It was at that point that one could make the ally touch the crystals to imbue them with power.

He warned us that there were other forces at large in those lava mountains, forces which did not resemble the allies; they did not make any noise, but appeared only as fleeting shadows, and did not have any power at all.

Don Juan added that a brilliantly colored feather or some highly polished quartz crystals would attract the attention of an ally, but in the long run any object whatever would be equally effective, because the important part was not to find the objects but to find the force that would imbue them with power.

"What's the use of having beautifully polished crystals if you never find the spirit giver of power?" he said. "On the other hand, if you don't have the crystals but do find the spirit you may put anything in his way to be touched. You could put your dicks in the way if you can't find anything else."

The young men giggled. The most daring of them, the one who talked to me first, laughed loudly.

I noticed that don Juan had crossed his legs and was sitting in a relaxed manner. All the young men had also crossed their legs. I tried to slip casually into a more relaxed posture, but my left knee seemed to have a pinched nerve or a sore muscle and I had to stand up and jog on the spot for a few minutes.

Don Juan made a joking comment. He said I was out of practice kneeling down, because I had not been to confession in years, ever since I had begun running around with him.

That produced a great commotion among the young men. They laughed in spurts. Some of them covered their faces and giggled nervously.

"I'm going to show you fellows something," don Juan said casually after the young men had stopped laughing.

My guess was that he was going to let us see some power objects he had in his pouch. For an instant I thought the young men were going to cluster around him, for they made a sudden movement in unison. All of them bent forward a little bit, as if they were going to stand up, but then they all tucked their left legs in and went back to that mysterious position that was so hard on my knees.

I tucked my left leg in as casually as possible. I found that if I did not sit on my left foot, that is, if I kept a half-kneeling position, my knees did not hurt as much.

Don Juan stood up and walked around the big boulder until he was out of sight.

He must have fed the fire before he stood up, while I was tucking in my leg, for the new sticks chirped as they ignited and long flames spurted out. The effect was extremely dramatic. The flames grew twice as big. Don Juan suddenly stepped out from behind the boulder and stood where he had been sitting. I had a moment of bewilderment. Don Juan had put on a funny black hat. It had peaks on the side, by the ears, and it was round on top. It occurred to me that it was actually a pirate's hat. He was wearing a long black coat with tails, fastened with a single shiny metallic button, and he had a peg leg.

I laughed to myself. Don Juan really looked silly in his pirate's costume. I began to wonder where he had gotten that outfit out there in the wilderness. I assumed that it must have been hidden behind the rock. I commented to myself that all don Juan needed was a patch over his eye and a parrot on his shoulder to be the perfect stereotype of a pirate.

Don Juan looked at every member of the group, sweeping his eyes slowly from right to left. Then he looked up above us and stared into the darkness behind us. He remained in that position for a moment and then he went around the boulder and disappeared.

I did not notice how he walked. Obviously he must have had his knee bent in order to depict a man with a wooden leg; when he turned around to walk behind the boulder I should have seen his bent leg, but I was so mystified by his acts that I did not pay any attention to details.

The flames lost their strength at the very moment don Juan went around the boulder. I thought that his timing had been superb; he must have calculated how long it would take for the sticks he had added to the fire to burn and had arranged his appearance and exit according to that calculation.

The change in the intensity of the fire was very dramatic for the group; there was a ripple of nervousness among the young men. As the flames diminished in size the young men went back in unison to a cross-legged sitting position.

I expected don Juan to step out from behind the boulder right away and sit down again but he did not. He remained out of sight. I waited impatiently. The young men were sitting with an impassive look on their faces.

I could not understand what don Juan had intended with all those histrionics. After a long wait I turned to the young man on my right and asked him in a low voice if any of the items don Juan had put on—the funny hat and the long tail coat—and the fact he was standing on a peg leg had any meaning to him.

The young man looked at me with a funny blank expression. He seemed confused. I repeated my question and the other young man next to him looked at me attentively in order to listen.

They looked at each other seemingly in utter confusion. I said that to me the hat and the stump and the coat made him into a pirate.

By then all four men had come closer together around me. They giggled softly and fretted nervously. They seemed to be at a loss for words. The most daring of them finally spoke to me. He said that don Juan did not have a hat on, was not wearing a long coat, and was certainly not standing on a stump, but that he had a black cowl or shawl over his head and a jet black tunic, like a friar's, that went all the way to the ground.

"No!" another young man exclaimed softly. "He didn't have a cowl."

"That's right," the others said.

The young man who had spoken first looked at me with an expression of total disbelief.

I told them that we had to review what had happened very carefully and very quietly, and that I was sure don Juan had wanted us to do so and thus he had left us alone.

The young man who was to my extreme right said that don Juan was in rags. He had on a tattered poncho, or some sort of Indian coat, and a most beat-up sombrero. He was holding a basket with things in it, but he was not sure what those things were. He added that don Juan was not really dressed as a beggar but rather as a man who was coming back from an interminable journey loaded with strange things.

The young man who had seen don Juan with a black cowl said that he had nothing in his hands but that his hair was long and wild, as if he were a wild man that had just killed a friar and had put on his clothes but could not hide his wildness.

The young man to my left chuckled softly and commented on the weirdness of it all. He said that don Juan was dressed as an important man who had just gotten off his horse. He had leather leggings for horseback riding, big spurs, a whip that he kept beating on his left palm, a Chihuahua hat with a conical crown, and two .45-caliber automatic pistols. He said that don Juan was the picture of a well-to-do "ranchero."

The young man to my extreme left laughed shyly and did not volunteer to reveal what he had seen. I coaxed him, but the others did not seem to be interested. He appeared to be rather too shy to talk.

The fire was about to be extinguished when don Juan came out from behind the boulder.

"We better leave the young men to their doings," he said to me. "Bid them goodbye."

He did not look at them. He began to walk away slowly to give me time to say goodbye.

The young men embraced me.

There were no flames in the fire, but the live coals reflected enough glare. Don Juan was like a dark shadow a few feet away and the young men were a circle of neatly defined static silhouettes. They were like a row of jet black statues set in a background of darkness.

It was at that point that the total event had an impact on me. A chill ran up my spine. I caught up with don Juan. He told me in a tone of great urgency not to turn around to look at the young men, because at that moment they were a circle of shadows.

My stomach felt a force coming from the outside. It was as if a hand had grabbed me. I screamed involuntarily. Don Juan whispered that there was so much power in that area that it would be very easy for me to use the "gait of power."

We jogged for hours. I fell down five times. Don Juan counted out loud every time I lost my balance. Then he came to a halt.

"Sit down, huddle against the rocks, and cover your belly with your hands," he whispered in my ear.

Sunday, April 15, 1962

As soon as there was enough light in the morning we started walking. Don Juan guided me to the place where I had left my car. I was hungry but I felt otherwise invigorated and well rested.

We ate some crackers and drank some bottled mineral water that I had in my car. I wanted to ask him some questions that were overwhelming me, but he put his finger to his lips.

By mid-afternoon we were in the border town where

he wanted me to leave him. We went to a restaurant to eat lunch. The place was empty; we sat at a table by a window looking out at the busy main street and ordered our food.

Don Juan seemed relaxed; his eyes shone with a mischievous glint. I felt encouraged and began a barrage of questions. I mainly wanted to know about his disguise.

"I showed you a little bit of my *not-doing*," he said and his eyes seemed to glow.

"But none of us saw the same disguise." I said. "How did you do that?"

"It's all very simple," he replied. "They were only disguises, because everything we do is in some way merely a disguise. Everything we do, as I have told you, is a matter of *doing*. A man of knowledge could hook himself to everyone's *doing* and come up with weird things. But they are not weird, not really. They are weird only to those who are trapped in *doing*.

"Those four young men and yourself are not aware yet of *not-doing*, so it was easy to fool all of you."

"But how did you fool us?"

"It won't make sense to you. There is no way for you to understand it."

"Try me, don Juan, please."

"Let's say that when every one of us is born we bring with us a little ring of power. That little ring is almost immediately put to use. So every one of us is already hooked from birth and our rings of power are joined to everyone else's. In other words, our rings of power are hooked to the *doing* of the world in order to make the world."

"Give me an example so I could understand it," I said.

"For instance, our rings of power, yours and mine, are hooked right now to the *doing* in this room. We are making this room. Our rings of power are spinning this room into being at this very moment."

"Wait, wait," I said. "This room is here by itself. I am not creating it. I have nothing to do with it."

Don Juan did not seem to be concerned with my argumentative protests. He very calmly maintained that the room we were in was brought to being and was kept in place because of the force of everybody's ring of power.

"You see," he continued, "every one of us knows the *doing* of rooms because, in one way or another, we have spent much of our lives in rooms. A man of knowledge, on the other hand, develops another ring of power. I would call it the ring of *not-doing*, because it is hooked to *not-doing*. With that ring, therefore, he can spin another world."

A young waitress brought our food and seemed to be suspicious of us. Don Juan whispered that I should pay her to show her that I had enough money.

"I don't blame her for distrusting you," he said and roared with laughter. "You look like hell."

I paid the woman and tipped her, and when she left us alone I stared at don Juan, trying to find a way to recapture the thread of our conversation. He came to my rescue.

"Your difficulty is that you haven't yet developed your extra ring of power and your body doesn't know *not-doing*," he said.

I did not understand what he had said. My mind was locked in quite a prosaic concern. All I wanted to know was whether or not he had put on a pirate's outfit.

Don Juan did not answer but laughed uproariously. I begged him to explain.

"But I've just explained it to you," he retorted.

"You mean, that you didn't put on any disguise?" I asked.

"All I did was to hook my ring of power to your own *doing*," he said. "You yourself did the rest and so did the others."

"That's incredible!" I exclaimed.

"We all have been taught to agree about *doing*," he said softly. "You don't have any idea of the power that that agreement brings with it. But, fortunately, *not-doing* is equally miraculous, and powerful."

I felt an uncontrollable ripple in my stomach. There was an unbridgeable abysm between my first-hand experience and his explanation. As an ultimate defense I

ended up, as I had always done, with a tinge of doubt
and distrust and with the question, "What if don Juan was
really in cahoots with the young men and he himself
had set it all up?"

I changed the subject and asked him about the four
apprentices.

"Did you tell me that they were shadows?" I asked.

"That's right."

"Were they allies?"

"No. They were apprentices of a man I know."

"Why did you call them shadows?"

"Because at that moment they had been touched by
the power of *not-doing,* and since they are not as stupid
as you are they shifted into something quite different from
what you know. I didn't want you to look at them for
that reason. It would have only injured you."

I did not have any more questions. I was not hungry
either. Don Juan ate heartily and seemed to be in an
excellent mood. But I felt dejected. Suddenly a consuming fatigue possessed me. I realized that don Juan's path
was too arduous for me. I commented that I did not have
the qualifications to become a sorcerer.

"Perhaps another meeting with Mescalito will help
you," he said.

I assured him that that was the farthest thing from my
mind, and that I would not even consider the possibility.

"Very drastic things have to happen to you in order
for you to allow your body to profit from all you have
learned," he said.

I ventured the opinion that since I was not an Indian
I was not really qualified to live the unusual life of a
sorcerer.

"Perhaps if I could disentangle myself from all my
commitments I could fare in your world a little better,"
I said. "Or if I would go into the wilderness with you and
live there. As it is now, the fact I have a foot in both
worlds makes me useless in either."

He stared at me for a long moment.

"This is your world," he said, pointing to the busy
street outside the window. "You are a man of that world.

And out there, in that world, is your hunting ground. There is no way to escape the *doing* of our world, so what a warrior does is to turn his world into his hunting ground. As a hunter, a warrior knows that the world is made to be used. So he uses every bit of it. A warrior is like a pirate that has no qualms in taking and using anything he wants, except that the warrior doesn't mind or he doesn't feel insulted when he is used and taken himself."

17

A WORTHY OPPONENT

Tuesday, December 11, 1962

My traps were perfect; the setting was correct; I saw rabbits, squirrels and other rodents, quail, and birds, but I could not catch anything at all during the whole day.

Don Juan had told me, as we left his house in the early morning, that I had to wait that day for a "gift of power," an exceptional animal that might be lured into my traps and whose flesh I could dry for "power food."

Don Juan seemed to be in a pensive mood. He did not make a single suggestion or comment. Near the end of the day he finally made a statement.

"Someone is interfering with your hunting," he said.

"Who?" I asked, truly surprised.

He looked at me and smiled and shook his head in a gesture of disbelief.

"You act as if you didn't know who," he said. "And you've known who all day."

I was going to protest but I saw no point in it. I knew he was going to say "la Catalina," and if that was the kind of knowledge he was talking about, then he was right, I did know who.

"We either go home now," he continued, "or we wait until dark and use the twilight to catch her."

He appeared to be waiting for my decision. I wanted to leave. I began to gather some thin rope that I was using but before I could voice my wish he stopped me with a direct command.

"Sit down," he said. "It would be a simpler and more sober decision to just leave now, but this is a peculiar case and I think we must stay. This show is just for you."

"What do you mean?"

"Someone is interfering with you, in particular, so that makes it your show. I know who and you also know who."

"You scare me," I said.

"Not me," he replied, laughing. "That woman, who is out there prowling, is scaring you."

He paused as if he were waiting for the effect of his words to show on me. I had to admit that I was terrified.

Over a month before, I had had a horrendous confrontation with a sorceress called "la Catalina." I had faced her at the risk of my life because don Juan had convinced me that she was after his life and that he was incapable of fending off her onslaughts. After I had come in contact with her, don Juan disclosed to me that she had never really been of any danger to him, and that the whole affair had been a trick, not in the sense of a malicious prank but in the sense of a trap to ensnare me.

His method was so unethical to me that I became furious with him.

Upon hearing my angry outburst don Juan had begun to sing some Mexican tunes. He imitated popular crooners and his renditions were so comical that I had ended up laughing like a child. He entertained me for hours. I never knew he had such a repertoire of idiotic songs.

"Let me tell you something," he had finally said on that

occasion. "If we wouldn't be tricked, we would never learn. The same thing happened to me, and it'll happen to anyone. The art of a benefactor is to take us to the brink. A benefactor can only point the way and trick. I tricked you before. You remember the way I recaptured your hunter's spirit, don't you? You yourself told me that hunting made you forget about plants. You were willing to do a lot of things in order to be a hunter, things you wouldn't have done in order to learn about plants. Now you must do a lot more in order to survive."

He stared at me and broke into a fit of laughter.

"This is all crazy," I said. "We are rational beings."

"You're rational," he retorted. "I am not."

"Of course you are," I insisted. "You are one of the most rational men I have ever met."

"All right!" he exclaimed. "Let us not argue. I am rational, so what?"

I involved him in the argument of why it was necessary for two rational beings to proceed in such an insane way, as we had proceeded with the lady witch.

"You're rational, all right," he said fiercely. "And that means you believe that you know a lot about the world, but do you? Do you really? You have only seen the acts of people. Your experiences are limited only to what people have done to you or to others. You know nothing about this mysterious unknown world."

He signaled me to follow him to my car and we drove to the small Mexican town nearby.

I did not ask what we were going to do. He made me park my car by a restaurant and then we walked around the bus depot and the general store. Don Juan walked on my right side, leading me. Suddenly I became aware that someone else was walking side by side with me to my left, but before I had time to turn to look, don Juan made a fast and sudden movement; he leaned forward, as if he were picking something from the ground, and then grabbed me by the armpit when I nearly stumbled over him. He dragged me to my car and did not let go of my arm even to allow me to unlock the door. I fumbled with the keys for a moment. He shoved me gently into the car and then got in himself.

"Drive slowly and stop in front of the store," he said.

When I had stopped, don Juan signaled me with a nod of his head to look. "La Catalina" was standing at the place where don Juan had grabbed me. I recoiled involuntarily. The woman took a couple of steps towards the car and stood there defiantly. I scrutinized her carefully and concluded that she was a beautiful woman. She was very dark and had a plump body but she seemed to be strong and muscular. She had a round full face with high cheekbones and two long braids of jet black hair. What surprised me the most was her youth. She was at the most in her early thirties.

"Let her come closer if she wants," don Juan whispered.

She took three or four steps towards my car and stopped perhaps ten feet away. We looked at each other. At that moment I felt there was nothing threatening about her. I smiled and waved at her. She giggled as if she were a shy little girl and covered her mouth. Somehow I felt delighted. I turned to don Juan to comment on her appearance and behavior, and he scared me half to death with a yell.

"Don't turn your back to that woman, damn it!" he said in a forceful voice.

I quickly turned to look at the woman. She had taken another couple of steps towards my car and was standing barely five feet away from my door. She was smiling; her teeth were big and white and very clean. There was something eerie about her smile, however. It was not friendly; it was a contained grin; only her mouth smiled. Her eyes were black and cold and were staring at me fixedly.

I experienced a chill all over my body. Don Juan began to laugh in a rhythmical cackle; after a moment's wait the woman slowly backed away and disappeared among people.

We drove away and don Juan speculated that if I did

not tighten up my life and learn, she was going to step
on me as one steps on a defenseless bug.

"She is the worthy opponent I told you I had found for
you," he said.

Don Juan said that we had to wait for an omen before
we knew what to do with the woman who was interfering
with my hunting.

"If we see or hear a crow, we'll know for sure that we
can wait, and we'll also know where to wait," he added.

He slowly turned around in a complete circle, scanning
all the surroundings.

"This is not the place to wait," he said in a whisper.

We began to walk towards the east. It was already
fairly dark. Suddenly two crows flew out from behind
some tall bushes and disappeared behind a hill. Don Juan
said that the hill was our destination.

Once we arrived there he circled it and chose a place
facing the southeast at the bottom of the hill. He cleaned
the dry twigs and leaves and other debris from a circular
spot five or six feet in diameter. I attempted to help him,
but he refused me with a strong movement of his hand.
He put his finger over his lips and made a gesture of silence. When he had finished he pulled me to the center
of the circle, made me face the south away from the
hill, and whispered in my ear that I had to imitate his
movements. He began a sort of dance, making a rhythmical thump with his right foot; it consisted of seven
even beats spaced by a cluster of three fast thumps.

I tried to adapt myself to his rhythm and after a few
clumsy attempts I was more or less capable of reproducing the same thumping.

"What's this for?" I whispered in his ear.

He told me, also in a whisper, that I was thumping like
a rabbit and that sooner or later the prowler would be
attracted by the noise and would show up to see what
was going on.

Once I had copied the rhythm, don Juan ceased to
thump himself but had me continue, marking the pace
with a movement of his hand.

From time to time he would listen attentively, with his head slightly tilted to the right, seemingly to pick out noises in the chaparral. At one point he signaled me to stop and he remained in a most alert position; it was as if he were ready to spring up and jump on an unknown and unseen assailant.

Then he motioned me to continue the thumping and after a while he stopped me again. Every time I stopped he listened with such a concentration that every fiber in his body seemed to be tense to the point of bursting.

Suddenly he jumped to my side and whispered in my ear that the twilight was at its full power.

I looked around. The chaparral was a dark mass, and so were the hills and the rocks. The sky was dark blue and I could not see the clouds any more. The whole world seemed to be a uniform mass of dark silhouettes which did not have any visible boundaries.

I heard the eerie distant cry of an animal, a coyote or perhaps a night bird. It happened so suddenly that I did not pay attention to it. But don Juan's body jerked a bit. I felt its vibration as he stood next to me.

"Here we go," he whispered. "Thump again and be ready. She's here."

I began to thump furiously and don Juan put his foot over mine and signaled me frantically to relax and thump rhythmically.

"Don't scare her away," he whispered in my ear. "Calm down and don't lose your marbles."

He again began to mark the pace of my thumping, and after the second time he made me stop I heard the same cry again. This time it seemed to be the cry of a bird which was flying over the hill.

Don Juan made me thump once more and just when I stopped I heard a peculiar rustling sound to my left. It was the sound a heavy animal would make while moving about in the dry underbrush. The thought of a bear crossed my mind, but then I realized that there were no bears in the desert. I grabbed on to don Juan's arm and he smiled at me and put his finger to his mouth in a gesture of silence. I stared into the darkness towards my left, but he signaled me not to. He repeatedly pointed directly above me and then he made me turn around slowly and silently until I was facing the dark mass of the hill. Don Juan kept his finger leveled at a certain point on the hill. I kept my eyes glued to the spot and suddenly, as if in a nightmare, a dark shadow leaped at me. I shrieked and fell down to the ground on my back. For a moment the dark silhouette was superimposed against the dark blue sky and then it sailed through the air and landed beyond us, in the bushes. I heard the sound of a heavy body crashing into the shrubs and then an eerie outcry.

Don Juan helped me up and guided me in the darkness to the place where I had left my traps. He made me gather and disassemble them and then he scattered the pieces away in all directions. He performed all this without saying a single word. We did not speak at all on our way back to his house.

"What do you want me to say?" don Juan asked after I had urged him repeatedly to explain the events I had witnessed a few hours before.

"What was it?" I asked.

"You know damn well who it was," he said. "Don't water it down with 'what was it?' It is who it was that is important."

I had worked out an explanation that seemed to suit me. The figure I had seen looked very much like a kite that someone had let out over the hill while someone else, behind us, had pulled it to the ground, thus the effect of a dark silhouette sailing through the air perhaps fifteen or twenty yards.

He listened attentively to my explanation and then laughed until tears rolled down his cheeks.

"Quit beating around the bush," he said. "Get to the point. Wasn't it a woman?"

I had to admit that when I fell down and looked up I saw the dark silhouette of a woman with a long skirt leaping over me in a very slow motion; then something seemed to have pulled the dark silhouette and it flew over me with great speed and crashed into the bushes. In fact, that movement was what had given me the idea of a kite.

Don Juan refused to discuss the incident any further.

The next day he left to fulfill some mysterious errand and I went to visit some Yaqui friends in another community.

Wednesday, December 12, 1962

As soon as I arrived at the Yaqui community, the Mexican storekeeper told me that he had rented a record player and twenty records from an outfit in Ciudad Obregon for the "fiesta" he was planning to give that night in honor of the Virgin of Guadalupe. He had already told everybody that he had made all the necessary arrangements through Julio, the traveling salesman who came to the Yaqui settlement twice a month to collect installments on a layaway plan for cheap articles of clothing which he had succeeded in selling to some Yaqui Indians.

Julio brought the record player early in the afternoon and hooked it to the dynamo that provided electricity for the store. He made sure that it worked; then he turned up the volume to its maximum, reminded the storekeeper not to touch any knobs, and began to sort the twenty records.

"I know how many scratches each of them has," Julio said to the storekeeper.

"Tell that to my daughter," the storekeeper replied.

"You're responsible, not your daughter."

"Just the same, she's the only one who'll be changing the records."

Julio insisted that it did not make any difference to him whether she or someone else was going to actually handle the record player as long as the storekeeper paid for any records that were damaged. The storekeeper began to argue with Julio. Julio's face became red. He turned from time to time to the large group of Yaqui Indians congregated in front of the store and made signs of despair or frustration by moving his hands or contorting his face in a grimace. Seemingly as a final resort, he demanded a cash deposit. That precipitated another long argument about what constituted a damaged record. Julio stated with authority that any broken record had to be paid for in full, as if it were new. The storekeeper became angrier and began to pull out his extension cords. He seemed bent upon unhooking the record player and canceling the party. He made it clear to his clients congregated in front of the store that he had tried his best to come to terms with Julio. For a moment it seemed that the party was going to fail before it had started.

Blas, the old Yaqui Indian in whose house I was staying, made some derogatory comments in a loud voice about the Yaquis' sad state of affairs that they could not even celebrate their most revered religious festivity, the day of the Virgin of Guadalupe.

I wanted to intervene and offer my help, but Blas stopped me. He said that if I were to make the cash deposit, the storekeeper himself would smash the records.

"He's worse than anybody," he said. "Let him pay the deposit. He bleeds us, so why shouldn't he pay?"

After a long discussion in which, strangely enough, everyone present was in favor of Julio, the storekeeper hit upon terms which were mutually agreeable. He did not pay a cash deposit but accepted responsibility for the records and the record player.

Julio's motorcycle left a trail of dust as he headed for some of the more remote houses in the locality. Blas said that he was trying to get to his customers before they came to the store and spent all their money buying booze. As he was saying this a group of Indians emerged from behind the store. Blas looked at them and began to laugh and so did everyone else there.

Blas told me that those Indians were Julio's customers and had been hiding behind the store waiting for him to leave.

The party began early. The storekeeper's daughter put a record on the turntable and brought the arm down; there was a terrible loud screech and a high-pitched buzz and then came a blasting sound of a trumpet and some guitars.

The party consisted of playing the records at full volume. There were four young Mexican men who danced with the storekeeper's two daughters and three other young Mexican women. The Yaquis did not dance; they watched with apparent delight every movement the dancers made. They seemed to be enjoying themselves just watching and gulping down cheap tequila.

I bought individual drinks for everybody I knew. I wanted to avoid any feelings of resentment. I circulated among the numerous Indians and talked to them and then offered them drinks. My pattern of behavior worked until they realized I was not drinking at all. That seemed to annoy everyone at once. It was as if collectively they had discovered that I did not belong there. The Indians became very gruff and gave me sly looks.

The Mexicans, who were as drunk as the Indians, also realized at the same time that I had not danced; and that appeared to offend them even more. They became very aggressive. One of them forcibly took me by the arm and dragged me closer to the record player; another served me a full cup of tequila and wanted me to drink it all in one gulp and prove that I was a "macho."

I tried to stall them and laughed idiotically as if I were actually enjoying the situation. I said that I would like to dance first and then drink. One of the young men called out the name of a song. The girl in charge of the record player began to search in the pile of records. She seemed to be a little tipsy, although none of the women had openly been drinking, and had trouble fitting a record on the turntable. A young man said that the record she had selected was not a twist; she fumbled with the pile, trying to find the suitable one, and everybody closed in around her and left me. That gave me time to run behind the store, away from the lighted area, and out of sight.

I stood about thirty yards away in the darkness of some bushes trying to decide what to do. I was tired. I felt it was time to get in my car and go back home. I began to walk to Blas's house, where my car was parked. I figured that if I drove slowly no one would notice that I was leaving.

The people in charge of the record player were apparently still looking for the record—all I could hear was the high-pitched buzzing of the loudspeaker—but then came the blasting sound of a twist. I laughed out loud, thinking that they had probably turned to where I had been and found out that I had disappeared.

I saw some dark silhouettes of people walking in the opposite direction, going towards the store. We passed each other and they mumbled, "Buenas noches." I recognized them and spoke to them. I told them that it was a great party.

Before I came to a sharp bend in the road I encountered two other people, whom I did not recognize, but I greeted them anyway. The blasting sound of the record player was almost as loud there on the road as it was in front of the store. It was a dark starless night, but the glare from the store lights allowed me to have a fairly good visual perception of my surroundings. Blas's house was very near and I accelerated my pace. I noticed then the dark shape of a person, sitting or perhaps squatting to my left, at the bend of the road. I thought for an instant that it might have been one of the people from the party who had left before I had. The person seemed to be defecating on the side of the road. That seemed odd. People in the community went into the thick bushes to perform their bodily functions. I thought that whoever it was in front of me must have been drunk.

I came to the bend and said, "Buenas noches." The person answered me with an eerie, gruff, inhuman howl. The hair on my body literally stood on end. For a second I was paralyzed. Then I began to walk fast. I took a quick glance. I saw that the dark silhouette had stood up halfway; it was a woman. She was stooped over, leaning forward; she walked in that position for a few yards and then she hopped. I began to run, while the woman hopped like a bird by my side, keeping up with my speed. By the time I arrived at Blas's house she was cutting in front of me and we had almost touched.

I leaped across a small dry ditch in front of the house and crashed through the flimsy door.

Blas was already in the house and seemed unconcerned with my story.

"They pulled a good one on you," he said reassuringly. "The Indians take delight in teasing foreigners."

My experience had been so unnerving that the next day I drove to don Juan's house instead of going home as I had planned to do.

Don Juan returned in the late afternoon. I did not give him time to say anything but blurted out the whole story, including Blas's commentary. Don Juan's face became somber. Perhaps it was only my imagination, but I thought he was worried.

"Don't put so much stock in what Blas told you," he said in a serious tone. "He knows nothing of the struggles between sorcerers.

"You should have known that it was something serious the moment you noticed that the shadow was to your left. You shouldn't have run either."

"What was I supposed to do? Stand there?"

"Right. When a warrior encounters his opponent and the opponent is not an ordinary human being, he must make his stand. That is the only thing that makes him invulnerable."

"What are you saying, don Juan?"

"I'm saying that you have had your third encounter with your worthy opponent. She's following you around, waiting for a moment of weakness on your part. She almost bagged you this time."

I felt a surge of anxiety and accused him of putting me in unnecessary danger. I complained that the game he was playing with me was cruel.

"It would be cruel if this would have happened to an average man," he said. "But the instant one begins to live like a warrior, one is no longer ordinary. Besides, I didn't find you a worthy opponent because I want to play

with you, or tease you, or annoy you. A worthy opponent might spur you on; under the influence of an opponent like 'la Catalina' you may have to make use of
everything I have taught you. You don't have any other
alternative."

We were quiet for a while. His words had aroused a
tremendous apprehension in me.

He then wanted me to imitate as close as possible the
cry I had heard after I had said "Buenas noches."

I attempted to reproduce the sound and came up with
some weird howling that scared me. Don Juan must
have found my rendition funny; he laughed almost uncontrollably.

Afterwards he asked me to reconstruct the total sequence; the distance I ran, the distance the woman was
from me at the time I encountered her, the distance she
was from me at the time I reached the house, and the
place where she had begun hopping.

"No fat Indian woman could hop that way," he said
after assessing all those variables. "They could not even
run that far."

He made me hop. I could not cover more than four
feet each time, and if I were correct in my perception,
the woman had hopped at least ten feet with each leap.

"Of course, you know that from now on you must be
on the lookout," he said in a tone of great urgency. "She
will try to tap you on your left shoulder during a moment when you are unaware and weak."

"What should I do?" I asked.

"It is meaningless to complain," he said. "What's important from this point on is the strategy of your life."

I could not concentrate at all on what he was saying.
I took notes automatically. After a long silence he asked
if I had any pain behind my ears or in the nape of my
neck. I said no, and he told me that if I had experienced an uncomfortable sensation in either of those two
areas it would have meant that I had been clumsy and
that "la Catalina" had injured me.

"Everything you did that night was clumsy," he said.

"First of all, you went to the party to kill time, as though there is any time to kill. That weakened you."

"You mean I shouldn't go to parties?"

"No, I don't mean that. You may go any place you wish, but if you do, you must assume the full responsibility for that act. A warrior lives his life strategically. He would attend a party or a reunion like that only if his strategy calls for it. That means, of course, that he would be in total control and would perform all the acts that he deems necessary."

He looked at me fixedly and smiled, then covered his face and chuckled softly.

"You are in a terrible bind," he said. "Your opponent is on your trail and for the first time in your life you cannot afford to act helter-skelter. This time you will have to learn a totally different *doing,* the *doing* of strategy. Think of it this way. If you survive the onslaughts of 'la Catalina' you will have to thank her someday for having forced you to change your *doing.*"

"What a terrible way of putting it!" I exclaimed. "What if I don't survive?"

"A warrior never indulges in thoughts like that," he said. "When he has to act with his fellow men, a warrior follows the *doing* of strategy, and in that *doing* there are no victories or defeats. In that *doing* there are only actions."

I asked him what the *doing* of strategy entailed.

"It entails that one is not at the mercy of people," he replied. "At that party, for instance, you were a clown, not because it served your purposes to be a clown, but because you placed yourself at the mercy of those people. You never had any control and thus you had to run away from them."

"What should I have done?"

"Not go there at all, or else go there to perform a specific act.

"After horsing around with the Mexicans you were weak and 'la Catalina' used that opportunity. So she placed herself in the road to wait for you.

"Your body knew that something was out of place, though, and yet you spoke to her. That was terrible. You must not utter a single word to your opponent during one of those encounters. Then you turned your back to her. That was even worse. Then you ran away from her, and that was the worst thing you could have done! Apparently she is clumsy. A sorcerer that is worth his salt would have mowed you down right then, the instant you turned your back and ran away.

"So far your only defense is to stay put and do your dance."

"What dance are you talking about?" I asked.

He said that the "rabbit thumping" he had taught me was the first movement of the dance that a warrior groomed and enlarged throughout his life, and then executed in his last stand on earth.

I had a moment of strange sobriety and a series of thoughts occurred to me. On one level it was clear that what had taken place between me and "la Catalina" the first time I had confronted her was real. "La Catalina" was real, and I could not discard the possibility that she was actually following me. On the other level I could not understand how she was following me, and this gave rise to the faint suspicion that don Juan might be tricking me, and that he himself was somehow producing the weird effects I had witnessed.

Don Juan suddenly looked at the sky and told me that there was still time to go and check the sorceress. He reassured me that we were running very little danger, because we were only going to drive by her house.

"You must confirm her shape," don Juan said. "Then there won't be any doubts left in your mind, one way or the other."

My hands began to sweat profusely and I had to dry them repeatedly with a towel. We got in my car and don Juan directed me to the main highway and then to a wide unpaved road. I drove in the center of it; heavy trucks and tractors had carved deep trenches and my car was too low to go on either the left or the right side of

the road. We went slowly amid a thick cloud of dust.
The coarse gravel which was used to level the road had
lumped with dirt during the rains, and chunks of dry
mud rocks bounced against the metal underside of my
car, making loud explosive sounds.

Don Juan told me to slow down as we were coming
to a small bridge. There were four Indians sitting there
and they waved at us. I was not sure whether or not I
knew them. We passed the bridge and the road curved
gently.

"That's the woman's house," don Juan whispered to
me as he pointed with his eyes to a white house with
a high bamboo fence all around it.

He told me to make a U-turn and stop in the middle
of the road and wait to see if the woman became suspicious enough to show her face.

We stayed there perhaps ten minutes. I thought it was
an interminable time. Don Juan did not say a word. He
sat motionless, looking at the house.

"There she is," he said, and his body gave a sudden
jump.

I saw the dark foreboding silhouette of a woman standing inside the house, looking through the open door. The
room was dark and that only accentuated the darkness
of the woman's silhouette.

After a few minutes the woman stepped out of the
darkness of the room and stood in the doorway and
watched us. We looked at her for a moment and then
don Juan told me to drive on. I was speechless. I could
have sworn that she was the woman I had seen hopping
by the road in the darkness.

About half an hour later, when we had turned onto
the paved highway, don Juan spoke to me.

"What do you say?" he asked. "Did you recognize
the shape?"

I hesitated for a long time before answering. I was
afraid of the commitment entailed in saying yes. I carefully worded my reply and said that I thought it had
been too dark to be completely sure.

He laughed and tapped me gently on my head.

"She was the one, wasn't she?" he asked.

He did not give me time to reply. He put a finger to his mouth in a gesture of silence and whispered in my ear that it was meaningless to say anything, and that in order to survive "la Catalina's" onslaughts I had to make use of everything he had taught me.

PART TWO

Journey to Ixtlan

18

THE SORCERER'S RING OF POWER

In May of 1971, I paid don Juan the last visit of my apprenticeship. I went to see him on that occasion in the same spirit I had gone to see him during the ten years of our association; that is to say, I was once again seeking the amenity of his company.

His friend don Genaro, a Mazatec Indian sorcerer, was with him. I had seen both of them during my previous visit six months earlier. I was considering whether or not to ask them if they had been together all that time, when don Genaro explained that he liked the northern desert so much that he had returned just in time to see me. Both of them laughed as if they knew a secret.

"I came back just for you," don Genaro said.

"That's true," don Juan echoed.

I reminded don Genaro that the last time I had been there, his attempts to help me to "stop the world" had been disastrous for me. That was my friendly way of letting him know that I was afraid of him. He laughed uncontrollably, shaking his body and kicking his legs like a child. Don Juan avoided looking at me and also laughed.

"You're not going to try to help me any more, are you, don Genaro?" I asked.

My question threw both of them into spasms of laughter. Don Genaro rolled on the ground, laughing, then lay on his stomach and began to swim on the floor. When I saw him doing that I knew I was lost. At that moment my body somehow became aware that I had arrived at the end. I did not know what that end was. My personal tendency to dramatization and my previous experience with don Genaro made me believe that it might be the end of my life.

During my last visit to them, don Genaro had attempted to push me to the brink of "stopping the world." His efforts had been so bizarre and direct that don Juan himself had had to tell me to leave. Don Genaro's demonstrations of "power" were so extraordinary and so baffling that they forced me to a total re-evaluation of myself. I went home, reviewed the notes that I had taken in the very beginning of my apprenticeship, and a whole new feeling mysteriously set in on me, although I had not been fully aware of it until I saw don Genaro swimming on the floor.

The act of swimming on the floor, which was congruous with other strange and bewildering acts he had performed in front of my very eyes, started as he was lying face down. He was first laughing so hard that his body shook as in a convulsion, then he began kicking, and finally the movement of his legs became coordinated with a paddling movement of his arms, and don Genaro started to slide on the ground as if he were lying on a board fitted with ball bearings. He changed directions various times and covered the entire area of the front of don Juan's house, maneuvering around me and don Juan.

Don Genaro had clowned in front of me before, and every time he had done it don Juan had asserted that I had been on the brink of "seeing." My failure to "see" was a result of my insistence on trying to explain every one of don Genaro's actions from a rational point of view. This time I was on guard and when he began to swim I did not attempt to explain or understand the event. I simply watched him. Yet I could not avoid the sensation of being dumbfounded. He was actually sliding on his stomach and chest. My eyes began to cross as I watched him. I felt a surge of apprehension. I was convinced that if I did not explain what was happening I would see," and that thought filled me with an extraordinary anxiety. My nervous anticipation was so great that in some way I was back at the same point, locked once more in some rational endeavor.

Don Juan must have been watching me. He suddenly tapped me; I automatically turned to face him, and for an instant I took my eyes away from don Genaro. When I looked at him again he was standing by me with his head slightly tilted and his chin almost resting on my right shoulder. I had a delayed startled reaction. I looked at him for a second and then I jumped back.

His expression of feigned surprise was so comical that I laughed hysterically. I could not help being aware, however, that my laughter was unusual. My body shook with nervous spasms originating from the middle part of my stomach. Don Genaro put his hand on my stomach and the convulsion-like ripples ceased.

"This little Carlos is always so exaggerated!" he exclaimed as if he were a fastidious man.

Then he added, imitating don Juan's voice and mannerisms, "Don't you know that a warrior never laughs that way?"

His caricature of don Juan was so perfect that I laughed even harder.

Then both of them left together and were gone for over two hours, until about midday.

When they returned they sat in the area in front of don Juan's house. They did not say a word. They seemed to be sleepy, tired, almost absentminded. They stayed motionless for a long time, yet they seemed to be so comfortable and relaxed. Don Juan's mouth was slightly opened, as if he were really asleep, but his hands were clasped over his lap and his thumbs moved rhythmically.

I fretted and changed sitting positions for a while, then I began to feel a soothing placidity. I must have fallen asleep. Don Juan's chuckle woke me up. I opened my eyes. Both of them were staring at me.

"If you don't talk, you fall asleep," don Juan said, laughing.

"I'm afraid I do," I said.

Don Genaro lay on his back and began to kick his legs in the air. I thought for a moment that he was going to start his disturbing clowning again, but he went back right away to his cross-legged sitting position.

"There is something you ought to be aware of by now," don Juan said. "I call it the cubic centimeter of chance. All of us, whether or not we are warriors, have a cubic centimeter of chance that pops out in front of our eyes from time to time. The difference between an average man and a warrior is that the warrior is aware of this, and one of his tasks is to be alert, deliberately waiting, so that when his cubic centimeter pops out he has the necessary speed, the prowess to pick it up.

"Chance, good luck, personal power, or whatever you may call it, is a peculiar state of affairs. It is like a very small stick that comes out in front of us and invites us to pluck it. Usually we are too busy, or too preoccupied, or just too stupid and lazy to realize that that is our cubic centimeter of luck. A warrior, on the other hand, is always alert and tight and has the spring, the gumption necessary to grab it."

"Is your life very tight?" don Genaro asked me abruptly.

"I think it is," I said with conviction.

"Do you think that you can pluck your cubic centimeter of luck?" don Juan asked me with a tone of incredulity.

"I believe I do that all the time," I said.

"I think you are only alert about things you know," don Juan said.

"Maybe I'm kidding myself, but I do believe that nowadays I am more aware than at any other time in my life." I said and really meant it.

Don Genaro nodded his head in approval.

"Yes," he said softly, as if talking to himself. "Little Carlos is really tight, and absolutely alert."

I felt that they were humoring me. I thought that per-

haps my assertion about my alleged condition of tightness
may have annoyed them.

"I didn't mean to brag," I said.

Don Genaro arched his eyebrows and enlarged his
nostrils. He glanced at my notebook and pretended to be
writing.

"I think Carlos is tighter than ever," don Juan said to
don Genaro.

"Maybe he's too tight," don Genaro snapped.

"He may very well be," don Juan conceded.

I did not know what to interject at that point so I remained quiet.

"Do you remember the time when I jammed your
car?" don Juan asked casually.

His question was abrupt and unrelated to what we
had been talking about. He was referring to the time
when I could not start the engine of my car until he said
I could.

I remarked that no one could forget such an event.

"That was nothing," don Juan asserted in a factual
tone.

"Nothing at all. True, Genaro?"

"True," don Genaro said indifferently.

"What do you mean?" I said in a tone of protest.
"What you did that day was something truly beyond my
comprehension."

"That's not saying much," don Genaro retorted.

They both laughed loudly and then don Juan patted
me on the back.

"Genaro can do something much better than jamming
your car," he went on. "True, Genaro?"

"True," don Genaro replied, puckering up his lips like
a child.

"What can he do?" I asked, trying to sound unruffled.

"Genaro can take your whole car away!" don Juan exclaimed in a booming voice; and then he added in the
same tone, "True, Genaro?"

"True!" don Genaro retorted in the loudest human
tone I had ever heard.

I jumped involuntarily. My body was convulsed by three or four nervous spasms.

"What do you mean, he can take my whole car away?" I asked.

"What did I mean, Genaro?" don Juan asked.

"You meant that I can get into his car, turn the motor on, and drive away," don Genaro replied with unconvincing seriousness.

"Take the car away, Genaro," don Juan urged him in a joking tone.

"It's done!" don Genaro said, frowning and looking at me askew.

I noticed that as he frowned his eyebrows rippled, making the look in his eyes mischievous and penetrating.

"All right!" don Juan said calmly. "Let's go down there and examine the car."

"Yes!" don Genaro echoed. "Let's go down there and examine the car."

They stood up, very slowly. For an instant I did not know what to do, but don Juan signaled me to stand up.

We began walking up the small hill in front of don Juan's house. Both of them flanked me, don Juan to my right and don Genaro to my left. They were perhaps six or seven feet ahead of me, always within my full field of vision.

"Let's examine the car," don Genaro said again.

Don Juan moved his hands as if he were spinning an invisible thread; don Genaro did likewise and repeated, "Let's examine the car." They walked with a sort of bounce. Their steps were longer than usual, and their hands moved as though they were whipping or batting some invisible objects in front of them. I had never seen don Juan clowning like that and felt almost embarrassed to look at him.

We reached the top and I looked down to the area at the foot of the hill, some fifty yards away, where I had parked my car. My stomach contracted with a jolt. The car was not there! I ran down the hill. My car was not anywhere in sight. I experienced a moment of great confusion. I was disoriented.

My car had been parked there since I had arrived early in the morning. Perhaps half an hour before, I had come down to get a new pad of writing paper. At that time I had thought of leaving the windows open because of the excessive heat, but the number of mosquitoes and other flying insects that abounded in the area had made me change my mind, and I had left the car locked as usual.

I looked all around again. I refused to believe that my car was gone. I walked to the edge of the cleared area. Don Juan and don Genaro joined me and stood by me, doing exactly what I was doing, peering into the distance to see if the car was somewhere in sight. I had a moment of euphoria that gave way to a disconcerting sense of annoyance. They seemed to have noticed it and began to walk around me, moving their hands as if they were rolling dough in them.

"What do you think happened to the car, Genaro?" don Juan asked in a meek tone.

"I drove it away," don Genaro said and made the most astounding motion of shifting gears and steering. He bent his legs as though he were sitting, and remained in that position for a few moments, obviously sustained only by the muscles of his legs; then he shifted his weight to his right leg and stretched his left foot to mimic the action on the clutch. He made the sound of a motor with his lips; and finally, to top everything, he pretended to have hit a bump in the road and bobbed up and down, giving me the complete sensation of an inept driver that bounces without letting go of the steering wheel.

Don Genaro's pantomime was stupendous. Don Juan laughed until he was out of breath. I wanted to join them in their mirth but I was unable to relax. I felt threatened and ill at ease. An anxiety that had no precedence in my life possessed me. I felt I was burning up inside and began kicking small rocks on the ground and ended up hurling them with an unconscious and unpredictable fury. It was as if the wrath was actually outside of myself and had suddenly enveloped me. Then the feeling of annoyance left me, as mysteriously as it had hit me. I took a deep breath and felt better.

I did not dare to look at don Juan. My display of anger embarrassed me, but at the same time I wanted to laugh. Don Juan came to my side and patted me on the back. Don Genaro put his arm on my shoulder.

"It's all right!" don Genaro said. "Indulge yourself. Punch yourself in the nose and bleed. Then you can get a rock and knock your teeth out. It'll feel good! And if that doesn't help, you can mash your balls with the same rock on that big boulder over there."

Don Juan giggled. I told them that I was ashamed of myself for having behaved so poorly. I did not know what had gotten into me. Don Juan said that he was sure I knew exactly what was going on, that I was pretending not to know, and that it was the act of pretending that made me angry.

Don Genaro was unusually comforting; he patted my back repeatedly.

"It happens to all of us," don Juan said.

"What do you mean by that, don Juan?" don Genaro asked, imitating my voice, mocking my habit of asking don Juan questions.

Don Juan said some absurd things like "When the world is upside down we are right side up, but when the world is right side up we are upside down. Now when the world and we are right side up, we think we are upside down. . . ." He went on and on, talking gibberish while don Genaro mimicked my taking notes. He wrote on an invisible pad, enlarging his nostrils as he moved his hand, keeping his eyes wide open and fixed on don Juan. Don Genaro had caught on to my efforts to write without looking at my pad in order to avoid altering the natural flow of conversation. His portrayal was genuinely hilarious.

I suddenly felt very at ease, happy. Their laughter was soothing. For a moment I let go and had a belly laugh. But then my mind entered into a new state of apprehension, confusion, and annoyance. I thought that whatever was taking place there was impossible; in fact, it was inconceivable according to the logical order by which I am accustomed to judge the world at hand. Yet, as the perceiver, I perceived that my car was not there. The thought occurred to me, as it always had happened when don Juan had confronted me with inexplicable phenomena, that I was being tricked by ordinary means. My mind had always, under stress, involuntarily and consistently repeated the same construct. I began to consider how many confederates don Juan and don Genaro would have needed in order to lift my car and remove it from where I had parked it. I was absolutely sure that I had compulsively locked the doors; the handbrake was on; it was in gear; and the steering wheel was locked. In order to move it they would have had to lift it up bodily. That task would have required a labor force that I was convinced neither of them could have brought together. Another possibility was that someone in agreement with them had broken into my car, wired it, and driven it away. To do that would have required a specialized knowledge that was beyond their means. The only other possible explanation was that perhaps they were mesmerizing me. Their movements were so novel to me and so suspicious that I entered into a spin of rationalizations. I thought that if they were hypnotizing me I was then in a state of altered consciousness. In my experience with don Juan I had noticed that in such states one is incapable of keeping a consistent mental record of the passage of time. There had never been an enduring order, in matters of passage of time, in all the states of nonordinary reality I had experienced, and my conclusion was that if I kept myself alert a moment would come when I would lose my order of sequential time. As if, for example, I were looking at a mountain at a given moment, and then in my next moment of awareness I found myself looking at a valley in the opposite direction, but without remembering having turned around. I felt that if something of that nature would happen to me I could then explain what was taking place with my car as, perhaps, a case of hypnosis. I decided that the only thing I could do was to watch every detail with excruciating thoroughness.

"Where's my car?" I asked, addressing both of them.

"Where's the car, Genaro?" don Juan asked with a look of utmost seriousness.

Don Genaro began turning over small rocks and looking underneath them. He worked feverishly over the whole flat area where I had parked my car. He actually turned over every rock. At times he would pretend to get angry and would hurl the rock into the bushes.

Don Juan seemed to enjoy the scene beyond words. He giggled and chuckled and was almost oblivious to my presence.

Don Genaro had just finished hurling a rock in a display of sham frustration when he came upon a good-sized boulder, the only large and heavy rock in the parking area. He attempted to turn it over but it was too heavy and too deeply imbedded in the ground. He struggled and puffed until he was perspiring. Then he sat on the rock and called don Juan to help him.

Don Juan turned to me with a beaming smile and said, "Come on, let's give Genaro a hand."

"What's he doing?" I asked.

"He's looking for your car," don Juan said in a casual and factual tone.

"For heaven's sake! How can he find it under the rocks?" I protested.

"For heaven's sake, why not?" don Genaro retorted and both of them roared with laughter.

We could not budge the rock. Don Juan suggested that we go to the house and look for a thick piece of wood to use as a lever.

On our way to the house I told them that their acts were absurd and that whatever they were doing to me was unnecessary.

Don Genaro peered at me.

"Genaro is a very thorough man," don Juan said with a serious expression. "He's as thorough and meticulous as you are. You yourself said that you never leave a stone unturned. He's doing the same."

Don Genaro patted me on the shoulder and said that don Juan was absolutely right and that, in fact, he wanted to be like me. He looked at me with an insane glint and opened his nostrils.

Don Juan clapped his hands and threw his hat to the ground.

After a long search around the house for a thick piece of wood, don Genaro found a long and fairly thick tree trunk, a part of a house beam. He put it across his shoulders and we started back to the place where my car had been.

As we were going up the small hill and were about to reach a bend in the trail from where I would see the flat parking area, I had a sudden insight. It occurred to me that I was going to find my car before they did, but when I looked down, there was no car at the foot of the hill.

Don Juan and don Genaro must have understood what I had had in mind and ran after me, laughing uproariously.

Once we got to the bottom of the hill they immediately went to work. I watched them for a few moments. Their acts were incomprehensible. They were not pretending that they were working, they were actually immersed in the task of turning over a boulder to see if my car was underneath. That was too much for me and I joined them. They puffed and yelled and don Genaro howled like a coyote. They were soaked in perspiration. I noticed how terribly strong their bodies were, especially don Juan's. Next to them I was a flabby young man.

Very soon I was also perspiring copiously. Finally we succeeded in turning over the boulder and don Genaro examined the dirt underneath the rock with the most maddening patience and thoroughness.

"No. It isn't here," he announced.

That statement brought both of them down to the ground with laughter.

I laughed nervously. Don Juan seemed to have true spasms of pain and covered his face and lay down as his body shook with laughter.

"In which direction do we go now?" don Genaro asked after a long rest.

Don Juan pointed with a nod of his head.

"Where are we going?" I asked.

"To look for your car!" don Juan said and did not crack a smile.

They again flanked me as we walked into the brush. We had only covered a few yards when don Genaro signaled us to stop. He tiptoed to a round bush a few steps away, looked in the inside branches for a few moments, and said that the car was not there.

We kept on walking for a while and then don Genaro made a gesture with his hand to be quiet. He arched his back as he stood on his toes and extended his arms over his head. His fingers were contracted like a claw. From where I stood, don Genaro's body had the shape of a letter S. He maintained that position for an instant and then virtually plunged headfirst on a long twig with dry leaves. He carefully lifted it up and examined it and again remarked that the car was not there.

As we walked into the deep chaparral he looked behind bushes and climbed small paloverde trees to look into their foliage, only to conclude that the car was not there either.

Meanwhile I kept a most meticulous mental record of everything I touched or saw. My sequential and orderly view of the world around me was as continuous as it had always been. I touched rocks, bushes, trees. I shifted my view from the foreground to the background by looking out of one eye and then out of the other. By all calculations I was walking in the chaparral as I had done scores of times during my ordinary life.

Next don Genaro lay down on his stomach and asked us to do likewise. He rested his chin on his clasped hands. Don Juan did the same. Both of them stared at a series of small protuberances on the ground that looked like minute hills. Suddenly don Genaro made a sweeping movement with his right hand and clasped something. He hurriedly stood up and so did don Juan. Don Genaro held his clasped hand in front of us and signaled us to come closer and look. Then he slowly began to open his hand. When it was half open a big black object flew away. The motion was so sudden and the flying object was so big that I jumped back and nearly lost my balance. Don Juan propped me up.

"That wasn't the car," don Genaro complained. "It was a goddamn fly. Sorry!"

Both of them scrutinized me. They were standing in front of me and were not looking directly at me but out of the corners of their eyes. It was a prolonged look.

"It was a fly, wasn't it?" don Genaro asked me.

"I think so," I said.

"Don't think," don Juan ordered me imperiously. "What did you see?"

"I saw something as big as a crow flying out of his hand," I said.

My statement was congruous with what I had perceived and was not intended as a joke, but they took it as perhaps the most hilarious statement that anyone had made that day. Both of them jumped up and down and laughed until they choked.

"I think Carlos has had enough," don Juan said. His voice sounded hoarse from laughing.

Don Genaro said that he was about to find my car, that the feeling was getting hotter and hotter. Don Juan said we were in a rugged area and that to find the car there was not a desirable thing. Don Genaro took off his hat and rearranged the strap with a piece of string from his pouch, then he attached his woolen belt to a yellow tassel affixed to the brim of the hat.

"I'm making a kite out of my hat," he said to me.

I watched him and I knew that he was joking. I had always considered myself to be an expert on kites. When I was a child I used to make the most complex kites and I knew that the brim of the straw hat was too brittle to resist the wind. The hat's crown, on the other hand, was too deep and the wind would circulate inside it, making it impossible to lift the hat off the ground.

"You don't think it'll fly, do you?" don Juan asked me.

"I know it won't," I said.

Don Genaro was unconcerned and finished attaching a long string to his kite-hat.

It was a windy day and don Genaro ran downhill as don Juan held his hat, then don Genaro pulled the string and the damn thing actually flew.

"Look, look at the kite!" don Genaro yelled.

It bobbed a couple of times but it remained in the air.

"Don't take your eyes off of the kite," don Juan said firmly.

For a moment I felt dizzy. Looking at the kite, I had had a complete recollection of another time; it was as if I were flying a kite myself, as I used to, when it was windy in the hills of my home town.

For a brief moment the recollection engulfed me and I lost my awareness of the passage of time.

I heard don Genaro yelling something and I saw the hat bobbing up and down and then falling to the ground, where my car was. It all took place with such speed that I did not have a clear picture of what had happened. I became dizzy and absent-minded. My mind held on to a very confusing image. I either saw don Genaro's hat turning into my car, or I saw the hat falling over on top of the car. I wanted to believe the latter, that don Genaro had used his hat to point at my car. Not that it really mattered, one thing was as awesome as the other, but just the same my mind hooked on that arbitrary detail in order to keep my original mental balance.

"Don't fight it," I heard don Juan saying.

I felt that something inside me was about to surface. Thoughts and images came in uncontrollable waves as if I were falling asleep. I stared at the car dumbfounded. It was sitting on a rocky flat area about a hundred feet away. It actually looked as if someone had just placed it there. I ran towards it and began to examine it.

"Goddamnit!" don Juan exclaimed. "Don't stare at the car. *Stop the world!*"

Then as in a dream I heard him yelling, "Genaro's hat! Genaro's hat!"

I looked at them. They were staring at me directly. Their eyes were piercing. I felt a pain in my stomach. I had an instantaneous headache and got ill.

Don Juan and don Genaro looked at me curiously. I

sat by the car for a while and then, quite automatically, I unlocked the door and let don Genaro get in the back seat. Don Juan followed him and sat next to him. I thought that was strange because he usually sat in the front seat.

I drove my car to don Juan's house in a sort of haze. I was not myself at all. My stomach was very upset, and the feeling of nausea demolished all my sobriety. I drove mechanically.

I heard don Juan and don Genaro in the back seat laughing and giggling like children. I heard don Juan asking me, "Are we getting closer?"

It was at that point that I took deliberate notice of the road. We were actually very close to his house.

"We're about to get there," I muttered.

They howled with laughter. They clapped their hands and slapped their thighs.

When we arrived at the house I automatically jumped out of the car and opened the door for them. Don Genaro stepped out first and congratulated me for what he said was the nicest and smoothest ride he had ever taken in his life. Don Juan said the same. I did not pay much attention to them.

I locked my car and barely made it to the house. I heard don Juan and don Genaro roaring with laughter before I fell asleep.

19

STOPPING THE WORLD

The next day as soon as I woke up I began asking don Juan questions. He was cutting firewood in the back of his house, but don Genaro was nowhere in sight. He said that there was nothing to talk about. I pointed out that I had succeeded in remaining aloof and had observed don Genaro's "swimming on the floor" without wanting or demanding any explanation whatsoever, but my restraint had not helped me to understand what was taking place. Then, after the disappearance of the car, I became automatically locked in seeking a logical explanation, but that did not help me either. I told don Juan that my insistence on finding explanations was not something that I had arbitrarily devised myself, just to be difficult, but was something so deeply ingrained in me that it overruled every other consideration.

"It's like a disease," I said.

"There are no diseases," don Juan replied calmly. "There is only indulging. And you indulge yourself in trying to explain everything. Explanations are no longer necessary in your case."

I insisted that I could function only under conditions of order and understanding. I reminded him that I had drastically changed my personality during the time of our association, and that the condition that had made that change possible was that I had been capable of explaining to myself the reasons for that change.

Don Juan laughed softly. He did not speak for a long time.

"You are very clever," he finally said. "You go back to where you have always been. This time you are finished though. You have no place to go back to. I will not explain anything to you any more. Whatever Genaro did to you yesterday he did it to your body, so let your body decide what's what."

Don Juan's tone was friendly but unusually detached and that made me feel an overwhelming loneliness. I expressed my feelings of sadness. He smiled. His fingers gently clasped the top of my hand.

"We both are beings who are going to die," he said softly. "There is no more time for what we used to do. Now you must employ all the *not-doing* I have taught you and *stop the world*."

He clasped my hand again. His touch was firm and friendly; it was like a reassurance that he was concerned and had affection for me, and at the same time it gave me the impression of an unwavering purpose.

"This is my gesture for you," he said, holding the grip he had on my hand for an instant. "Now you must go by yourself into those friendly mountains." He pointed with his chin to the distant range of mountains towards the southeast.

He said that I had to remain there until my body told me to quit and then return to his house. He let me know that he did not want me to say anything or to wait any longer by shoving me gently in the direction of my car.

"What am I supposed to do there?" I asked.

He did not answer but looked at me, shaking his head.

"No more of that," he finally said.

Then he pointed his finger to the southeast.

"Go there." he said cuttingly.

I drove south and then east, following the roads I had always taken when driving with don Juan. I parked my car around the place where the dirt road ended and then I hiked on a familiar trail until I reached a high plateau. I had no idea what to do there. I began to meander, looking for a resting place. Suddenly I became aware of a small area to my left. It seemed that the chemical composition of the soil was different on that spot, yet when I focused my eyes on it there was nothing visible that would account for the difference. I stood a few feet away and tried to "feel" as don Juan had always recommended I should do.

I stayed motionless for perhaps an hour. My thoughts began to diminish by degrees until I was no longer talking to myself. I then had a sensation of annoyance. The feeling seemed to be confined to my stomach and was more acute when I faced the spot in question. I was repulsed by it and felt compelled to move away from it. I began scanning the area with crossed eyes and after a short walk I came upon a large flat rock. I stopped in front of it. There was nothing in particular about the rock that attracted me. I did not detect any specific color or any shine on it, and yet I liked it. My body felt good. I experienced a sensation of physical comfort and sat down for a while.

I meandered in the high plateau and the surrounding mountains all day without knowing what to do or what to expect. I came back to the flat rock at dusk. I knew that if I spent the night there I would be safe.

The next day I ventured farther east into the high mountains. By late afternoon I came to another even higher plateau. I thought I had been there before. I looked around to orient myself but I could not recognize any of the surrounding peaks. After carefully selecting a suitable place I sat down to rest at the edge of a barren rocky area. I felt very warm and peaceful there. I tried to pour out some food from my gourd, but it was empty. I drank some water. It was warm and stale. I thought that I had nothing else to do but to return to don Juan's house and began to wonder whether or not I should start on my way back right away. I lay down on my stomach and rested my head on my arm. I felt uneasy and changed positions various times until I found myself facing the west. The sun was already low. My eyes were tired. I looked down at the ground and caught sight of a large black beetle. It came out from behind a small rock, pushing a ball of dung twice its size. I followed its movements for a long time. The insect seemed unconcerned with my presence and kept on pushing its load over rocks, roots, depressions, and protuberances on the ground. For all I knew, the beetle was not aware that I was there. The thought occurred to me that I could not possibly be sure that the insect was not aware of me; that thought triggered a series of rational evaluations about the nature of the insect's world as opposed to mine. The beetle and I were in the same world and obviously the world was not the same for both of us. I became immersed in watching it and marveled at the gigantic strength it needed to carry its load over rocks and down crevices.

I observed the insect for a long time and then I became aware of the silence around me. Only the wind hissed between the branches and leaves of the chaparral. I looked up, turned to my left in a quick and involuntary fashion, and caught a glimpse of a faint shadow or a flicker on a rock a few feet away. At first I paid no attention to it but then I realized that that flicker had been to my left. I turned again suddenly and was able to clearly perceive a shadow on the rock. I had the weird sensation that the shadow instantly slid down to the ground and the soil absorbed it as a blotter dries an ink blotch. A chill ran down my back. The thought crossed my mind that death was watching me and the beetle.

I looked for the insect again but I could not find it. I thought that it must have arrived at its destination and then had dropped its load into a hole in the ground. I put my face against a smooth rock.

The beetle emerged from a deep hole and stopped a few inches away from my face. It seemed to look at me and for a moment I felt that it became aware of my presence, perhaps as I was aware of the presence of my death. I experienced a shiver. The beetle and I were not that different after all. Death, like a shadow, was stalking both of us from behind the boulder. I had an extraordinary moment of elation. The beetle and I were on a par. Neither of us was better than the other. Our death made us equal.

My elation and joy were so overwhelming that I began

to weep. Don Juan was right. He had always been right.
I was living in a most mysterious world and, like everyone else, I was a most mysterious being, and yet I was
no more important than a beetle. I wiped my eyes and as
I rubbed them with the back of my hand I saw a man, or
something which had the shape of a man. It was to my
right about fifty yards away. I sat up straight and strained
to see. The sun was almost on the horizon and its yellowish glow prevented me from getting a clear view. I heard
a peculiar roar at that moment. It was like the sound of
a distant jet plane. As I focused my attention on it, the
roar increased to a prolonged sharp metallic whizzing
and then it softened until it was a mesmerizing, melodious sound. The melody was like the vibration of an electrical current. The image that came to my mind was that
two electrified spheres were coming together, or two
square blocks of electrified metal were rubbing against
each other and then coming to rest with a thump when
they were perfectly leveled with each other. I again
strained to see if I could distinguish the person that
seemed to be hiding from me, but I could only detect a
dark shape against the bushes. I shielded my eyes by
placing my hands above them. The brilliancy of the sunlight changed at that moment and then I realized that
what I was seeing was only an optical illusion, a play of
shadows and foliage.

I moved my eyes away and I saw a coyote calmly trotting across the field. The coyote was around the spot
where I thought I had seen the man. It moved about fifty
yards in a southerly direction and then it stopped, turned,
and began walking towards me. I yelled a couple of times
to scare it away, but it kept on coming. I had a moment
of apprehension. I thought that it might be rabid and I
even considered gathering some rocks to defend myself
in case of an attack. When the animal was ten or fifteen
feet away I noticed that it was not agitated in any way;
on the contrary, it seemed calm and unafraid. It slowed
down its gait, coming to a halt barely four or five feet
from me. We looked at each other, and then the coyote
came even closer. Its brown eyes were friendly and clear.

I sat down on the rocks and the coyote stood almost touching me. I was dumbfounded. I had never seen a wild coyote that close, and the only thing that occurred to me at that moment was to talk to it. I began as one would talk to a friendly dog. And then I thought that the coyote "talked" back to me. I had the absolute certainty that it had said something. I felt confused but I did not have time to ponder upon my feelings, because the coyote "talked" again. It was not that the animal was voicing words the way I am accustomed to hearing words being voiced by human beings, it was rather a "feeling" that it was talking. But it was not like a feeling that one has when a pet seems to communicate with its master either. The coyote actually said something; it relayed a thought and that communication came out in something quite similar to a sentence. I had said, "How are you, little coyote?" and I thought I had heard the animal respond, "I'm all right, and you?" Then the coyote repeated the sentence and I jumped to my feet. The animal did not make a single movement. It was not even startled by my sudden jump. Its eyes were still friendly and clear. It lay down on its stomach and tilted its head and asked, "Why are you afraid?" I sat down facing it and I carried on the weirdest conversation I had ever had. Finally it asked me what I was doing there and I said I had come there to "stop the world." The coyote said, "Que bueno!" and then I realized that it was a bilingual coyote. The nouns and verbs of its sentences were in English, but the conjunctions and exclamations were in Spanish. The thought crossed my mind that I was in the presence of a Chicano coyote. I began to laugh at the absurdity of it all and I laughed so hard that I became almost hysterical. Then the full weight of the impossibility of what was happening struck me and my mind wobbled. The coyote stood up and our eyes met. I stared fixedly into them. I felt they were pulling me and suddenly the animal became iridescent; it began to glow. It was as if my mind were replaying the memory of another event that had taken place ten years before, when under the influence of peyote I witnessed the metamorphosis of an ordinary dog into an unforgettable iridescent being. It was as though the coyote had triggered the recollection, and the memory of that previous event was summoned and became superimposed on the coyote's shape; the coyote was a fluid, liquid, luminous being. Its luminosity was dazzling. I wanted to cover my eyes with my hands to protect them, but I could not move. The luminous being touched me in some undefined part of myself and my body experienced such an exquisite indescribable warmth and wellbeing that it was as if the touch had made me explode. I became transfixed. I could not feel my feet, or my legs, or any part of my body, yet something was sustaining me erect.

I have no idea how long I stayed in that position. In the meantime, the luminous coyote and the hilltop where I stood melted away. I had no thoughts or feelings. Everything had been turned off and I was floating freely.

Suddenly I felt that my body had been struck and then it became enveloped by something that kindled me. I became aware then that the sun was shining on me. I could vaguely distinguish a distant range of mountains towards the west. The sun was almost over the horizon. I was looking directly into it and then I saw the "lines of the world." I actually perceived the most extraordinary profusion of fluorescent white lines which crisscrossed everything around me. For a moment I thought that I was perhaps experiencing sunlight as it was being refracted by my eyelashes. I blinked and looked again. The lines were constant and were superimposed on or were coming through everything in the surroundings. I turned around and examined an extraordinarily new world. The lines were visible and steady even if I looked away from the sun.

I stayed on the hilltop in a state of ecstasy for what appeared to be an endless time, yet the whole event may have lasted only a few minutes, perhaps only as long as the sun shone before it reached the horizon, but to me it seemed an endless time. I felt something warm and soothing oozing out of the world and out of my own body. I knew I had discovered a secret. It was so simple. I experienced an unknown flood of feelings. Never in my life had I had such a divine euphoria, such peace, such an encompassing grasp, and yet I could not put the discovered secret into words, or even into thoughts, but my body knew it.

Then I either fell asleep or I fainted. When I again became aware of myself I was lying on the rocks. I stood up. The world was as I had always seen it. It was getting dark and I automatically started on my way back to my car.

Don Juan was alone in the house when I arrived the next morning. I asked him about don Genaro and he said that he was somewhere in the vicinity, running an errand. I immediately began to narrate to him the extraordinary experiences I had had. He listened with obvious interest.

"You have simply *stopped the world,*" he commented after I had finished my account.

We remained silent for a moment and then don Juan said that I had to thank don Genaro for helping me. He seemed to be unusually pleased with me. He patted my back repeatedly and chuckled.

"But it is inconceivable that a coyote could talk," I said.

"It wasn't talk," don Juan replied.

"What was it then?"

"Your body understood for the first time. But you failed to recognize that it was not a coyote to begin with and that it certainly was not talking the way you and I talk."

"But the coyote really talked, don Juan!"

"Now look who is talking like an idiot. After all these years of learning you should know better. Yesterday you *stopped the world* and you might have even *seen.* A magical being told you something and your body was capable of understanding it because the world had collapsed."

"The world was like it is today, don Juan."

"No, it wasn't. Today the coyotes do not tell you anything, and you cannot *see* the lines of the world. Yesterday you did all that simply because something had stopped in you."

"What was the thing that stopped in me?"

"What stopped inside you yesterday was what people have been telling you the world is like. You see, people tell us from the time we are born that the world is such and such and so and so, and naturally we have no choice but to see the world the way people have been telling us it is."

We looked at each other.

"Yesterday the world became as sorcerers tell you it is," he went on. "In that world coyotes talk and so do deer, as I once told you, and so do rattlesnakes and trees and all other living beings. But what I want you to learn is *seeing*. Perhaps you know now that *seeing* happens only when one sneaks between the worlds, the world of ordinary people and the world of sorcerers. You are now smack in the middle point between the two. Yesterday you believed the coyote talked to you. Any sorcerer who doesn't *see* would believe the same, but one who *sees* knows that to believe that is to be pinned down in the realm of sorcerers. By the same token, not to believe that coyotes talk is to be pinned down in the realm of ordinary men."

"Do you mean, don Juan, that neither the world of ordinary men nor the world of sorcerers is real?"

"They are real worlds. They could act upon you. For example, you could have asked that coyote about anything you wanted to know and it would have been compelled to give you an answer. The only sad part is that coyotes are not reliable. They are tricksters. It is your fate not to have a dependable animal companion."

Don Juan explained that the coyote was going to be my companion for life and that in the world of sorcerers to have a coyote friend was not a desirable state of affairs. He said that it would have been ideal for me to have talked to a rattlesnake, since they were stupendous companions.

"If I were you," he added, "I would never trust a

coyote. But you are different and you may even become a coyote sorcerer."

"What is a coyote sorcerer?"

"One who draws a lot of things from his coyote brothers."

I wanted to keep on asking questions but he made a gesture to stop me.

"You have seen the lines of the world," he said. "You have seen a luminous being. You are now almost ready to meet the ally. Of course you know that the man you saw in the bushes was the ally. You heard its roar like the sound of a jet plane. He'll be waiting for you at the edge of a plain, a plain I will take you to myself."

We were quiet for a long time. Don Juan had his hands clasped over his stomach. His thumbs moved almost imperceptibly.

"Genaro will also have to go with us to that valley," he said all of a sudden. "He is the one who has helped you to *stop the world.*"

Don Juan looked at me with piercing eyes.

"I will tell you one more thing," he said and laughed. "It really does matter now. Genaro never moved your car from the world of ordinary men the other day. He simply forced you to look at the world like sorcerers do, and your car was not in that world. Genaro wanted to soften your certainty. His clowning told your body about the absurdity of trying to understand everything. And when he flew his kite you almost *saw.* You found your car and you were in both worlds. The reason we nearly split our guts laughing was because you really thought you were driving us back from where you thought you had found your car."

"But how did he force me to see the world as sorcerers do?"

"I was with him. We both know that world. Once one knows that world all one needs to bring it about is to use that extra ring of power I have told you sorcerers have. Genaro can do that as easily as snapping his fingers. He kept you busy turning over rocks in order to distract your thoughts and allow your body to *see.*"

I told him that the events of the last three days had done some irreparable damage to my idea of the world. I said that during the ten years I had been associated with him I had never been so moved, not even during the times I had ingested psychotropic plants.

"Power plants are only an aid," don Juan said. "The real thing is when the body realizes that it can *see*. Only then is one capable of knowing that the world we look at every day is only a description. My intent has been to show you that. Unfortunately you have very little time left before the ally tackles you."

"Does the ally have to tackle me?"

"There is no way to avoid it. In order to *see* one must learn the way sorcerers look at the world and thus the ally has to be summoned, and once that is done it comes."

"Couldn't you have taught me to *see* without summoning the ally?"

"No. In order to *see* one must learn to look at the world in some other fashion, and the only other fashion I know is the way of a sorcerer."

20

JOURNEY TO IXTLAN

Don Genaro returned around noon and at don Juan's suggestion the three of us drove down to the range of mountains where I had been the day before. We hiked on the same trail I had taken but instead of stopping in the high plateau, as I had done, we kept on climbing until we reached the top of the lower range of mountains, then we began to descend into a flat valley.

We stopped to rest on top of a high hill. Don Genaro

picked the spot. I automatically sat down, as I have always done in their company, with don Juan to my right and don Genaro to my left, making a triangle.

The desert chaparral had acquired an exquisite moist sheen. It was brilliantly green after a short spring shower.

"Genaro is going to tell you something," don Juan said to me all of a sudden. "He is going to tell you the story of his first encounter with his ally. Isn't that so, Genaro?"

There was a tone of coaxing in don Juan's voice. Don Genaro looked at me and contracted his lips until his mouth looked like a round hole. He curled his tongue against his palate and opened and closed his mouth as if he were having spasms.

Don Juan looked at him and laughed loudly. I did not know what to make out of it.

"What's he doing?" I asked don Juan.

"He's a hen!" he said.

"A hen?"

"Look, look at his mouth. That's the hen's ass and it is about to lay an egg."

The spasms of don Genaro's mouth seemed to increase. He had a strange, crazy look in his eyes. His mouth opened up as if the spasms were dilating the round hole. He made a croaking sound in his throat, folded his arms over his chest with his hands bent inward, and then unceremoniously spat out some phlegm.

"Damn it! It wasn't an egg," he said with a concerned look on his face.

The posture of his body and the expression on his face were so ludicrous that I could not help laughing.

"Now that Genaro almost laid an egg maybe he will tell you about his first encounter with his ally," don Juan insisted.

"Maybe," don Genaro said, uninterested.

I pleaded with him to tell me.

Don Genaro stood up, stretched his arms and back. His bones made a cracking sound. Then he sat down again.

"I was young when I first tackled my ally," he finally said. "I remember that it was in the early afternoon. J had been in the fields since daybreak and I was returning to my house. Suddenly, from behind a bush, the ally came out and blocked my way. He had been waiting for me and was inviting me to wrestle him. I began to turn around in order to leave him alone but the thought came to my mind that I was strong enough to tackle him. I was afraid though. A chill ran up my spine and my neck became stiff as a board. By the way, that is always the sign that you're ready, I mean, when your neck gets hard."

He opened up his shirt and showed me his back. He stiffened the muscles of his neck, back, and arms. I noticed the superb quality of his musculature. It was as if the memory of the encounter had activated every muscle in his torso.

"In such a situation," he continued, "you must always close your mouth."

He turned to don Juan and said, "Isn't that so?"

"Yes," don Juan said calmly. "The jolt that one gets from grabbing an ally is so great that one might bite off one's tongue or knock one's teeth out. One's body must be straight and well-grounded, and the feet must grab the ground."

Don Genaro stood up and showed me the proper position: his body slightly bent at the knees, his arms hanging at his sides with the fingers curled gently. He seemed relaxed and yet firmly set on the ground. He remained in that position for an instant, and when I thought he was going to sit down he suddenly lunged forward in one stupendous leap, as if he had springs attached to his heels. His movement was so sudden that I fell down on my back; but as I fell I had the clear impression that don Genaro had grabbed a man, or something which had the shape of a man.

I sat up again. Don Genaro was still maintaining a tremendous tension all over his body, then he relaxed his muscles abruptly and went back to where he had been sitting before and sat down.

"Carlos just *saw* your ally right now," don Juan remarked casually, "but he's still weak and fell down."

"Did you?" don Genaro asked in a naïve tone and enlarged his nostrils.

Don Juan assured him that I had "seen" it.

Don Genaro leaped forward again with such a force that I fell on my side. He executed his jump so fast that I really could not tell how he had sprung to his feet from a sitting position in order to lunge forward.

Both of them laughed loudly and then don Genaro changed his laughter into a howling indistinguishable from a coyote's.

"Don't think that you have to jump as well as Genaro in order to grab your ally," don Juan said in a cautioning tone. "Genaro jumps so well because he has his ally to help him. All you have to do is to be firmly grounded in order to sustain the impact. You have to stand just like Genaro did before he jumped, then you have to leap forward and grab the ally."

"He's got to kiss his medallion first," don Genaro interjected.

Don Juan, with feigned severity, said that I had no medallions.

"What about his notebooks?" don Genaro insisted. "He's got to do something with his notebooks—put them down somewhere before he jumps, or maybe he'll use his notebooks to beat the ally."

"I'll be damned!" don Juan said with seemingly genuine surprise. "I have never thought of that. I bet it'll be the first time an ally is beaten down to the ground with notebooks."

When don Juan's laughter and don Genaro's coyote howling subsided we were all in a very fine mood.

"What happened when you grabbed your ally, don Genaro?" I asked.

"It was a powerful jolt," don Genaro said after a moment's hesitation. He seemed to have been putting his thoughts in order.

"Never would I have imagined it was going to be like that," he went on. "It was something, something, something . . . like nothing I can tell. After I grabbed it we began to spin. The ally made me twirl, but I didn't let go. We spun through the air with such speed and force that I couldn't see any more. Everything was foggy. The spinning went on, and on, and on. Suddenly I felt that I was standing on the ground again. I looked at myself. The ally had not killed me. I was in one piece. I was myself! I knew then that I had succeeded. At long last I had an ally. I jumped up and down with delight. What a feeling! What a feeling it was!

"Then I looked around to find out where I was. The surroundings were unknown to me. I thought that the ally must have taken me through the air and dumped me somewhere very far from the place where we started to spin. I oriented myself. I thought that my home must be towards the east, so I began to walk in that direction. It was still early. The encounter with the ally had not taken too long. Very soon I found a trail and then I saw a bunch of men and women coming towards me. They were Indians. I thought they were Mazatec Indians. They surrounded me and asked me where I was going. 'I'm going home to Ixtlan,' I said to them. 'Are you lost?' someone asked. 'I am,' I said. 'Why?' 'Because Ixtlan is not that way. Ixtlan is in the opposite direction. We ourselves are going there,' someone else said. 'Join us!' they all said. 'We have food!' "

Don Genaro stopped talking and looked at me as if he were waiting for me to ask a question.

"Well, what happened?" I asked. "Did you join them?"

"No. I didn't," he said. "Because they were not real. I knew it right away, the minute they came to me. There was something in their voices, in their friendliness that gave them away, especially when they asked me to join them. So I ran away. They called me and begged me to come back. Their pleas became haunting, but I kept on running away from them."

"Who were they?" I asked.

"People," don Genaro replied cuttingly. "Except that they were not real."

"They were like apparitions," don Juan explained. "Like phantoms."

"After walking a while," don Genaro went on, "I became more confident. I knew that Ixtlan was in the direction I was going. And then I saw two men coming down the trail towards me. They also seemed to be Mazatec Indians. They had a donkey loaded with firewood. They went by me and mumbled, 'Good afternoon.'

" 'Good afternoon!' I said and kept on walking. They did not pay any attention to me and went their way. I slowed down my gait and casually turned around to look at them. They were walking away unconcerned with me. They seemed to be real. I ran after them and yelled, 'Wait, wait!'

"They held their donkey and stood on either side of the animal, as if they were protecting the load.

" 'I am lost in these mountains,' I said to them. 'Which way is Ixtlan?' They pointed in the direction they were going. 'You're very far,' one of them said. 'It is on the other side of those mountains. It'll take you four or five days to get there.' Then they turned around and kept on walking. I felt that those were real Indians and I begged them to let me join them.

"We walked together for a while and then one of them got his bundle of food and offered me some. I froze on the spot. There was something terribly strange in the way he offered me his food. My body felt frightened, so I jumped back and began to run away. They both said that I would die in the mountains if I did not go with them and tried to coax me to join them. Their pleas were also very haunting, but I ran away from them with all my might.

"I kept on walking. I knew then that I was on the right way to Ixtlan and that those phantoms were trying to lure me out of my way.

"I encountered eight of them; they must have known that my determination was unshakable. They stood by the road and looked at me with pleading eyes. Most of them even displayed food and other goods that they were supposed to be selling, like innocent merchants by the side of the road. I did not stop nor did I look at them.

"By late afternoon I came to a valley that I seemed to

recognize. It was somehow familiar. I thought I had been there before, but if that was so I was actually south of Ixtlan. I began to look for landmarks to properly orient myself and correct my route when I saw a little Indian boy tending some goats. He was perhaps seven years old and was dressed the way I had been when I was his age. In fact, he reminded me of myself tending my father's two goats.

"I watched him for some time; the boy was talking to himself, the same way I used to, then he would talk to his goats. From what I knew about tending goats he was really good at it. He was thorough and careful. He didn't pamper his goats, but he wasn't cruel to them either.

"I decided to call him. When I talked to him in a loud voice he jumped up and ran away to a ledge and peeked at me from behind some rocks. He seemed to be ready to run for his life. I liked him. He seemed to be afraid and yet he still found time to herd his goats out of my sight.

"I talked to him for a long time; I said that I was lost and that I did not know my way to Ixtlan. I asked the name of the place where we were and he said it was the place I had thought it was. That made me very happy. I realized I was no longer lost and pondered on the power that my ally had in order to transport my whole body that far in less time than it takes to bat an eyelash.

"I thanked the boy and began to walk away. He casually came out of his hiding place and herded his goats into an almost unnoticeable trail. The trail seemed to lead down into the valley. I called the boy and he did not run away. I walked towards him and he jumped into the bushes when I came too close. I commended him on being so cautious and began to ask him some questions.

" 'Where does this trail lead?' I asked. 'Down,' he said. 'Where do you live?' 'Down there.' 'Are there lots of houses down there?' 'No, just one.' 'Where are the other houses?' The boy pointed towards the other side of the valley with indifference, the way boys his age do. Then he began to go down the trail with his goats.

" 'Wait,' I said to the boy. 'I'm very tired and hungry. Take me to your folks.'

" 'I have no folks,' the little boy said and that jolted me. I don't know why but his voice made me hesitate. The boy, noticing my hesitation, stopped and turned to me. 'There's nobody at my house,' he said. 'My uncle is gone and his wife went to the fields. There is plenty of food. Plenty. Come with me.'

"I almost felt sad. The boy was also a phantom. The tone of his voice and his eagerness had betrayed him. The phantoms were out there to get me but I wasn't afraid. I was still numb from my encounter with the ally. I wanted to get mad at the ally or at the phantoms but somehow I couldn't get angry like I used to, so I gave up trying. Then I wanted to get sad, because I had liked that little boy, but I couldn't, so I gave up on that too.

"Suddenly I realized that I had an ally and that there was nothing that the phantoms could do to me. I followed the boy down the trail. Other phantoms lurched out swiftly and tried to make me trip over the precipices, but my will was stronger than they were. They must have sensed that, because they stopped pestering me. After a while they simply stood by my path; from time to time some of them would leap towards me but I stopped them with my will. And then they quit bothering me altogether."

Don Genaro remained quiet for a long time.

Don Juan looked at me.

"What happened after that, don Genaro?" I asked.

"I kept on walking," he said factually.

It seemed that he had finished his tale and there was nothing he wanted to add.

I asked him why was the fact that they offered him food a clue to their being phantoms.

He did not answer. I probed further and asked whether it was a custom among Mazatec Indians to deny that they had any food, or to be heavily concerned with matters of food.

He said that the tone of their voices, their eagerness to lure him out, and the manner in which the phantoms talked about food were the clues—and that he knew that because his ally was helping him. He asserted that by himself alone he would have never noticed those peculiarities.

"Were those phantoms allies, don Genaro?" I asked.

"No. They were people."

"People? But you said they were phantoms."

"I said that they were no longer real. After my encounter with the ally nothing was real any more."

We were quiet for a long time.

"What was the final outcome of that experience, don Genaro?" I asked.

"Final outcome?"

"I mean, when and how did you finally reach Ixtlan?"

Both of them broke into laughter at once.

"So that's the final outcome for you," don Juan remarked. "Let's put it this way then. There was no final outcome to Genaro's journey. There will never be any final outcome. Genaro is still on his way to Ixtlan!"

Don Genaro glanced at me with piercing eyes and then turned his head to look into the distance, towards the south.

"I will never reach Ixtlan," he said.

His voice was firm but soft, almost a murmur.

"Yet in my feelings . . . in my feelings sometimes I think I'm just one step from reaching it. Yet I never will. In my journey I don't even find the familiar landmarks I used to know. Nothing is any longer the same."

Don Juan and don Genaro looked at each other. There was something so sad about their look.

"In my journey to Ixtlan I find only phantom travelers," he said softly.

I looked at don Juan. I had not understood what don Genaro had meant.

"Everyone Genaro finds on his way to Ixtlan is only an ephemeral being," don Juan explained. "Take you, for instance. You are a phantom. Your feelings and your eagerness are those of people. That's why he says that he encounters only phantom travelers on his journey to Ixtlan."

I suddenly realized that don Genaro's journey was a metaphor.

"Your journey to Ixtlan is not real then," I said.

"It is real!" don Genaro interjected. "The travelers are not real."

He pointed to don Juan with a nod of his head and said emphatically, "This is the only one who is real. The world is real only when I am with this one."

Don Juan smiled.

"Genaro was telling his story to you," don Juan said, "because yesterday you *stopped the world,* and he thinks that you also *saw,* but you are such a fool that you don't know it yourself. I keep on telling him that you are weird, and that sooner or later you will *see.* At any rate, in your next meeting with the ally, if there is a next time for you, you will have to wrestle with it and tame it. If you survive the shock, which I'm sure you will, since you're strong and have been living like a warrior, you will find yourself alive in an unknown land. Then, as is natural to all of us, the first thing you will want to do is to start on your way back to Los Angeles. But there is no way to go back to Los Angeles. What you left there is lost forever. By then, of course, you will be a sorcerer, but that's no help; at a time like that what's important to all of us is the fact that everything we love or hate or wish for has been left behind. Yet the feelings in a man do not die or change, and the sorcerer starts on his way back home knowing that he will never reach it, knowing that no power on earth, not even his death, will deliver him to the place, the things, the people he loved. That's what Genaro told you."

Don Juan's explanation was like a catalyst; the full impact of don Genaro's story hit me suddenly when I began to link the tale to my own life.

"What about the people I love?" I asked don Juan. "What would happen to them?"

"They would all be left behind," he said.

"But is there no way I could retrieve them? Could I rescue them and take them with me?"

"No. Your ally will spin you, alone, into unknown worlds."

"But I could go back to Los Angeles, couldn't I? I could take the bus or a plane and go there. Los Angeles would still be there, wouldn't it?"

"Sure," don Juan said, laughing. "And so will Manteca and Temecula and Tucson."

"And Tecate," don Genaro added with great seriousness.

"And Piedras Negras and Tranquitas," don Juan said, smiling.

Don Genaro added more names and so did don Juan; and they became involved in enumerating a series of the most hilarious and unbelievable names of cities and towns.

"Spinning with your ally will change your idea of the world," don Juan said. "That idea is everything; and when that changes, the world itself changes."

He reminded me that I had read a poem to him once and wanted me to recite it. He cued me with a few words of it and I recalled having read to him some poems of Juan Ramon Jimenez. The particular one he had in mind was entitled "El Viaje Definitivo" (The Definitive Journey). I recited it.

> . . . and I will leave. But the birds will stay, singing:
> and my garden will stay, with its green tree,
> with its water well.
>
> Many afternoons the skies will be blue and placid,
> and the bells in the belfry will chime,
> as they are chiming this very afternoon.
>
> The people who have loved me will pass away,
> and the town will burst anew every year.
> But my spirit will always wander nostalgic
> in the same recondite corner of my flowery garden.

"That is the feeling Genaro is talking about," don Juan said. "In order to be a sorcerer a man must be passionate. A passionate man has earthly belongings and things dear to him—if nothing else, just the path where he walks."

"What Genaro told you in his story is precisely that Genaro left his passion in Ixtlan: his home, his people, all the things he cared for. And now he wanders around in his feelings; and sometimes, as he says, he almost reaches Ixtlan. All of us have that in common. For Genaro it is Ixtlan; for you it will be Los Angeles; for me . . ."

I did not want don Juan to tell me about himself. He paused as if he had read my mind.

Genaro sighed and paraphrased the first lines of the poem.

"I left. And the birds stayed, singing."

For an instant I sensed a wave of agony and an indescribable loneliness engulfing the three of us. I looked at don Genaro and I knew that, being a passionate man, he must have had so many ties of the heart, so many things he cared for and left behind. I had the clear sensation that at that moment the power of his recollection was about to landslide and that don Genaro was on the verge of weeping.

I hurriedly moved my eyes away. Don Genaro's passion, his supreme loneliness, made me cry.

I looked at don Juan. He was gazing at me.

"Only as a warrior can one survive the path of knowledge," he said. "Because the art of a warrior is to balance the terror of being a man with the wonder of being a man."

I gazed at the two of them, each in turn. Their eyes were clear and peaceful. They had summoned a wave of overwhelming nostalgia, and when they seemed to be on the verge of exploding into passionate tears, they held back the tidal wave. For an instant I think I *saw*. I *saw* the loneliness of man as a gigantic wave which had been frozen in front of me, held back by the invisible wall of a metaphor.

My sadness was so overwhelming that I felt euphoric. I embraced them.

Don Genaro smiled and stood up. Don Juan also stood up and gently put his hand on my shoulder.

"We are going to leave you here," he said. "Do what

you think is proper. The ally will be waiting for you at the edge of that plain."

He pointed to a dark valley in the distance.

"If you don't feel that this is your time yet, don't keep your appointment," he went on. "Nothing is gained by forcing the issue. If you want to survive you must be crystal clear and deadly sure of yourself."

Don Juan walked away without looking at me, but don Genaro turned a couple of times and urged me with a wink and a movement of his head to go forward. I looked at them until they disappeared in the distance and then I walked to my car and drove away. I knew that it was not my time, yet.